CLOWN PRINCE OF SOCCER?

The Len Shackleton Story

CLOWN PRINCE OF SOCCER?

The Len Shackleton Story

COLIN MALAM

DEDICATION

In memory of Neville Holtham, former sports editor of
The People and dedicated Len Shackleton fan, who died
before he could make the contribution to this book
that he intended.

Published in 2004 by Highdown,
an imprint of Raceform Ltd
Compton, Newbury, Berkshire, RG20 6NL
Raceform Ltd is a wholly-owned subsidiary of Trinity Mirror plc

A CIP catalogue record for this book is available from the British Library.

ISBN 1-904317-74-X

Designed by Fiona Pike
Printed by Creative Print & Design, Wales

CONTENTS

ACKNOWLEDGEMENTS

Len Shackleton was such an unusual and fascinating character that this book has been a pleasure to research and write. Although Shack died in 2000, at the age of 78, enough of his friends and contemporaries are still around to provide an illuminating, first-hand account of the man and his extraordinary life as a brilliantly gifted but flawed footballer, talented all-round sportsman, radical thinker, influential journalist and general good egg.

I interviewed so many of those friends and contemporaries that there isn't room here to list them all; but I should like to thank every one of them, and a number of journalists, again for their kindness and patience in giving me so much of their time to talk about Shack. It would be remiss of me, however, not to mention one or two of them in particular. Without the help of former *Sunday Mirror* man Vince Wilson, for example, it would have been a great deal more difficult, perhaps even impossible, to complete this book on time. The recollections, advice, guidance and contacts provided by my, and Shack's, old chum in somewhat difficult circumstances were absolutely invaluable.

Roger Shackleton, Len's middle son, was also a great help – up to a point. He was planning a biography of his father himself so it was understandable that he felt he could give me only limited assistance; but that proved sufficient to provide a clear and touching picture of Shack's family life. I am glad to say there was no holding back at all by the officials of Bradford Park Avenue, who were enormously helpful and welcoming at all times. Thanks are due, too, to Jim Bruce-Ball, in the *Sunday Telegraph* sports room, for all his delving into the 'big red book' for me.

Colin Malam

SIR STANLEY MATTHEWS
ON LEN SHACKLETON

Len Shackleton was unpredictable, brilliantly inconsistent, flamboyant, radical and mischievous; in short, he possessed all the attributes of a footballing genius, which he undoubtedly was. But such a character would not go down well with the blazer brigade who ran English football and had such an important say in the selection of the England team. Len would often say or do something to upset authority and I believe this predilection of his to shock was something the FA and England management were always uneasy about, and thus they never warmed to him.

Outspoken comments about coaching and his contempt for officialdom didn't endear Len to the England hierarchy and, despite his undoubted genius, this most talented of inside-forwards won only five caps in what was to all intents and purposes a fine footballing career with Bradford Park Avenue, Newcastle United and Sunderland. Len was a continuous exasperation and affront to the conventional and the conformists of English football, of whom there were many…

Len played to the gallery and, in so doing, fully demonstrated what I have always believed about football – that it is not only a superbly dramatic and exciting game, but can be a wonderfully clever one. For long periods in a match, Len would be quiet, often contributing little, but the two or three minutes when he turned it on and did something unpredictable and outrageous would be the moments of the game that provided the supporters with a golden memory to cherish for ever. As one supporter once told me, 'Two minutes of Shack's genius is worth the admission price alone'...

Len Shackleton's talents were extravagant in the extreme, he was inordinately clever and, despite playing to the crowd, I never saw him being selfish to team-mates. He was no mean goalscorer himself, and made many a goal for his fellow forwards, a fact that only those who had the pleasure of playing alongside him now seem to remember. For all his individuality, he did buckle down to team play when the mood took him, especially in his time at Sunderland. However, in the latter stages of a match, when it was evident the game was either won or lost, it was if he said to himself, 'Stuff this for a game of soldiers,' and he would proceed to amuse himself and the crowd. To apply himself fully to a game plan or a task for 90 minutes seemed beyond him. His capacity to shock and entertain in equal measures won him that dubious title, 'The Clown Prince of Soccer', which I feel belies his true genius.

STANLEY MATTHEWS
Extract from *The Way It Was*
(Copyright © 2000 Sir Stanley Matthews).
Reproduced by kind permission of
Headline Book Publishing Ltd.

INTRODUCTION

ON 1 December 1954, England played West Germany at Wembley. It was an historic game in many ways: for one thing, it was the first time since the post-war partition of Germany that the two countries had met. Not only that, but having upset the odds by beating hot favourites Hungary in the final of the World Cup five months earlier, the West Germans came to London as the new world champions. So England were absolutely desperate to win: not just for the prestige it would bring, but to close the open wound in their pride after having been humiliated twice, home and away, by the Hungarians during the preceding twelve months. In short, the last vestiges of England's fading reputation as masters of the game were at stake.

And win the game they did, thanks largely to superlative displays by two of the oldest players in the England team, Stanley Matthews and Len Shackleton. The Methuselah-like Matthews was only two months away from his 40th birthday that day, while Shackleton was deep into his 33rd year. Between them, they bemused an under-strength West Germany with their exceptional skill and were chiefly responsible for an impressive 3-1 victory. But although

Shackleton, recalled following a controversial, five-year absence from international football, also finished the world champions off with a magnificent goal, he never played for England again. In other words, that memorable match was the pinnacle of an extraordinary playing career in which Shack did not win a thing, received less than his due, yet created a legend that has us talking about him still today, nearly half a century after he hung up his boots.

Len Shackleton was a phenomenon; a complete one-off. In the decade immediately after the Second World War, when he was in his prime as a footballer, clever, talented inside-forwards (today's attacking midfielders, that is) abounded in English football. England had Raich Carter, Wilf Mannion, Jimmy Hagan, Ivor Broadis, Ernie Taylor and Eddie Baily, to name but a few, while Wales could point to the likes of Bryn Jones and Ivor Allchurch, Scotland to Billy Steel and Jimmy Logie, Northern Ireland to Peter Doherty and Jimmy McIlroy. Yet, even in such exalted company, Shackleton stood out.

He did so for several reasons. At a time when individualism and skilful manipulation of the ball were commonplace, Shack's expertise in that area was just mind-boggling. The tricks he could do with a football – and the old, heavy, leather 'casey', remember, not today's plastic-coated 'beach-ball' – were little short of magical. Len Shackleton was a natural-born showman, too. He loved to parade his skills in front of a big crowd; indeed, he believed it was his duty to entertain. Hence the well-documented stories about him sitting on the ball in the middle of a game or standing with one foot on it pretending to look at his watch. His behaviour on the field of play could be absolutely outrageous, and the fans loved him for it.

There was a more serious side to Shackleton's personality, however. As befits a Yorkshireman, he was acutely aware of his monetary value as a performer and, with complete justification, complained long and loud about the poor pay footballers were receiving at a time in the game's history when attendances were booming and the clubs were coining it in. An intelligent man and original thinker, Shack was also scornful of authority when he deemed it to be unworthy of his respect. The most famous, or infamous, example of that was the blank page in his autobiography, *Clown Prince of Soccer*, under the chapter heading, 'The Average Director's Knowledge of Football'.

Insubordination of that kind hardly endeared Shackleton to English football's establishment, which was even more stuffy and sensitive then than it is now. Indeed, his unconventionality, on and off the field, was almost certainly responsible for the scandalous fact that he, one of the finest footballers of his generation, won only five England caps. Yet, on the credit side, it is more than likely that his willingness to challenge the status quo contributed significantly to the groundswell of dissatisfaction and rebellion that eventually swept away the iniquitous maximum wage and inflicted serious damage on the feudal retain and transfer system in the early 1960s. Those early, liberating steps, of course, led eventually to the sky-high wages and complete freedom of contract we have today.

Shackleton's influence on the game did not end with his abrupt retirement at the start of the 1957-58 season, when he was thirty-five. Recruited quickly by the *Daily Express*, he began a new career as a football writer; and it was in his capacity as a journalist that he helped Brian Clough to obtain his first two managerial jobs, at Hartlepool and Derby County. How different might Clough's glittering, controversial career have been, not to mention the histories of Derby and Nottingham Forest, had Shack not pulled a few strings with Derby's chairman at that time, Sam Longson?

So there you have Len Shackleton – ball-artist supreme, self-confessed clown, natural rebel and, improbably, influential journalist. He may not have been the finest, most disciplined or most consistent player English football has ever seen but, as the rest of this book is designed to show, he was certainly one of the most entertaining and interesting characters to have contributed to the pageant. He was, if you like, the first and the finest of the game's many post-war mavericks.

CHAPTER ONE
'LIGHTNING SHACK'
– WONDER LAD

EXACTLY where Leonard Francis Shackleton got his extraordinary ball skills from is anybody's guess. Since both his father and grandfather were enthusiastic and talented sportsmen, those skills must have originated somewhere in the family genes. Their precise location is not so easy to find, however. His grandfather, Francis Shackleton, after whom he was given his second name, was a gifted amateur cricketer, while his father, Leonard Price Shackleton, shone as an amateur footballer, cricketer and track athlete. But while both obviously passed on their athleticism and aptitude for sport to young Len, there was little in Shackleton senior's own sporting career to suggest he would sire one of the cleverest and most audacious manipulators of a football the game has ever seen.

It is true that LPS, as we shall have to refer to him to avoid confusion, was sufficiently talented at football to think of taking it up professionally until a First World War wound put paid to the idea. On the other hand, LPS was anything but a ball-artist. As LFS revealed in his celebrated autobiography, *Clown Prince of Soccer*, his father's type of football pleased the 'get stuck in' spectators. Seemingly, LPS revelled in hard tackling and almost made a boast of the fact that he had been sent off the field frequently. In fact, as LFS pointed out, all of his family regarded sport as an occupation for he-men. David Steward, an uncle, was captain of Bradford Northern Rugby League club, for example, and LFS was honest enough to wonder whether he would have been a better footballer if he had possessed some of the 'devil' of his father and his Uncle David.

So, in that sense at least, the boy who was to go on to delight the crowds at Bradford Park Avenue, Newcastle United and Sunderland with his amazing tricks and outrageous showmanship was something of a freak. Certainly, Shackleton's younger brother, John, does not seem to have been blessed with anything like the same level of skill. A physical training instructor during his National Service days, John was taken on by Sunderland for a few years but failed to make the grade. Thereafter, he settled for coaching tennis while also pursuing a career as a chiropodist. Little sister Irene, youngest of the three Shackleton children, does not really come into the equation; but the fact that she played netball for her school and swam for the county underlines the strong sporting nature of the whole family.

Like most of his football contemporaries, Shack was self-taught. Born in Bradford in 1922 and growing up in the Depression-blighted 1930s, a time when there was not always enough money for the cinema and when multi-channel television and personal computers were just fanciful thoughts in some boffin's mind, young Leonard Francis was one of the thousands of boys who amused themselves with a ball wherever and whenever they could. There was no official football practice at his primary school, but he spent all his spare time kicking a ball about in the schoolyard, in the fields near his home and even in the house. Since the latter was done with full parental approval, there can be little doubt that Shack's family gave him every encouragement to develop his magical footwork. 'Youngsters manufactured their own entertainment with a tennis ball,' he said. 'From May to August we were all budding Herbert Sutcliffes or Hedley Veritys. In the winter we became Cliff Bastins and Dixie Deans.'

Wherever he went, Shack took a tennis ball with him. If his mother asked him to go on an errand, he would make sure he had a pal to keep him company so that they could pass and re-pass the ball all the way to the shops and back. That way, he said, he hardly noticed he had performed 'the loathsome task of shopping'. Darkness did not deter young Len and his friends from pursuing their favourite occupation, either. Refusing to be robbed of football time, his gang played many a tense match in front of a well-lit grocery shop; although what the shopkeeper thought of that is not recorded.

This was the golden age of 'street football', the loss of which many a modern coach blames for the perceived decline in the technical ability of English footballers. Indeed, Shackleton himself was bemoaning its disappearance from all over the country as long ago as 1955, when he published his autobiography. 'How many lads today carry muddy tennis balls in their jacket pockets, head for the fields and parks the moment they finish school, or sit through their lessons in shirts soaked with the sweat of half an hour's honest endeavour in the school playground?' he asked. 'Not many. It is no longer normal to do as we did. There are too many counter-attractions: manufactured merriment for the millions is laid on without our having to search for it.'

I had always imagined that the demise of street football came in the 1960s with that decade's marked increase in car ownership and the greater risk of road accidents it brought with it. However, Shackleton's version of events suggests the age-old recreational habits of football-mad boys were beginning to change as long ago as the early 1950s, the period when – thanks largely to the televised coronation of Queen Elizabeth II – television was starting to claim the attention of the populace, and not least the young.

But back in 1929, when Shack was seven, the budding footballer's main concern was how to get hold of some proper boots. He says he could not afford a pair, which one takes to mean that his parents could not. Having survived being shot twice in the death-traps that were the First World War trenches, Shackleton's father became a self-employed painter and decorator when he was demobbed, and the business flourished to some extent during the inter-war years. His wife, Martha, was particularly proud of the fact that they had managed to afford the rent of a semi-detached house at Horton Bank Top, a respectable working-class district in one of the highest parts of Bradford. Even so, when it came to a first pair of football boots for young Len, it was a case of make-do-and-mend.

Len's Uncle John, who always wanted Len to be a footballer, bought some studs and hammered them into an old pair of shoes for the boy. He loved them and could not wait to try them out in one of the games of indoor football that took place in the Shackleton household every evening, Sundays included. This football-crazy family used to clear the decks in the living room by removing chairs and pushing bulkier furniture into a corner. As a concession to the landlord's window panes, though, a ball of paper bound with elastic bands was substituted for the tennis ball.

Even so, there was an unfortunate accident on the first occasion that young Len wore his new 'boots'. He was having the time of his life when the ball rolled under the sideboard. As his father bent down to fish it out, Shack aimed a mighty kick and connected with his father's eye. That bloody experience frightened the life out of the boy; but such was LPS' enthusiasm for the game, reported LFS, he treated the incident 'as a normal hazard in the football education of son Leonard'.

Academically, too, Shackleton's education was proceeding apace. Although, in later life, one of his favourite aphorisms was 'Most footballers' brains are in their feet', he provided early proof that not all of his were by passing the secondary school scholarship exam when the time came to move on from elementary school. That notable scholastic success gave him the choice of half a dozen schools in Bradford, and he plumped unhesitatingly for Carlton High, a grammar school where the playing of football was encouraged. It was no contest, really: the alma mater of former Preston North End winger Dicky Watmough, Carlton had the best schoolboy football team in the city. So it hardly mattered to Shack that his new school was a 20-minute tram-ride away on the other side of Bradford, when he could have walked to two other schools from his home.

It was at Carlton High that he was first introduced to organised football as part of the school syllabus; and it came as such a shock that he wondered what he had been playing previously. He confessed that, until then, he had imagined the inside-right marked the inside-right, the left-back was responsible for the opposing left-back and so on, while everyone on the field – bar the goalkeepers – chased the ball. 'In those days,' he added, 'youngsters seldom sat at home discussing the tactics of soccer; we were too busy playing it, after our own fashion.'

Encouraged by his sports master, Walter Hodgson, who quickly spotted the natural ability in his new pupil, the little ball juggler was soon playing for Carlton's First XI. 'He had a terrific shot,' recalls Ken Teasdale, a friend and contemporary of Shackleton's, who went on to play in goal for Bradford City and had the misfortune to oppose the great man from schoolboy level onwards. Teasdale, who attended Drummond Road School, recalls playing against Shackleton's Carlton High in one game in particular. 'In those days, the crossbar was a bar resting on two angle irons, and Len hit it this time with a perfect shot. It was so hard, it lifted the bar off the angle irons and dropped it on my shoulders! It was such a shock! And they were big, heavy footballs then, too. Not the ping-pong balls they are now.'

The next step up for Shack was selection for Bradford Schools against Stoke Boys at Stoke City's old home, the Victoria Ground. He remembered his first representative match for Bradford as a wonderful experience made all the more memorable by the presence of City's England internationals, Frank Soo and Stanley Matthews, who were persuaded to act as linesmen. He reflected later that, had anyone told him then that he would play for England in 1954 with the same Stanley Matthews, it would have seemed too ridiculous for words.

As the graph of Shackleton's budding career continued to zoom upwards with what he saw as 'a few reasonable games' for Bradford Schoolboys, he was nominated for an England trial. Selected to play for the North against the Midlands at York, he did well enough to earn a second trial at Walsall. As a result of that, he was chosen to play for The Rest v England Boys at Kettering.

By this time, the local paper, the *Bradford Telegraph and Argus*, had cottoned on to the fact that they had a young footballer of considerable potential in their midst. 'According to experts,' read one of their reports, 'the boy Shackleton is a great football star of the future…This season, he has been chosen for the forward line in three schoolboy international trial matches, the final one of which is to be played at Kettering next Saturday. Naturally, Shackleton is the hero of his school, but he is a lad without a swelled head. He knows his own mind, however. He wants to be a "crack" footballer when he grows up. As the school's sports master told me today, he is an intelligent lad, with a football brain. He has scored in each of the two trial matches this season. "Lightning Shack" his pals call him.'

Lightning or not, the Kettering trial must have been a daunting experience for the young Shack, if only because of his extremely small stature at that point in his physical development. He never grew to be a giant, 5ft 8-9in being the most generous estimate of his adult height, but at 13 years of age he stood only 4ft 11in tall and weighed just 6st 2lb. However, despite being the smallest boy on view, he made enough of an impression on the selectors to be named at outside-right for England Schoolboys in their game against Wales at Aberdare, thus becoming the first Bradford schoolboy to gain international honours.

But while acclaiming the chosen team as 'very fine', one newspaper preview did presciently question the selection of our hero on the wing. 'One wonders whether the selectors have done wise in placing Shackleton at outside-right,' wrote its football correspondent. 'This midget genius from Bradford – he stands only 5ft and weighs 6st – won the distinction of being the cleverest forward in the game (at Kettering) by dint of his amazing powers of working the ball to advantage from the inside berth. His clever creative qualities may not be fully called into action on the wing. Still, Shackleton is a wonder lad, just the type likely to shine in any position… in 14 school representative matches, he has scored 40 goals, twice registering six in one match.'

Undeterred by the fact that he had never played at outside-right before, and having overcome an injury to his big toe sustained in a school match a few days before his international debut, Shackleton duly starred in the game against Wales. He scored two goals, and made others, as England romped home 6-2. Without doubt, he played so well largely because he spent most of the game in his normal inside-right position.

One newspaper report explained the switch thus: 'Shackleton was chosen for the outside-right position, but an early injury to Davis caused him to go inside, where he was such a success that most of the England goals came from his openings. Shackleton showed real football intelligence.' Another read: 'The success of the (forward) line came when Davis and Shackleton interchanged positions. Shackleton became the spearhead of all the attacks and his through passes were always a delight.' What Shack did not realise until many years later, when he joined Sunderland from Newcastle, was that the boy with whom he had switched positions so fruitfully in Aberdare had gone on to become the Sunderland centre-forward, Dickie Davis.

Nobody was prouder of young Leonard than his father after that memorable international debut against Wales. Shack recalls that when he returned home to Bradford from Aberdare that night, his dad, who normally tried to hide his enthusiasm for his son's performances, immediately collared the boy's first international cap. He then made a tour of the neighbourhood, knocking on doors, showing off the cap and telling everybody that young Len had scored two goals for England against Wales. It was not until the early hours that Shackleton senior crept back indoors, still clutching that precious souvenir of the first of his son's many great days.

Two more schoolboy caps followed. At Villa Park, Shack's England won 4-2 against a Scotland team containing that future idol of Anfield, Billy Liddell; then they thumped Northern Ireland 8-3 in Belfast. His international career at schoolboy level ended when he reached the age of 14. After that, there was just the occasional opportunity for him to play representative football. But at least it gave him a taste of the big time, Bradford Secondary Schools taking on Glasgow Schools at Hampden Park, before the professional clubs came calling.

Young Len was still at Carlton High when there was a knock one day on the door of his home at 38 Soaper Lane, Horton Bank Top. He opened the door himself and recognised the caller as Billy

Hardy, the manager of Bradford Park Avenue. In those days, schoolboys were allowed to discuss terms with professional clubs; so when Hardy invited him to join Park Avenue as an amateur, Shack jumped at the chance. Father was not so keen, however. Shackleton senior pointed out to Hardy that he and his brothers were fans of Park Avenue's fierce local rivals, Bradford City, and said that it seemed all wrong for Len to be joining the other lot. Wrong or not, the family did not prevent Shack from signing the forms proffered by Hardy, who told the youngster that he wanted him to come to Park Avenue as often as possible, especially on the training nights: Tuesdays and Thursdays.

While Shackleton's family encouraged him every inch of the way in his desire to become a professional footballer, others did not. Those who tried to discourage him included a Sunday School teacher who sounded a bit of a snob. When this killjoy asked each member of his class in turn what they would like to be when they grew up, young Len told him he was going to be a footballer. Unimpressed, the teacher dismissed the boy's ambition as nonsense. He said there might be some money in it for a few lucky ones but, for the most part, footballers took up the game professionally only when they could not earn their livings at a better job. 'You would find yourself mixing with all kinds of people – not a course I would recommend,' he added pompously. Fortunately, Shack saw the teacher for the idiot he was and refused to be put off.

Mr Know-it-all would probably have had an attack of the vapours, then, when he heard that the mighty Arsenal had also homed in on the gifted youngster, who, at 15, was still on amateur forms with Bradford Park Avenue, but playing for Kippax United in the Leeds League. Although training with Park Avenue on Tuesdays and Thursdays, Shackleton was not as closely connected with his hometown club as some imagined. Indeed, he claimed in his autobiography there had been no firm indication that Park Avenue were going to take him on as a professional when he came of age at 17. Nevertheless, it was taken for granted that would happen; so Shack was rather surprised when he was told by John Plows, a schoolmaster who took an interest in Kippax United, that he had recommended him to Arsenal.

In fact, it sounds as if he nearly swooned at the news. As Shackleton pointed out, it was every youngster's dream then to play for the famous London club and he could not quite believe that one of their scouts was coming to have a look at him playing for Kippax United. The report must have been favourable because, a few days before the end of the 1937-38 season, the arrival of a beautiful car – Shack could not remember whether it was a Chrysler or a Rolls – outside number 38 caused a sensation in Soaper Lane. While the neighbours congregated to have a look at this phenomenon, out stepped none other than George Allison himself, secretary-manager of the mighty Arsenal.

The fact that Allison had gone all the way up to Bradford to ask Len Shackleton in person to join the famous London club spoke volumes for the talent and the promise of the gifted youngster. Allison's grand gesture certainly impressed Shack and his parents, but was hardly necessary. 'He had no need to "sell" Arsenal to me,' confessed Len later. 'At that time, any 15-year-old boy, invited to join the greatest club in the world, would have been out of his mind to think twice. So it was that I accepted his offer of a job on the ground-staff and signed as an amateur.'

Given the monumental success the Gunners have enjoyed in recent years under the management of, first, George Graham, then Arsene Wenger, it should not be difficult for younger readers to understand the teenaged Shackleton's eagerness to join a club of their standing. Even so, largely because of Manchester United's preeminence, Arsenal have been unable to loom quite as large in English football during the past decade as they did during the 1930s. Back then, by dint of winning the League Championship five times and the FA Cup twice, between 1930 and 1938, Arsenal were the Manchester United or Liverpool of the years immediately before the Second World War.

That image-making run of success had been started, of course, by the legendary Herbert Chapman, first of the 'modern' football managers, whose bust still graces the marble halls of Highbury in recognition of his establishment of Arsenal as one of the most successful and famous clubs in the world. Having already transformed Huddersfield Town from a run-of-the-mill club into the first to pull off a hat-trick of League Championships, Chapman did much the same for Arsenal, who were a very moderate outfit when he took over in 1925. Nine years later, when he died suddenly of pneumonia, the Gunners were well on the way to their third First Division title in four years. Then, under Allison, Chapman's successor, they won the title twice more.

So being asked to join them, as young Shack had been, was a very big deal indeed. The importance of the invitation was reflected in the headlines. 'Given Big Chance by Arsenal – Bradford Ex-Schoolboy International Seeks Football Fame,' screamed the *Bradford Telegraph and Argus*. 'A Bradford schoolboy international footballer has been given an opportunity to make a name for himself in first-class football,' read the story below. 'He is 16-year-old Leonard Francis Shackleton, of 38, Soaper Lane, Horton Bank Top, until recently a scholar at Carlton High School for Boys, and who today left to join Arsenal Football Club, where he will be given a job in the office and will receive the necessary coaching and training. He cannot sign professional forms until he is 17 years of age.

'Shackleton was at Horton Bank Top School before proceeding

to Carlton Street, where he was an outstanding player. He not only captained the school football team and the Bradford Boys team, but also had the honour of gaining three schoolboy international "caps" when he played for England against Wales, Scotland and Ireland. He secured the three caps in one season and was the first Bradford high-school boy to win international honours. As a forward, he has been regarded by many good judges as one of the cleverest schoolboy footballers Bradford has produced for years. Although only slightly built, he has been a prolific scorer…

'Shackleton's mother today told a "*Telegraph and Argus*" reporter that Mr George Allison (manager of Arsenal A.F.C.) visited their home recently and made arrangements for Leonard to leave for London. Mrs Shackleton said they had decided to give the boy a chance. Several well-known clubs in first-class football had been interested in him… Today, Leonard set off on his great adventure. Perhaps he will follow in the footsteps of that other Bradford schoolboy footballer, Albert Geldard, who became a full-fledged international with Everton after having played with Bradford (Park Avenue) [sic].'

So no pressure there, then, as, in the full glare of local publicity, the 16-year-old set off alone for the big city in August 1938. One guesses it was to his considerable relief and delight that Shack was met at King's Cross by Jack Lambert, 'centre-forward hero of so many Arsenal triumphs', as Shackleton called the goalscoring spearhead of Chapman's all-conquering side, who had gone on to become the club's youth coach following his retirement as a player. Lambert installed him in digs at Highbury Hill, then took him along for a look at the famous Arsenal stadium.

Shackleton found it a real eye-opener. He had thought Villa Park, where he had played as a schoolboy international, was soccer perfection; but now he decided that even that fine stadium looked shabby in comparison with Highbury. And as he took in 'the mighty stands, the spotlessly-clean terracing, reaching, to my eyes, into the clouds, the emerald green turf', he spotted four of the star players – Ted Drake, Wilf Copping, Cliff Bastin and George Male – 'who had helped to make Arsenal great, helped, in fact, to make Arsenal "The" Arsenal.' They were within hailing distance, but he, 'the bumpkin from Bradford', dared not even wish them good morning.

Sadly, that is about as good as it got for Shackleton. Next morning, he was disappointed to be handed a pair of overalls, instead of boots, shirt and shorts, and told to follow the motor mower all over the famously well-tended pitch clipping any long stalks of grass missed by the machine. Enviously, he watched the 'real' players doing their training stint (no fancy training grounds out in the countryside then, note) while pretending to rake the gravel or cut the turf, without having the heart for either task.

Publicly, though, the youngster put on a brave face. 'It's wonderful,' he told the *Bradford Telegraph and Argus*, when interviewed about his first day at Highbury. 'A fortnight ago,' the report continued, 'Leonard was at school. Today he began a new course of education – as a footballer – and, as the youngest member of the Arsenal staff, he naturally began at the bottom.

'I met him on the oasis of rich green turf which Jack Campbell (clerk of works) has conjured out of the ground at Highbury… He was toiling in the hot sunshine cutting down the long stalks of grass which the mowing machine had passed over. "It's grand to be here," said Leonard, as he brushed the perspiration from his forehead. "Mr Allison has fixed me in comfortable lodgings, and everyone is friendly and helpful." Then, looking at the turf, he added: "If I get on well, I shall be playing on this pitch one day. I've got a wonderful opportunity and now it's up to me." '

Well, not exactly. It is almost as if Arsenal went out of their way to break Shackleton's spirit, rather than to encourage him. In 1938, the Gunners caused quite a furore in English football by paying a British record fee of £14,000 – described by many as the height of lunacy, believe it or not – to sign the Wales international inside-forward, Bryn Jones, from Wolverhampton Wanderers. As a result, one newspaper thought it would be a good idea to get a picture of Jones, Arsenal's costliest player, alongside their cheapest. Amazingly, the club went along with the suggestion and, you guessed it, nominated young Leonard for the job. It is not difficult to imagine how the lad must have felt when a wonderful action picture of Jones with the caption, 'He cost £14,000' was juxtaposed with one of Shack in overalls, stalk-shortening with a pair of grass clippers and reading, 'He cost nothing'.

Undoubtedly humiliated by Arsenal's insensitivity, Shackleton insisted that he bore Bryn Jones no ill-will for what had happened. However, it was clearly difficult for him to disguise his pleasure many years later at the thought that, when he was transferred from Newcastle United to Sunderland for a record £20,050 in 1948, Jones, then a veteran, moved from Highbury to Norwich City for a fee of less than £3,000.

In other, face-to-face circumstances, Shack showed that he was not one to be pushed around. Maybe the contempt for authority – at least, authority he did not feel merited his respect – that was to characterise much of his playing career had its origins in the kind of incident that occurred at Highbury one day. George Allison, having come out to do some training with the staff, called out to Shackleton, who was sweeping the terraces with other ground-staff boys. 'He shouted, "Come over here, son",' Shack recalled in later life, 'and put his foot up on the railing. "Fasten that!" he said, pointing to his shoelace. So I said, "Fasten the bloody thing yourself!" I'd have cleaned his boots for him, never mind fastened the lace; but he'd no reason to talk to me like that, even if he was the manager of Arsenal.'

Almost certainly, that show of defiance did not improve Shackleton's prospects of making a career at Highbury. For the moment, though, his main concern was to avoid work by hiding, along with other ground-staff boys, from the Arsenal groundsman, Bert Rudd. Shack, Bobby Daniel, brother of Ray Daniel, the Welsh international centre-half, who became one of Shackleton's team-mates and closest friends at Sunderland, and Harry Ward, like Shack a product of the Leeds League, used to kick a tennis ball about in the passages, snack bars and empty terraces of Highbury when they should have been assisting Rudd. One of their hiding places was alongside the asphalt training pitch behind the terracing, and they used to sit there for hours watching Arsenal's star players train.

Strangely, considering the marked difference in their positions, Eddie Hapgood, 'the finest left-back ever to play for England,' in Shackleton's words, was young Leonard's favourite. Perhaps it was Hapgood's self-possession that struck a chord in the budding genius. 'Hapgood,' he recalled, 'had such tremendous faith in his own ability that his confidence affected everything he did, and it spread through any team in which he played.'

Shack was allowed few opportunities by Arsenal to prove he had the same qualities as Hapgood. During the one season he spent with the Gunners, 1938-39, he wore the famous red and white shirt only twice – against Oxford University and Bristol Rovers. Like a lot of other boys, he played Athenian League football for Enfield most of the time: there were just so many youngsters on the books it was impossible for Arsenal to give more than a fraction of them regular match practice.

The nearest Shackleton got to the big time at Highbury was when he was again sweeping the terracing one day. Suddenly, Allison shouted to him to go and get stripped. The manager wanted someone to make up the numbers in a trial match featuring Arsenal's senior players. Shack found himself at outside-left, another position in which he'd never played before, and up against George Male, England's first-choice right-back. He got through the ordeal without mishap, he says, largely because of the brilliance of his partner at inside-left, Gordon Bremner, 'who, with minimum of assistance from me, managed to "paralyse" the normally cool and capable George Male.'

Then, a week or two before the end of the season, came the hammer blow. Harry Ward, the other lad from the Leeds League, and Shack were told the manager wanted to see them in his office. Both of them thought they were to be told off about neglecting some of their ground-staff duties and hoped it would have nothing to do with the playing side of the job; but they could not have been more wrong. This was where their short spell with Arsenal came to an end.

Shackleton says that Allison handled the situation diplomatically, and could not have been kinder, as he broke the bad news. Even so, it is not difficult to imagine how crushed the little Yorkshire lad must have felt as he stood there on the thick pile carpet in the manager's palatial office being told that all his dreams of fame and fortune with the most famous club in the land had come to nothing. Allison explained to Shack that he was not keeping him on because he considered him, at only 5ft 2in, to be too small to make the grade as a professional footballer with Arsenal or any other League club. He suggested that the boy should return home to Bradford and look for a job. Become a miner, an engineer or a commercial traveller instead, he suggested.

As is usually the norm in such cases, the Arsenal manager stressed that he was advising Shackleton in his own best interests. He even went so far as to claim that the boy would thank him for his advice one day. But young Shack was hardly listening. Fighting back the tears, his only thoughts were of the shame he would face when he returned home a failure after having been given a hero's send-off when he had left Bradford for London. Then Allison went just a little bit too far.

Anger was Shackleton's next emotion. What really stuck in the lad's craw was the Arsenal manager's ill-advised decision to patronise him, albeit unintentionally. Just before the chastened, downcast youth left the office, the Arsenal manager invited him to come next door and proudly showed him that newest of status symbols, a television set. The gesture seems to have been a well-meant attempt to cheer Shack up, but he took it badly. So far as he was concerned, it was just a matter of being given 'one last glimpse of the greatness of Arsenal before I returned to the back streets of Bradford ... so that I could go home and tell my "country-bumpkin" chums in Yorkshire about the miracles of modern science.'

It was a psychological error by Allison that would come back to haunt Arsenal down the years. Although Shackleton denied absolutely that he pursued any kind of vendetta against the London club when he became a famous and successful footballer with Newcastle and Sunderland, it had to be more than coincidence that Shack always seemed to reserve his finest performances for games against the club who had sacked him, written him off and patronised him at such a young age. Especially when those games were at Highbury. But more of that later.

Frankly, Allison does not sound like the sort of person you would want to know. Not, certainly, after reading *Football Memories*, the recent volume of memoirs by Brian Glanville, one of the outstanding British football writers of the post-war years. Glanville, a lifelong Arsenal fan, but always irreverent and entertaining, describes the man who managed the Gunners between 1934 and 1947 in these unflattering terms: 'During the war, one would see him in propaganda films: a squat, plump, rumbling figure, who had eliminated all trace of his original north-east accent. He came, in fact, from Middlesbrough, and had attached himself to Arsenal in their Woolwich days, when he was making his way as a young journalist, eventually representing the USA's Hearst newspapers. His accent, now, aped the received English of the period, the A's carefully if perversely pronounced as E's, as per the Prime Minister, Neville Chamberlain, himself, when war was declared: "I am speaking to you from the kebinet room in 10 Downing Street."

'By the time of the death of the incomparable Herbert Chapman in March, 1934, when a bad cold turned into irresistible pneumonia, George Allison had become a director of the club. As a publicist and journalist, he was unquestionably effective. To make him the new manager seemed an extraordinary choice. His knowledge of the game was scant; his relations with his players uneasy. Where he and Arsenal were so fortunate was in the presence "below stairs" of Tom Whittaker, an extraordinary trainer.'

In fairness to Allison in his misjudgement of Shackleton's potential at 16-17, it has to be said that the teenager did not cut a particularly impressive figure then. Not only did he stand only 5ft 2in in height, he was very much one-footed at that stage of his development. Looking back at the trial match he played in as a ground-staff boy, Shackleton confessed that he didn't think he had the strength to reach the penalty area with a corner kick taken with his stronger, right foot, never mind with the left. 'My main worry,' he wrote, 'was a "doubtful" left foot, or, to be more truthful, a practically useless one.'

Main worry in a playing sense, that is. Overriding everything else in Shackleton's mind now was concern about the future. There he was in May 1939, just 17 years old, jobless and far from home. Worse still, he felt he had let everybody down back in Bradford by not making the grade with Arsenal and was reluctant to return under those circumstances.

Harry Ward, the Yorkshire lad sacked along with Shack, felt the same. So they decided they would do anything to avoid returning to their native county. It was a decision that led to a curious and little-known episode in Shackleton's career. The two youths had a stroke of luck when somebody tipped Shack off that anyone capable of playing a reasonable game of football would be fixed up with a job in the London Paper Mills at Dartford, provided he turned out for the works team in the Kent League. So they packed their bags, spent their last few shillings on train tickets and tried their luck down in Kent.

However, London Paper Mills did not exactly welcome them with open arms. Frank Langan, the man who interviewed them, was disappointed to learn that they had no skills for anything other than football, even though he had been eager to employ them both when he had heard they were former Arsenal ground-staff boys. It meant that all that was available to them were menial jobs, which paid no more than seventeen shillings and sixpence (about 80p in today's money) a week. That would not have provided them with a bed and was considerably less than the fifty shillings they had been getting at Arsenal.

Fortunately for the two homeless, penniless young adventurers, Langan was a generous man and took pity on them. He offered to find them lodgings, pay them enough to cover the rent and give them a few shillings on top for spending money. The offer was equivalent to double the normal pay for boys of their age doing that particular job, and they jumped at it. 'It saved me from returning home with my tail between my legs,' Shack said gratefully.

With Europe rumbling ominously towards a second world war in the spring of 1939, the football season was just about over. So young Len turned his attention to cricket, another ball game for which he had a rare gift, on behalf of London Paper Mills throughout the summer. He also played for the works football team during the early part of the 1939-40 season until, with the "phoney" war gradually developing into the real thing and his mother pleading with him to rejoin the rest of the family, he returned to Bradford. 'I went back when I'd got enough courage to go home and tell them I was a failure,' he said.

It was with some annoyance, then, that Shack, in 1947 heard Tom Whittaker, who had succeeded Allison as manager of Arsenal, trying to blame the outbreak of hostilities for the departure from Highbury of someone who had emerged, post-war, as a player of immense talent. 'Shackleton would have been an Arsenal player still,' Whittaker claimed, 'had it not been for the war. He had left the club at the start of the war and decided to settle in Bradford.' Shackleton's response to that attempted cover-up was terse: 'Arsenal are entitled to their opinion,' he said,' but there was no war in progress that day in May when I was called into the manager's office and given marching orders!'

Something more pleasant that Shack never forgot was the kindness shown him in his hour of need by Frank Langan and London Paper Mills. Once the player had become famous, Langan used to send him good luck telegrams whenever he played in big games; so Shackleton went out of his way to make a sentimental return journey to Dartford in 1946 after playing in the FA v Army PT XI international trial at Wembley. It was, in fact, the day Shack heard he was to play for England for the first time at senior level, against Scotland in one of the so-called Victory Internationals.

When he and his wife, Marjorie, turned up at the paper mills, the workforce made a great fuss of them. To Shack's great embarrassment, they were swamped with congratulations and asked to pose for photographs with mill workers who had played football for the Dartford side when he was there. He told Frank Langan that

London Paper Mills had been as kind then as when, in 1939, he had been 'an unwanted nobody'. That kindness, he added, was why Dartford had to be his first call after England had picked him to play against Scotland.

By 1955, the year *Clown Prince of Soccer* was first published, Shackleton had become very worldly-wise. That much is clear from the tribute he paid his former boss at Dartford Paper Mills. What it amounted to was that everyone wants to know you and help you when you are at the top of the tree; but not too many remain friendly or come to your aid, like Langan, when you are down on your luck and your career starts to nosedive. 'He alone saved me the ignominy of scuttling home, a heart-broken flop,' said Shack. 'Perhaps Frank played as big a part in the football career of Len Shackleton as anyone … So many different things might have happened without his assistance.'

CHAPTER TWO
BACK HOME

IT was not long after Len Shackleton's return to Bradford in April 1940 and just before his 18th birthday, that Bradford Park Avenue got back in touch with the football prodigy they had let slip through their fingers a couple of years earlier. Hearing Shack was back in town, manager David Steele, who had been in charge at Park Avenue when Arsenal spirited the Carlton High School boy away to London, invited him up to the ground for a chat. The upshot of that meeting was his reappearance in the red, black and amber hoops of Bradford as an amateur. Making a living by assembling aircraft radios for the telecommunications firm, GEC, during the week, he played a couple games for Park Avenue at the end of the 1939-40 season, trained with them all through the close season and decided that the following season would be 'make or break' for him.

At the start of that season, 1940-41, Shackleton was a regular in the side from August until Christmas, when Steele finally asked him to sign professional forms for the club. Shackleton's confidence in his own ability had remained undiminished by George Allison's crushing appraisal of him and he jumped at the chance. He was so keen to sign on, in fact, that he and his father walked the four miles from the family home at Horton Bank Top to Park Avenue.

Shack was soon reminded, though, that he was not on easy street. Having signed the forms, he was told by an apologetic Steele that, under Football League rules, he ought to be receiving a £10 signing-on fee, but that the club did not have that much money in the kitty. Instead, he got a down payment of ten shillings (twenty shillings to the old pound, remember), followed by fifteen shillings a week later, seven and sixpence after that and sundry other small payments from time to time. 'Transfer fees are often paid on hire purchase,' Shack remarked ruefully, 'but I imagine this was the only time a club had paid a signing-on fee on the "never-never". There is not much glamour in hire purchase!' Not only that, but he was never quite sure whether he had received the full £10 to which he was entitled.

Nevertheless, Shackleton always had a high opinion of Steele. He said the players respected him as a man who was prepared to stand up to the directors on their behalf and who worked always in the best interests of the club. They also admired him for being able himself to do in training what he was telling others to do. 'I was very lucky when I started at Bradford at 15 years of age,' said Billy Elliott, one of Shack's contemporaries at Park Avenue, 'because the manager then was the ex-Scottish international, David Steele. He knew the game, there's no doubt about that. He taught me a lot and he taught Shackleton a lot as well. There weren't many people who could handle Shack; but if Steele told him not to do a thing, he'd not do it – if he was that way out.'

Shackleton celebrated his new professional status by playing immediately for Park Avenue against Leeds United at Elland Road on Christmas morning. Then, at the invitation of Park Avenue's local rivals, Bradford City, he turned out for them as a guest player at Huddersfield in the afternoon. The second match was notable for that rarity, a headed goal by Shack. It went in like a rocket from 15 yards, apparently. Christmas Day, 1940, always stood out in his memory because it saw him become a professional footballer, play for two clubs in one day and actually head a goal.

It was possible to play for more than one club during the Second World War because, in a complete reversal of the game's feudally restrictive employment rules in peacetime, players were allowed to move freely from club to club and turn out for whomever they wished. Significantly, it was not until half a century later, and the Bosman case, that English professional footballers achieved anything like the same degree of freedom. One reason for the delay, perhaps, was the chaos that ensued when clubs and players began to take advantage of a situation in which many footballers were called up for duty in the armed services while others remained at home working in what were called 'reserved occupations' – jobs that, like the one Shackleton had with GEC, were considered important to the war effort.

As Jack Rollin explains in his definitive history of the period, *Soccer At War, 1939-45*, the wartime game would have collapsed as an organised entity without the introduction of guest players. Unfortunately, clubs began to abuse it once they realised the advantage this new freedom could give them. Initially, the guest player system was brought in as an emergency measure to help out clubs who found themselves short of players; but it soon became the custom for some to seek a guest at the expense of their own registered and available members. As Rollin says, 'The higher the status of the club in question, the more likely it was that they were able to attract 'star' guests. It might have been questionable ethics, but it was good box office. It caused bad feeling and even led to some players asking for a transfer… But as the war went on and problems mounted, the fact that the game was continuing on organised lines was regarded as the overriding consideration.'

My own father, Albert Malam, was involved in one of the disputes caused by the guest player system. Rollin tells the story as follows: 'With an internationally-accepted reputation like that of Manchester City's Peter Doherty, it was obvious that he would be eagerly sought. The usual practice was for the player to inform his club whether he was likely to be around on a particular Saturday. "I wired Mr Wilfred Wild (the City manager) to say I had an unexpected short leave and would be available on the Saturday, requesting him to send instructions to my Blackpool home," said Doherty. "When I arrived there, I found a letter from the manager informing me that the team had been selected and that Albert Malam had been chosen as inside-left. I could understand this, of course, as Malam was available every week and I was not. What annoyed me was the fact that after a long, overnight journey made with the specific intention of playing, no assistance was given to me in the matter of expenses. It was a thoughtless omission and one that remained in my mind for a long time." '

It was the start of many problems between Doherty and City that led ultimately to the great Northern Ireland international's departure from the club. You have to feel for a star player like him coming home from the armed forces and finding himself kept out of his own club side by a guest player from elsewhere. But in defence of my father and Wilfred Wild, I have to point out that Dad was a talented inside-forward who had played for Chesterfield, Huddersfield Town and Doncaster Rovers before the war and had been in particularly good form at Maine Road. He was always available during the war because, as a qualified coachbuilder, he worked in the heavily bombed Liverpool docks, helping to turn ocean liners into troopships.

On at least one other occasion the boot was on the other foot for Doherty, so to speak. When the Ulsterman went to Blackpool one day to watch Liverpool and called in at the dressing-room to chat to one or two friends, he found himself being asked to turn out for the

Merseysiders. It was only afterwards that he discovered George Ainsley, the Leeds United forward who was later to join Bradford Park Avenue, had been left out of the team to make room for him. The decision caused ructions because the RAF had given Ainsley permission to obtain leave for the game. Angered, the RAF said they would release no more players for Liverpool, who had to apologise to them and to the Football League.

Structurally, English football was reorganised on a regional basis by the League following the declaration of war in September 1939. Divided first into ten regional mini-leagues, four of them in the south, the participating clubs (several, including Aston Villa, Sunderland, Derby County, Ipswich Town and Norwich City, closed down or opted out at various points) were then split roughly on a north-south basis for the remainder of the hostilities. Previous status did not count for anything: Bradford Park Avenue, proud members of the old Second Division, for example, found themselves lumped together with Bradford City, next to bottom of the Third Division North, whether they liked it or not. The FA Cup was replaced by the League War Cup, then the League North Cup and League South Cup, until normal service was restored on and off the field in 1945-46.

This, then, was the tense, confused, makeshift context in which Len Shackleton, at 18, began his career as a professional footballer with Park Avenue. In some respects, it was ideal for somebody starting to make his way in the game. Although there were still honours to be won, be it as winners of your regional league or the ersatz cup competitions, the pressures of peacetime football were considerably reduced. For one thing, there was no promotion or relegation; for another, Second Division Park Avenue found themselves playing regularly against big First Division clubs, such as Liverpool, Manchester United and Sunderland, whom they would never have met under normal circumstances. So, as Jack Rollin points out, the standard of play remained pretty high.

'Arguments,' he wrote in *Soccer At War*, 'have reverberated about the quality of performance at top level in what were unusual circumstances, but sound reasoning has echoed its praises. Selection of players was frequently restricted by the availability of servicemen since the large proportion of international players came from military sources. It did not inhibit enterprise. The players were probably physically fitter than they had been as peacetime professionals, and while the rigours of service training were not necessarily conducive to improving football skills, the heavy programme of games at service and civilian level for the privileged few meant that the players were certainly match fit as well.'

There were other benefits, too: benefits that relate more directly to the subject of this biography. 'Universally,' adds Rollin, 'there was every incentive to express individual ability, from the encouragement from older players who continually passed experience gained over the years to the youngsters. They had no fear of being dropped. Unrestricted, they developed their own styles, which, by frequent exposure, became like the repertoire of a jazz musician whose impromptu solo performances are easily accommodated because of the knowledge of the main theme and overall accomplishment of his fellow artists.'

Arguably, no English footballer, before or since, has produced performances that were more dazzlingly impromptu than Len Shackleton's. If we continue the jazz motif here, then he was the Charlie Parker of our game, a genius who thrilled audiences with an unprecedented mastery of his instrument – the ball – and constantly pushed back the boundaries of improvisation. Equally, he was a flawed crowd-pleaser who could not be relied on to deliver the goods every single time.

That, though, was Shack, the finished article: between 1940 and 1945, he was simply young Len, the teenage sensation growing into manhood with Bradford Park Avenue in wartime football, learning his trade at thirty shillings (£1.50 in new money) a game and beginning to discover just how cleverly he could manipulate a football for the benefit of his team and to the delight of the crowd.

Shackleton's development was also helped by the fact that Bradford Park Avenue did not rely on guest players as heavily as some other clubs. Ivor Broadis, the Manchester City, Newcastle United and England inside-forward who was later to rejoin Shack at Sunderland, and Leslie Compton, the Arsenal and England centre-half and brother of Denis, were just about the only big-name players from other clubs who turned out for Park Avenue during the war years. Broadis, who was in the RAF, did so only because he was stationed near Bradford. As a result, Shackleton found himself playing in a fairly settled team, in which he and team-mates such as Scottish international Jimmy Stephen and the future England international, Billy Elliott, became regulars.

The youngster positively flourished in such favourable circumstances. If you look at the official records, they will say that Len Shackleton played just seven times for Park Avenue and scored only four goals. But those statistics are nonsense: they are confined to the 1946-47 season, the first in which English football returned fully to its pre-war normality and the one in which Shack was transferred to Newcastle United. In other words, they give no indication at all of this blossoming player's astonishing exploits in the wartime game.

He played six full seasons, and part of a season either side, for Park Avenue between 1940 and 1946, scoring 171 league and cup goals in 209 appearances. That total, as hardly needs saying, is getting on for a goal a game and, unsurprisingly, still stands as a club record. His most prolific season was 1944-45, when he actually exceeded the goal-a-game target by finishing with 40 in 39 appearances. That haul included the five he scored in a 6-1 win against Hull City on 23 December 1944. Park Avenue were also pretty severe on their local rivals. The biggest win of many against Bradford City was a 10-0 victory at Valley Parade, City's ground, on 19 December 1942.

Since he was in goal for City that day, it is a hammering Ken Teasdale has never forgotten. Unexpectedly, though, Shackleton's friend and fellow-Bradfordian looks back on it as something of a personal triumph. 'Every time we played against each other at school, Len put lots of goals past me,' he said. 'But it was rather funny that, on that one occasion, I restricted him to just one out of the ten!' Sadly, that is not quite right. Tim Clapham, Park Avenue's official historian, informs me that Shackleton actually scored twice that day. But as Ken was 81 when he told me this story, he can be forgiven a small, self-congratulatory lapse of memory.

Oddly enough, Shack himself rather glossed over this early, formative part of his career. In *Clown Prince of Soccer*, he devoted no more than a couple of pages to his record-breaking spell with Park Avenue in a way that suggested he did not rate its importance very highly and/or was still experiencing some measure of guilt about having carried on playing while other footballers were away from home serving their country in the armed forces. He certainly chafed at the thought of having become, almost by accident, an essential part of the domestic war effort instead of a serviceman. Shack found himself in a frustrating situation where he wanted to join his pals in the Army, Navy or Air Force, so quashing any suggestion that he was trying to dodge the fighting, yet was itching to devote all his time to becoming a professional footballer.

All his efforts to join up came to naught. He volunteered for the

RAF but as soon as the authorities learned what his employment was, they turned him down. He tried for the Fleet Air Arm, too, only to be frustrated when GEC refused to release him. He kept haunting each recruiting office in Bradford in turn, but when the Army acted like the other Services, he finally decided he was wasting his time.

So he turned for consolation to the thing he was better at than most people. 'I had my football at the weekends,' he mused. 'It was wartime substitute soccer, the regional stuff with over-familiar opponents, but at least I was getting more match practice than other players overseas in uniform. It was good fun, wartime football, with little at stake, no reputations to be considered, and nothing more than petty cash as the reward for playing.'

Others, however, remember rather more fondly the six years Shack spent at Park Avenue. Frank Thornton, the current chairman of the club, was just 12 when he first watched one of their games. It was a wartime cup-tie against Blackpool in 1943, and he remembers clearly that Stanley Matthews was playing for Blackpool, while Leslie Compton was at left-back for Park Avenue. He is not so sure whether Shackleton was on the field that day, but thinks he probably was. 'I was a bit too short, really, and I didn't see much of it,' he explains, 'but I certainly caught the atmosphere. The roar when Shack got the ball was incredible – and there was plenty of that, so he must have been playing that day. Every time, the crowd expected something – and quite often they got it!

'Len was one of those players that you only see once in a lifetime, and I don't think you see them at all these days. His ball control was mesmeric: he had this wonderful backspin and I saw him, many times, go up to a classy defender and apparently lose control of the ball, which went two or three yards ahead of him. The defender would think, "Right, I've got him!" and go for the ball; but it would suddenly disappear because he had put loads of backspin on it. A bit like a cricket ball, it would bounce back to Len and he would be past them before they could recover. It was fantastic stuff!

'The other thing was that he had a wonderful ability to aim the ball over short distances. More than once, I saw him beat a defender by bouncing the ball off a corner flag. I mean, this was quite incredible stuff! He also became quite expert at dropping corner kicks on to the crossbar. The idea was for it to come out into the goalmouth. As a result, we scored quite a few goals from corners.

'Then there was the famous incident when he sat on the ball. I was there and saw it for myself. I can't remember who we were playing, but Shack suddenly stopped moving with the ball and sat on it. Everybody else stopped, and rumour has it that when the referee went up to him and asked if he was OK, Len replied, "Yes, I'm fine," and continued to sit there. Then up he got and ran off with the ball while the opposing defence was trying to make sense of it all.'

There is any number of other witnesses only too willing to testify that it was during the six years Shackleton spent with Bradford Park Avenue that he perfected the ball skills and developed the showmanship that were to make him unique. Ken Teasdale, who knew Shack as a rival in both schoolboy and wartime football, insists it was not until he joined Park Avenue that he began to do tricks with the ball and play to the crowd. Certainly, by the time centre-half/wing-half Ron Greenwood was transferred from Chelsea to Park Avenue for £3,500 towards the end of the war, Shackleton's personality as a footballer seems to have been set in stone.

'Len Shackleton was also a key member of the side, a player with lovely, almost unbelievable skills,' recalled the former West Ham United and England manager in his autobiography. 'There was no one quite like our Len. He was a showman, a crowd-pleaser, a character who was larger than life. Some of the things he did had nothing to do with the winning and losing of a game, but the crowds loved him. He could even cut his foot under the ball so sharply that it would spin towards an opponent and then come back to him as if on a piece of string.

'Len also had an instinct for being in the right place at the right time, something which was often illustrated in practice, when he liked to keep goal. He would stand between the posts and use everything but his hands to stop the ball. He would use a heel or thigh, his head or chest, a shoulder or his backside to stop shots, just to prove he was different. During a game, this same instinct told him exactly the right moment to stick a leg out to intercept the ball.

'I used to play right-half behind him in the early days and he always liked to have me behind him for support; but when I was defending and under the whip I never got much help from Len. "How about lending a hand?" I used to shout... Some players give their team all they have all the time, and they demand everything in return. Len Shackleton was always just himself.'

Both Greenwood and Shackleton played in one of the most famous games in Park Avenue's history. It was the second, away leg of a fourth round FA Cup tie against Manchester City in 1945-46. Each round was played on a home and away basis in that first season after the war, and Park Avenue went to Manchester with little prospect of going through after losing the first leg 3-1. Greenwood takes up the story: 'Our cause seemed hopeless and, to rub things in, our coach ran into a blizzard right on top of the Pennines on our way to Maine Road for the second leg. The wind howled, the snow swirled, our coach struggled. Len Shackleton said to me, "Let's turn back... we don't stand a chance anyway." That seemed a fair assessment, but we pushed on and eventually got to the ground with less than 20 minutes to spare. Our trouble proved worthwhile. We won by eight goals to two on a pitch covered with pools of water – and Jack Gibbons scored six. The sight of the great Frank Swift picking the ball out of his net eight times is something I shall never forget. Everything went right for us. It was one of those days.'

Carried away a bit, no doubt, by the memory of that momentous and unlikely victory, Greenwood did not get his facts quite right. According to the record books, Gibbons scored only four of Park Avenue's goals that day. The others were claimed by Dix (two), Knott and Farrell. But the odd thing is that Len Shackleton, usually their leading scorer, did not get a single one. Johnny Downie, the Scottish inside-forward who went on from Park Avenue to play for Manchester United, was amazed by that. 'Shack and I never got a goal between us!' he exclaimed when I talked to him. 'But it [the victory at Maine Road] was wonderful. I couldn't believe it, nor could my father. He had come down from Scotland for the first leg, so when a fellow told him after the second leg, "They've lost 8-2!" he said, "I'm not surprised." "No, no," said the other chap, "Park Avenue won 8-2!" '

As the war drew to a close, Len Shackleton was faced with two choices, one difficult, the other not so difficult. The latter involved GEC, the firm for whom he had been assembling aircraft radios. They had moved to Bradford from Coventry to escape the heavy bombing of that Midlands city; but now the hostilities were nearly over, they decided to return to their former home and Shack was asked to go with them. With no desire to leave Bradford, and 'real' football just around the corner, he had no hesitation in turning down flat the invitation to work in a Midlands factory.

A major consideration here was the fact that David Steele had been quietly putting together a good team at Park Avenue. The recruitment of players of the quality of Ron Greenwood, Billy Elliott, Jimmy Stephen and Johnny Downie, Shackleton felt, offered every chance of success on the resumption of normal league and cup football after the war. Not only that, but he had begun to attract the attention of England's international selectors, who had been blooding him in FA and Football League teams. So there was every reason for Shack to believe he could make a name for himself in the game, and GEC's offer of continued employment never had a chance of succeeding.

Even less enthusiastic was his response to the notification, soon afterwards, that he would be required to join the Army and do two years' National Service. For the benefit of those not old enough to remember that quaint peacetime institution, all fit and healthy young men between 18 and 25 were duty-bound to leave their jobs, occupations or whatever and put in two years' service with the Army, Navy or RAF. With the international political situation still unstable at a time when many servicemen were being demobilised, and with Britain's manpower resources taxed by the occupation of Germany and other military obligations elsewhere in the world, the government was anxious to make up the numbers of the military.

But Shackleton was 23 in 1945, and that was not an ideal age for a footballer to be interrupting his career for two years – especially when the game was just about to return to normality. He had seen many players have the best years of their careers taken from them by the war, and he was determined to avoid being damaged in the same way if he could. 'Keen enough during the war,' said Shack, 'after VJ-Day with all my friends returning on demob leave, I had no desire to join up. And unlike a person doing an ordinary job of work, two or three years' Army service after the war could easily have ruined all my hopes of a career in soccer.'

Desperate to avoid National Service, Shackleton enquired as to whether there was any alternative and found a way, of sorts, out of his dilemma. It was to go down the mines and become a 'Bevin Boy'. Bevin Boys, named after Ernest Bevin, Minister of Labour in the wartime coalition government and the man who initiated the scheme, were soldiers in a 48,000-strong army of young men recruited in a desperate attempt to strengthen an industry weakened by the questionable wartime decision to call up experienced miners for service in the armed forces.

Realising that if he could work in one of the many Yorkshire pits, he would be fairly close to home and Bradford Park Avenue, he decided to have a crack at it. Assigned to Fryston Colliery, near Castleford, he got kitted out in the necessary equipment – overalls, boots, helmet and lamp – and, accompanied by Park Avenue team-mate Jimmy Stephen, began making the 60-mile round trip to Fryston each day.

But Shack did not like what he found there: in fact, he hated it. Struggling just to cope with having to leave home at six o'clock in the morning, he got a nasty shock when required to descend in the pit cage for the first time. Calling the cages 'torture boxes' he described that first descent as a terrifying experience. It was like being suspended on a piece of elastic, he said. One minute you were rushing into the bowels of the earth; the next, you would stop suddenly and just dangle there. At the end of the first day, he realised he had made a terrible mistake by volunteering for the mines and resolved to find ways and means of 'dodging the column' without being reported for absenteeism.

Johnny Downie can vouch for the fact that Shackleton did not overwork himself as a Bevin Boy. Another of the young Park Avenue players who opted for the mines instead of National Service, Downie says he enjoyed the experience up to a point. 'I stayed for quite a while,' he told me. 'We were all in the Fryston Colliery at Castleford. They looked after us quite well there and allowed us to come home to Bradford. Each day, I got the bus to Leeds, Leeds to Pontefract, Pontefract to the colliery; and it was very good. I wouldn't like to do it again, though: I wasn't happy down below. Up on top was all right, but we were a long way down below, most of us. I was at the loading end of the operation. When they got the coal out, we put it into trolleys. That was all the skill we had, really, for mining. To be fair, they couldn't allow us to be in a position where we could jeopardise others. So there was no working at the coalface, or anything like that.'

And where, pray, was Len Shackleton while all this was going on? 'He was at the pit (shaft) bottom, away up along the road,' recalls Downie. And what was he doing, exactly? 'Oh, I don't know. Wasting his time, I would think. He didn't go very often: he didn't go as often as us. Geoff Walker (yet another Park Avenue player-turned Bevin Boy) and I went to live there in Fryston for a short while; but they (Shackleton and Stephen) travelled every day.'

When Shack did turn up for his shift at the colliery, he worked with Stephen in the joiners' shop at the pit bottom. 'There is a certain amount of joinery to be done down the pit, you know – doors and that sort of thing – and we were doing odd jobs there,' explained Stephen, who lives in retirement in Portsmouth, where he finished his playing career in fine style. But although the pit manager even put on a special, nine-to-five shift for Shackleton and Stephen, it still could not take the sting out of the six-hour round trip they faced each day. 'It was an horrendous journey,' recalled Stephen. 'Len was living at Queensbury, on the outskirts of Bradford, and I was also living on the outskirts of the city, but in another part. We had to get a bus from home to the centre of Bradford. Then we got a bus to Leeds, a bus from Leeds to Castleford and, finally, a bus from Castleford to Fryston. We used to leave our homes at six o'clock in the morning to start work at nine; and it was the same coming back, of course. It was a dreadful way of life, really.'

Little wonder, then, that Shack did not always present himself for duty at Fryston. Not that his penchant for skiving – more evidence of which we shall see later – seemed to make him any less popular with his team-mates. 'All right,' Johnny Downie adds, 'the colliery could have been better. I hated going down the shaft, really. Oh, it's terrible, that coming up and down. Once I was down, I was not bad: there was a little lamp and that was it. But Shack never came down into the real depths: he stayed behind in the pit bottom, and I don't blame him.'

As for Jimmy Stephen, he missed Shackleton so much when his pal was transferred to Newcastle United in 1946 that he just stopped going to Fryston. 'When Len left, that was the end of our friendship – going to work and that – and I was so sick of it, I became what you'd call an "absentee". As such, I was then called up into the RAF and did my National Service with them.'

Needless to say, Stephen thought Shack a wonderful fellow. 'Oh, he was a great lad, Len,' said the Scottish international full-back. 'He was a great character – quick witted, comical. He pulled everybody's leg something shocking.' Stephen also obviously revered Shackleton as a footballer: 'He was clever: clever with the ball, clever in his head, a great player. And didn't he score some goals! He certainly wasn't a defensive-minded inside-forward. Some inside-forwards were up and down the park and they were back in defence helping out, but Len wasn't too keen on doing that. Nevertheless, he was worth his weight in gold up front. You could always find him with the ball, and you were on the attack again. He was a great player, there's no doubt about it.'

Johnny Downie, another Scot, heartily agrees: 'As a footballer, I think he was the best fellow I ever played with, without any shadow of doubt. He and George Best were the best two players I've ever seen. Shack was wonderful to me off the field as well. I was very young when he was at Park Avenue – they brought me down from Scotland in 1942, when I was 17 – and he looked after most of the young people at the club. So I couldn't say a word against him. He was a wonderful gentleman and a very, very good friend.

'Because I was so young I wasn't always in the same team as him; but when I played with him, it was always very enjoyable. He had all the tricks, you know – taking the ball out to the corner flag and then sitting on it (the ball, that is). It was funny, but we were winning when he did it, of course. One thing he taught me was that we only passed the ball if we drew a man. "If we don't draw the man, we don't pass it," he used to say. When I watch football nowadays, they pass the ball as soon as look at you!

'I know people have suggested that he didn't always take the game as seriously as he might have done, and that's possibly correct, but he did think deeply about his football. Two other good pieces of advice he gave me as a fellow inside-forward were: "Always play yourself onside with a man you can see: don't run forward and hope there's somebody at your back" and "We only pass it up the wings when we can't get it up the middle. If you can't get it up the middle, pass it out to the wing." '

Sadly, Len Shackleton's formative, record-breaking, six-year spell with Bradford Park Avenue ended on a discordant note – quite literally – in October 1946. He claimed that, in part, he was driven out by the barracking he received from a section of the club's fans. If true, it suggests a lot of ingrates or idiots were supporting the club at that time. According to Shack, not everybody on the terraces at Park Avenue approved of his inventive, highly individualistic approach to the game and let him know it in no uncertain terms.

Looking back at that episode with the benefit of hindsight, Shackleton came to the conclusion that any player who held on to the ball in an attempt to do something constructive with it, rather than passing the buck to a team-mate, always ran the risk of barracking by the 'knowledgeable ones' on the terraces. 'Ball players, call them jugglers if you like,' he reflected, 'must expect to antagonise the "get rid of it" faction while trying to inject fresh ideas into the bloodstream of modern mass-production soccer.'

In his case, he said, the barracking he received in those early days was chiefly responsible for his transfer from Bradford Park Avenue to Newcastle United. 'At any rate,' he added, 'I was helped on my way by the bob-enders.' The normally placid Stanley Matthews was so angered by the behaviour of the Park Avenue fans that he was quoted in a Sunday newspaper as saying, 'The £13,000 transfer of Len Shackleton from Bradford to Newcastle United is another proof of the harm unsporting spectators can do to players and clubs.'

Shack does admit, though, that he had already made up his mind to move on. He had decided he had gone as far as he could with Park Avenue and, at 24, was seeking greater security for his new family. He had a wife, Marjorie, by then and Graham, the eldest of their three sons, was born in Bradford in 1946. 'Call me callous if you will,' he said, 'but Bradford was just a stepping-stone for me. I had other ideas.'

Despite that 1955 show of bravado, Shackleton retained a deep affection for his home-town club for the rest of his life. Even in his declining years, he did not miss Park Avenue's annual dinners if he could help it. 'Oh, yes, he always came to the dinners,' says Frank Thornton. 'Mind you, he expected star treatment. He had to have the best car and a chauffeur, and we were quite willing to accommodate him. After all, people would come to our events just to talk to Len! He was very special. Once, I was talking to a Yorkshireman who said: "Bloody hell! Who does he think he is?" "Well," I said, "I'll tell you exactly who he is!" and proceeded to do so in no uncertain terms.'

John Helm, the ITV football commentator and interviewer, also has cause to remember Shack's appearances at those annual dinners. 'He always used to sit alongside me at the top table,' said Helm, who is a vice-president of Park Avenue. 'He was deaf as a post and only laughed in the wrong places. I had to explain all the jokes to him because he'd got so deaf. But he had a very loud voice – "What was that one about?" he'd say – and everyone would laugh.

'He was a wonderful character, and he just loved to come to the dinners. He was still very youthful for his age and he came year on year. He came with his old pal, Billy Elliott, for a few years, and he had a terrific memory for all his matches. He had a wicked sense of humour as well. He used to play games with the waiters at the dinner: he'd pretend not to hear when they were asking for the money, and things like that. He'd cough up eventually, but he always had the same little patter.'

It caused Shack great distress, then, to see Park Avenue's sad decline after the war. But it could be said to have been accelerated by his own departure in 1946. 'The Bradford team was virtually falling apart,' reasons Thornton, 'and he probably felt that he had to get somewhere else to progress his career. I never did find out what the problem was at Park Avenue, why they lost so many players, because they did have some cracking results.

'They won 8-2 at Manchester City in the FA Cup when he played, of course; and then there was the famous trio of games against Manchester United [in 1948-49, the mighty Old Trafford club needed three attempts to knock Second Division Park Avenue out of the fourth round of the FA Cup] when Johnny Downie played a blinder just before he joined United. We had a cracking side that could compete with the best.'

Ron Greenwood remembered with a warm glow one game at Highbury in the 1947-48 season. 'Arsenal won the League championship by a clear seven points (that season),' he said. 'They headed the First Division from start to finish, but in the third round of the Cup at Highbury we beat them by a goal to nil. I was Bradford PA's captain and without any shadow of doubt, it was one of the most marvellous afternoons of my career. Our win was so unexpected but so honestly deserved that even now it seems unreal.'

Incidentally, Frank Thornton was such an avid Park Avenue fan that he actually cycled from his home in Bradford to London and back – a round trip of 400 miles – to see that Cup tie at Highbury. Now that's what I call a supporter! Even now, at 72, he makes another 400-mile round trip – though not by bike – from his home in Oxford, where he is in business, to Bradford whenever possible. 'I don't go as much these days,' he confesses. 'I'm finding that long round trip for an hour and half of football a bit much; but I do go as often as I can.'

Despite that level of support – Thornton was one of 1500 fans who followed Park Avenue to Highbury – and occasional FA Cup heroics, Bradford's once pre-eminent club continued to sink towards the bottom of the table. They were eventually relegated in 1949-50 to the Third Division North, where they found themselves competing again with Bradford City. They stayed there, mostly sloshing about near the foot of the table, until 1958, when the bottom 12 clubs in the Third Division North and the Third Division South were thrown together to form the new, 24-club Fourth Division. Promotion to the Third Division in 1960-61 sparked new hope and brought some much-needed respite from the downward spiral; but Park Avenue went down again two seasons later. That relegation in 1962-63 was their death-knell. Seven years later, after finishing bottom for three seasons running, they were voted out of the Football League after a 62-year stay.

'We dropped into the Northern Premier League, and were there for four seasons,' says the Park Avenue historian, Tim Clapham, charting the decline of an ailing club. 'The old Park Avenue ground was sold at the end of the '72-73 season because there were mounting debts. All the sale did, really, was clear the debts: it didn't leave the club with any money. They then moved in with Bradford

City at Valley Parade for one season, '73-74; but the crowd dropped by half when they did that – it was like Manchester United moving in with Manchester City – because half the fans wouldn't be seen dead at Valley Parade. So, having lost half the support and many of the players, the directors decided at the end of that season it wasn't worth carrying on, especially as they were having to pay Bradford City a substantial rent. They decided that was it, pulled the plug and went into voluntary liquidation.'

John Helm, a Park Avenue supporter all his life, particularly regrets the demolition of the club's old ground. 'It was shared by Yorkshire County Cricket Club,' he recalled. 'So you could actually sit in a stand there, watch the football on one side and then, if you went through a little hole sort of exit, watch Fred Trueman running up and down as well. Many a time that happened. A wonderful aerial photo exists of the ground when both cricket and football were going on: Yorkshire playing at one side and Park Avenue at the other. It broke my heart when they just knocked it down. It was a wonderful ground, it really was. Everybody says it was a much nicer ground than Valley Parade.'

Park Avenue did not go completely out of existence, however. They played Sunday football until 1988, when the club was officially re-formed. The moving spirit behind the re-formation was a chap called Bob Robinson. He called a public meeting in Bradford to see if people were interested in getting Park Avenue going again and prompted an encouraging response. When the decision was taken to go ahead with the project, Robinson was interviewed by the *Telegraph and Argus*. 'We've got no players,' he said famously, 'we've got no manager, we've got no ground and we've got no money. We've just got to make steady progress.'

That is exactly what Park Avenue have done in the past 16 years, with the West Riding County Amateur League as their starting point.

'We were there for just one season,' explains Tim Clapham. 'We resigned and joined the Central Midlands League. We stayed there for just one season, too, before resigning again and going into the North West Counties League. That gave us a foothold on the football pyramid, and we climbed pretty fast from there. Having gone through that league from the lower divisions to the top, we won the championship in 1995 and were promoted into the Unibond League, where we've been ever since. We won promotion from the lower division to the Premier Division in 2001, so we've never taken a step back yet. We've been moving forward all the time.'

At the time of writing, Park Avenue had their eyes fixed on the next rung of the ladder, the Nationwide Football Conference, and they took a step closer towards it in 2004 by qualifying for Nationwide North, one of the two feeder leagues for the Conference. From there, of course, it would be possible to reclaim the Football League status they lost so painfully earlier. And Len Shackleton is still with them in spirit, if not in body, as they continue to pursue that long-held aim. These days, their fall from grace is underlined by the fact that they play at the tiny Horsfall Stadium in – would you believe it? – Cemetery Road out in the southern suburbs. A former athletics track owned by Bradford City Council, it has just one stand. That is more than enough for their needs considering the average gate is only about 500.

Even so, they cling fiercely to memories of a more glorious past. There is a Len Shackleton Suite in their modest clubhouse, and one wall is devoted entirely to the career of the greatest player ever to have pulled on the shirt. It is covered with newspaper cuttings and photographs, and even includes one of the few England shirts he wore and was allowed to keep. (After his full international debut against Denmark in Copenhagen in September 1948, Shack asked for his shirt as a memento and was told that he could not have it).

When, in retirement, Shack lived at Grange-over-Sands in Cumbria, he used to go to watch Park Avenue play whenever he could. Frank Thornton remembers one such occasion in particular: 'He came to see one of our games two or three years ago. We were playing up in Kendal against Netherfield, who are now Kendal Town. He was a guest of their club because he didn't live very far away. Anyway, he came over at half-time, and I don't think I saw any of the second half because Len was telling me about football and his adventures. He could talk the hind legs off a donkey! But what a wonderful guy! I'm just very sad that I didn't meet him many years before.'

CHAPTER THREE
SIX-GOAL SHACK

ALTHOUGH Shackleton had been asking Park Avenue for a transfer for some time without success, it was not until the last minute that he learned he was being sold to Newcastle United, who were also in the old Second Division at the time. The move proved a humiliating experience that infuriated him and, almost certainly, intensified the rebelliousness and contempt for authority that, just as much as his brilliant footwork and unconventional behaviour, characterised a controversial career. As a result of the way the transfer was conducted, Newcastle and Shack got off on the wrong foot from the start and never really got back on the right one.

The first, unfortunate episode in a series of clashes began when, out of the blue, Fred Emery, who had taken over from David Steele as Park Avenue's manager in 1943, instructed Shack to report at a Bradford hotel at two o'clock one afternoon without explaining why. The player guessed a transfer might be in the offing, but did not know to which club. There was no instant enlightment, either, when he turned up at the hotel. He recognised nobody, was approached by nobody and waited uncomfortably in the lounge for an hour pretending not to notice the strange looks he was being given by a hovering waiter. Then a stranger, later identified as Sunderland manager Bill Murray, came up to him and said, 'I couldn't get you. The fee is too high.' Only then did Shackleton know for sure he was about to be transferred.

Several prosperous-looking individuals finally descended the stairs and one of them, the Bradford Park Avenue chairman, Stanley Waddilove, pointed at Shack and told one of the other men: 'There he is. He's all yours, Stan.' The person to whom the remark was directed turned out to be the Newcastle United director-manager, Stan Seymour. Seymour then shook Shackleton's hand, introduced himself and asked if he would like to join his club. Shack agreed readily enough, although he was too young at the time to know that he was not compelled to go along with the deal.

The whole affair, he said many years later, left a nasty taste in the mouth because it had been too reminiscent of a cattle market, with him on show as the prize bull. 'I may be wrong,' he grumbled, 'but it seems rather absurd to have people bartering in human flesh, without so much as permitting the object of their bids to be present at the sale. Even harem-bound girls were permitted to sum up their prospective employers while the bidding was taking place.'

Shackleton complained, too, that he did not even know what the fee for his transfer was. He had to wait for the evening paper to discover that he had been sold to Newcastle for a record £13,000. In actual fact, it was £13,000 and threepence. The latest transfer record of £13,000 had just been established by the sale of free-scoring centre-forward Albert Stubbins from Newcastle to Liverpool; but Park Avenue wanted to beat that, so Newcastle director Wilf Taylor threw a threepenny bit on the table to tip the balance. However, the news that he was replacing Stubbins disturbed even Shack's massive self-confidence. 'I'm not as good as him!' he confessed to thinking in a rare moment of self-doubt.

Shackleton had not been completely overawed by events in that

Bradford hotel, though. With a boldness that was to become second nature to him, he asked Stan Seymour straight what he would be getting out of the deal. When the answer was '£500', he was delighted because, at that point, he imagined his transfer fee would be in the region of only £5,000. Even £500 was a small fortune in those days, but Shack swore he never did receive it – an omission that hardly improved his stormy, two-year relationship with Newcastle or his opinion of football club directors. He said he thought he was joining a great club and did so intending to end his career at St James' Park; but, blaming infighting among the board, administrative inefficiency and poor man-management for his disillusionment, he got away as soon as he could.

Paying 10 per cent of the fee to the player, as Stan Seymour seemed to propose, would have been completely against Football League regulations at the time. To the disgust of Shackleton and most other professional footballers, all they were entitled to then was a measly signing-on fee of £10 – no matter how large the transfer fee. So an old lady was simply rubbing salt in the wound when she approached Shack after his first game for Newcastle and told him how lucky he was to be getting £13,000 for joining the club.

The old lady's primary intention, however, had been to congratulate Shackleton for scoring no fewer than six goals on his debut for Newcastle at St James' Park on 5 October 1946, when they beat Newport County by a staggering 13-0. Three of them came in the space of 155 breathtaking seconds and, typically, he knocked in the last of the six with his backside. Cheeky, eh?

There may have been more sensational first public appearances by a footballer for his new club, but it is extremely difficult, if not impossible, to think of one. Even allowing for the fact that Newport shipped a total of 81 goals that season and finished bottom of the Second Division, six points adrift of their fellow-countrymen,

Swansea Town, it was an extraordinary personal performance in an extraordinary victory. If nothing else, it illustrated the enormous self-possession and confidence – arrogance even – Shackleton had acquired by now on the field of play.

'If you could go to bed at night and write your own dream,' he told Brian Moore in an interview for Sky Sports more than 50 years later, 'you couldn't do better than write yourself scoring six goals on your debut. In fact, you wouldn't write it because nobody would believe that. I'm still waiting for the ball, by the way!'

Desperate to celebrate, Shack had to wait until the following day because his wife, Marjorie, was still back in Bradford expecting their first child and they had decided not to move to Newcastle until she and the baby were well enough to do so. That meant he did not have anyone close with whom he could share his new-found fame as 'Six-Goal Shack', the nickname given him by the Geordies. So he boarded the train from Newcastle to Bradford on the Sunday morning, keen to hear what Marjorie and, to an even greater extent, his father, thought about his massive contribution to the goal-fest against Newport.

He was particularly anxious about his dad's reaction, because Shackleton senior seems to have made a point of never praising his son's performances – a tough-love policy that Shack loyally felt helped to keep 'my feet on the ground and my head out of the clouds'. One extraordinary example of his father's intransigence on the matter followed that wartime game when Shack had scored five of Bradford Park Avenue's goals against Hull City. Arriving home that evening, he found his father in his armchair in front of the fire. Knowing it had been one of those days when everything had come off for him, young Shack was convinced that this was one occasion when Shackleton senior simply could not avoid complimenting him.

Some hope! Driven to distraction by his father's stubborn silence,

Shack could not help asking him whether he thought he had had a good match. That was a mistake. 'Your sister Irene could have back-heeled another three into the net!' came the dismissive reply. It was a relief for the son, then, to be greeted with just silence from the old man after his six-goal debut for Newcastle. 'As long as he was uncomplaining, I was satisfied I had done everything expected of me,' concluded Shack, rather sheepishly.

All on the field continued to go swimmingly until his fourth game with Newcastle took him back to Park Avenue. There, with his wife Marjorie overdue with their first baby, attending the match against doctor's orders and assuring their Bradford friends that her Len would hit the headlines that day, he missed a penalty in a 2-1 defeat by his old club. Typically, he tried to make a positive out of the negative. Failing like that, he consoled himself, was a valuable lesson: it taught him that no footballer should expect to be on top all the time – a lesson that ought to be driven home to every player, preferably when young enough to appreciate it.

The surprising thing about that game is that it was one of the few occasions on which Shack seems to have lost his customary self-possession and decisiveness. What threw this masterly manipulator of the ball was the fact that he was facing one of his old mates, in Chick Farr, the Park Avenue goalkeeper. Having spent hours with Farr practising penalty kicks, Shackleton was not sure in his own mind how to approach this, their first confrontation in a League match. Since he normally hit a penalty with his right foot to the goalkeeper's right, he thought Farr would expect that; so he decided to aim for his left instead. But then he thought the goalkeeper would expect him to change his normal kick, and wondered whether he should stick to his normal routine. Still debating in his mind which side to put it, he was all of a dither as he ran up to take the kick and Farr saved easily.

Defeat at Park Avenue was one of the comparatively few setbacks suffered by Newcastle in what was turning out to be an encouraging season for them. The purchase of Shackleton completed a formidable forward line that read Jackie Milburn, Roy Bentley, Charlie Wayman, Len Shackleton and Tommy Pearson. The firepower it carried was reflected in the number of League goals they scored. Newcastle's total of 95 was easily the highest and way ahead of those registered by the two clubs, Manchester City (78) and Burnley (65), promoted from the Second Division in 1946-47. However, 62 goals conceded and 13 defeats suffered meant they had to settle for fifth place.

Shackleton was not only playing alongside Milburn, but working with him. Still a Bevin Boy at the time of his transfer, Shack turned down offers of jobs from nearly every pit in Northumberland and Durham, all of them eager to enjoy the prestige of employing Newcastle's new, £13,000 signing. Instead, he agreed to go and work with Milburn, a real pitman from the famous mining town of Ashington, who had told him he had a 'smashing' job at the Gosforth pit. Shackleton was Milburn's labourer at the Hazlerigg workshops, where 'Wor Jackie' had moved after leaving Ashington colliery. Milburn had a motor bike, and he and Shack – still wearing their pit gear – travelled to St James' Park on it three times a week for training.

Working with an authentic and conscientious miner like Milburn came as an unpleasant surprise to Shackleton after the cushy number he had fiddled for himself at Fryston. Shack was a bit taken aback when Milburn told him he worked every day, from half-past seven in the morning until six o'clock in the evening, but did not take him too seriously. He soon discovered his mistake. Keen to make a good impression, and hoping the boss would not expect him to do it often, he reported at the pit dead on time for his first day's work. It was pitch dark, and there was six inches of snow on the ground; but Shack perked up a little when the foreman told him that he could work with Milburn, who would look after him while he was at the colliery.

This was the winter of 1946-47, one of the coldest on record, and everything was frozen solid. Milburn, though, kept insisting he was on a 'smashing' job, so Shackleton thought he must have some sort of dodge up his sleeve. That was another mistake. Milburn promptly led him into a snow-covered field, where the two of them had to wade through snow and ice to reach a half-submerged pile of steel girders. The 'smashing' job, it turned out, involved lifting those girders and carrying them across the field. Whenever he wanted a good nightmare, Shackleton joked in later life, he would just go to sleep thinking about Gosforth Colliery, and about his days as a Bevin Boy in general.

Despite the fact that two of their key players were slinging girders around in their spare time, Newcastle also enjoyed a long run in the FA Cup the first season Shackleton was with them. Decisive victories over Crystal Palace and Southampton in the third and fourth rounds were followed by a tight, two-game struggle to overcome Leicester City in the fifth. Then a 2-0 win against Sheffield United, the favourites, took Newcastle into the semi-finals, where they were to meet Charlton Athletic at the Leeds United ground, Elland Road. And, oddly enough, it was at that exciting and promising point in their season that the relationship between Newcastle United and Len Shackleton went a little more sour.

Shack thought the preparations for the semi-final were all wrong. For a start, he believed it was a bad move to keep the team closeted away in special training at Seahouses, on the Northumberland coast, during the long period between the sixth round and the semi-final. The only time they were permitted to break camp was for League matches once a week. As a result, Shackleton felt, Newcastle's play lost some of its smooth rhythm.

The directors were running the team themselves at this point, with one of them, Stan Seymour, as honorary manager – whatever that meant; and Shack argued that they blundered by trying to keep the cup team intact and refusing to rest several players who obviously needed a break. He was convinced that, in particular, centre-forward Charlie Wayman, who was struggling to regain lost form, needed a rest; but they kept picking him to play. Picking him to play in every game but the semi-final, that is.

Along with most of Tyneside, Shackleton was aghast when it was decided to replace Wayman with George Stobbart for the game at Elland Road. This crucial change, combined with the monastic special training, seems to have undermined Newcastle's form and confidence totally: at any rate, they were thumped 4-0 by Charlton, the eventual winners of the tournament, in the semi-final and the affronted Wayman slapped in a transfer request – a reaction Shack thought thoroughly justified.

That was only the half of it. Immediately after the semi-final, Shackleton and club captain Joe Harvey went on strike. The reason was the difficulties both were experiencing over housing in Newcastle. In Shackleton's case, he claimed that the board had failed to honour a promise to allow him to rent a semi-detached house similar to the one he had given up in Bradford. Angry about being let down, he decided to stay in Yorkshire after the semi-final – regardless of the result – until something was done about his house. For similar reasons, fellow-Bradfordian Harvey also declined to return to Newcastle with the team.

There followed a short stand-off between players and club before Shack was ordered to appear before the Newcastle directors on the Thursday following the semi-final. When, on entering the boardroom, he found himself confronted by a 'stern-looking collection of businessmen turned soccer sages', he kept telling himself that he was in the right and had nothing to fear. But the prosecutor-in-chief was solicitor Willie McKeag, later to become Lord Mayor of Newcastle, and his courtroom expertise was such that Shackleton was soon beginning to believe he, and not the club, was the villain of the piece. Indeed, only the intervention of another director, John Lee, saved the day for Shack.

Lee, whom Shack described as a very good friend of all the United players, made the sensible suggestion that the meeting should be adjourned so that Stan Seymour could be asked to confirm or deny the player's claim that he had been promised the tenancy of a semi-detached house. Why this simple check had not been made in the first place is rather baffling; but now Shackleton's future at the club seemed to hang on the word of one man. Understandably, he was worried that Seymour might deny making the promise. If that proved to be the case, he knew the board would believe one of their fellow directors rather than him, a mere professional footballer.

Although temporarily suspended, along with Joe Harvey, Shackleton went along to St James' Park to watch the Good Friday game against Birmingham City. There, to his great relief, Seymour tipped him the wink that he had nothing to worry about. Then, after a directors' meeting following the game, Lee came out to say: 'You shall have your house, Len. It is up to us to keep our word.' That was not quite the end of the matter, though. Anxious that it should not look to the supporters as if Shackleton and Harvey's strike action had forced the club to give way, Newcastle issued a statement to the press in which it was suggested that the housing difficulties of both players had been sorted out because they were in the wrong and had apologised. Shack was willing to bite the bullet because Newcastle took him and his wife house-hunting within minutes of the meeting ending. They were installed in a new home at Gosforth by the following Wednesday, and the speed with which the club had acted, he felt, proved the justice of his case.

It was not long before there was another clash between Shackleton and Newcastle, however. At Christmas, 1947, he and his best friend in football, goalkeeper Jack Fairbrother, incurred the wrath of new manager George Martin. They did so by refusing to accompany the other players, as ordered, to watch Charlton Athletic, their opponents in the third round of the FA Cup, play a League game at Middlesbrough over the holiday period. Shack, who had been given permission to join his wife at the home of friends in Leicester, and Fairbrother stubbornly refused to change the plans they had made to be with their families. 'The events of Christmas 1947,' Shackleton acknowledged, 'had the effect of widening the gap already opened between the club and myself.'

Given the fractiousness of the relationship between Shackleton and Newcastle, it is not entirely impossible to believe what sounds very much like an apocryphal story that Malcolm Macdonald says he was told by Joe Harvey. According to 'Supermac', it happened when Newcastle were playing Manchester City, then a very good side captained by Don Revie. Before the game, the Newcastle manager, George Martin, is said to have told Shack in front of the other players: 'Today's a bloody important game. We need the points, we need to win it! If you get a hat-trick, you can come off.'

'It's one of those things you say, isn't it?' adds Macdonald. 'Anyway, Len only went and scored a hat-trick in the first 20 minutes, then walked off. After 20 minutes, Newcastle are 3-0 up, with all three of the goals scored by Shackleton, and he's walked off! There were no substitutes in those days, of course, and the manager was furious. 'What the bloody hell are you doing?' he yelled at Shack. To which Len replied: 'You said to me ...' That is how Len was: he would take people at their word, then turn their words back against them. Man. City, left with most of the game still to play against ten men, came back from 3-0 down to win 4-3.'

Since none of the facts fits any of the results between Newcastle and City during Shackleton's two years at St James' Park, what is said to have happened cannot have involved the Manchester club. Perhaps the opponents were different; perhaps it never really happened at all. The point here, though, is that Shackleton's personality was so unusual and unconventional – and his talent so exceptional – that people would have no difficulty in believing that it might have happened, that he could have been capable of such bloody-minded behaviour simply to make the manager and directors suffer. As Macdonald observes: 'Which footballer today could go and create a story, even if it is mythical, by scoring goals as and when he wanted? There isn't one: not even Alan Shearer.' It is worth adding, I think, that it is unlikely Shack, spiteful and lazy as he could be, would have been so unprofessional as to leave his team-mates in the lurch like that.

Shackleton's fraught relationship with Newcastle was not helped by circumstances beyond his control. In January 1948, on the day before his club were due to travel down to London to play Charlton at The Valley in the third round of the FA Cup, Shackleton's 15-month-old son, Graham, was taken seriously ill. But not wanting to worsen things between himself and the club, Shack reluctantly left his wife to wait for the doctor while he made a late dash to catch the train with the rest of the team. Having telephoned Marjorie as soon as he arrived at King's Cross, the worried father was told that his young son had been taken to hospital. Then, in the middle of a night of torment, Shackleton was informed that Graham had undergone an emergency operation, but that it was too early to tell whether it had been a success.

Understandably, Shack did not get much sleep that night. The telephone kept ringing with messages about his son's condition, which remained stable. Even so, he was unsure the following morning whether to return to Newcastle for what could have been a last look at young Graham or play in the match at Charlton. Unwisely, you cannot help but feel, he decided to play: he could not possibly have had his mind fully on a game that Charlton won 2-1. Straight after it, Shack jumped into a waiting taxi, headed for King's Cross and made the journey back to Newcastle that the club ought to have arranged for him a lot earlier.

Arriving at the hospital where his son was being treated, he was relieved to find the operation had been a success. Even so, he was warned by Marjorie not to be shocked by the sight that awaited him. Graham, surrounded by glass screens, had both legs in splints and both arms spread-eagled. The boy looked terrible, and Shack must have uttered a silent prayer of thanks when the doctor told him what a narrow escape his son had had. The problem had been a knot in the intestine, which had been untied – but only just in time: another hour and it might have been too late. The doctor also explained that Graham's 'stringing-up' was intended merely to stop him scratching.

Having gone through all this trauma, Shack was not best pleased to be treated unsympathetically by Newcastle on the Monday morning. When captain Joe Harvey was doling out a pound note each to the players to cover the cost of a theatre ticket, taxi fare and a meal in London (my, how the cost of living in the capital has changed during the past 56 years!), he told Shackleton that he had been ordered not to give him any expenses. While Shack conceded that Newcastle were well within their rights to deny him the money, since he had not stayed over on the Saturday night, he felt it very mean to withhold this single pound note just because he had rushed home to see his son in hospital.

He also had trouble getting his fare for the taxi from Charlton to

King's Cross. That amounted to 25 shillings plus a half-a-crown tip (which translates as one pound, seven shillings and sixpence in all). It was exactly the amount he had paid out, and he was annoyed that there were hints he was over-charging. While admitting that, in other circumstances, he might have claimed more than he had actually spent, he stressed that he wanted no profit from rushing home to see his sick son. 'Twenty five shillings means nothing to a football club,' he grumbled, 'so the dispute over the taxi fare was obviously just one more effort by Newcastle to antagonise me.'

Shackleton claims there were so many 'little, nasty things' happening at St James' Park between 1946 and 1948 that they prompted frequent transfer requests from players who might have been expected to be contented. He cites, in particular, the case of left-winger Tommy Pearson. According to Shack, 'loveable' Tommy, who in dressing-room discussions invariably went out of his way to be fair to the directors, was treated badly by them. It was hinted that there was a troublesome clique at Newcastle and that Pearson was the ringleader. That sort of shabby treatment shattered Pearson's loyalty to the club, claimed Shackleton, and hastened a return to his native Scotland as an Aberdeen player.

Shackleton's turn to leave came before that. He was playing golf with Pearson and Jack Fairbrother, his close friends, at Tynemouth on a cold February day in 1948, when a messenger from the clubhouse told him he was to report immediately to St James' Park. Shack took his time, of course. He and his two regular partners finished the remaining 17 holes before Pearson drove him to the ground, both of them knowing that Shackleton was almost certainly about to be transferred. Only a week earlier, he had slapped in a transfer request after being dropped from the first team following a defeat. He knew it would be accepted because an unnamed Newcastle official had virtually told him so not long before. 'Get wise, Len. There's only one way to make money in football,' the official had advised him privately one day. Puzzled, Shack asked Jack Fairbrother what that meant. 'He's advising you to ask for a transfer and he'll help you get it,' his friend told him.

As Shackleton and Pearson parted at St James' Park, the latter told him he was doing the right thing and predicted correctly he himself would be following quite soon. 'I realised then just how badly Newcastle players were being handled,' said Shack, returning mercilessly to his favourite gripe, 'because, although it does not matter very much when a player of my temperament wants to move, there must be something seriously wrong if a loyal club man like Tommy Pearson decides he has had enough.'

Having seen Shackleton score 26 goals in 57 League appearances, plus another three in the FA Cup, and been entertained royally into the bargain, the Newcastle fans were a lot more reluctant than the directors to see him go. Hundreds of letters to the local newspapers made that much clear, and the workers at the huge Vickers Armstrong factory on Tyneside went so far as to stage a 'Keep Shack' protest meeting. It was all in vain, of course. With no fewer than 12 clubs said to be queuing up to buy the free-scoring inside-forward, the Newcastle board were eager to cash in on their gifted, but troublesome asset.

There was quite a queue for his services. One paper reported that Arsenal were ready to pay £20,000, a statement Shack found very amusing after having been kicked out of Highbury nine years previously, when the London club could have signed him for nothing; but the Gunners were said to have many rivals. Hull City, Portsmouth, Blackpool, Bolton Wanderers, Liverpool, Manchester City, Bury, Aston Villa and Sunderland were all said to be keen to sign him. All but Hull of those clubs were in the old First Division, the elite of English football, at the time; and Third Division (North)

Hull, with the legendary Raich Carter about to take over as manager of his old club from Major Frank Buckley, were very ambitious.

Shack, however, had eyes for only one of his suitors – Sunderland. Paying little heed to the bitter local rivalry between them and Newcastle, he made it clear his main consideration was to be able to 'go on living among the grand folk in Northumberland and Durham – the best people in the world.' He got his wish. As soon as he entered the Newcastle offices, Shackleton was informed that they had accepted an offer for him from Sunderland. That offer, it turned out, had been a shrewd, deal-clinching £20,050.

The extra £50 was the idea of one of the three Sunderland negotiators, Colonel Joe Prior, who calculated correctly that the other interested clubs would be frightened off if they heard the opening bid was in excess of £20,000, the maximum to which Sunderland's rivals were prepared to go. Thus, in February 1948, Len Shackleton became the first British footballer to crack the £20,000 barrier and left Second Division Newcastle for First Division Sunderland.

Although there had been a great clamour for Shack's services from a number of clubs, in reality it was no contest. That was largely because Sunderland had cleverly – not to mention illegally – outmanoeuvred all their rivals before the bidding even started. It was real cloak and dagger stuff. Shackleton first became aware of Sunderland's interest in him when 'a funny little man with his collar turned up and his trilby pulled down over his face' turned up on the doorstep of his Gosforth home one night.

The mysterious caller proved to be Sunderland scout Jack Hall, who told Shackleton that Bill Murray, the Sunderland manager, was around the corner in his car and wanting to speak to him. Shack, as cheeky as ever and perhaps wanting to test Murray's resolve to go through with this illegal approach, decided to make him wait.

Telling Hall that he was going out, when he'd had no intention of doing so previously, Shackleton and his wife, Marjorie, went through the motions of having a night out before hastening back home a couple of hours later hoping their little subterfuge had not ruined everything.

It was gone ten o'clock now, but Murray had not been deterred. There was another knock on the door by Hall, who took Shackleton to the next street, where the Sunderland manager was waiting. He had taken so much care not to be spotted that his car was parked in the shadows between lamp-posts. Once face-to-face with his quarry, though, Murray came straight to the point. He told Shack that Sunderland wanted to sign him and got a favourable response. This was a couple of days before the deadline for the auction planned by Newcastle, and Prior had discovered through a 'contact' at St James' Park that the bidding was expected to be around the £20,000 mark. His informant had also told him that if Sunderland could beat that figure, the player was virtually theirs. Hence the extra £50 on the fee. What amused Shack about it all was that the £20,050 Sunderland paid for him was £7,000 more than the figure they had decided they could not afford when he had been up for sale at Bradford Park Avenue only two years earlier.

Long after Shackleton had bridged the deepest football divide of the North-East, the relationship between him and Newcastle continued to fester. Having encountered so much trouble in getting his previous employers to honour their promise to let him rent a semi-detached house like the one he had had in Bradford, Shackleton immediately took the three Sunderland officials, directors Prior and Syd Collings and manager Billy Murray, to see his wife at their Gosforth home. There, he made the trio promise Marjorie that he and she would be able to rent one 'just as nice' in Sunderland. In response, Murray gave him cast-iron assurances on the subject, so much so that the expensive, demanding newcomer came to the conclusion that this was one club which knew the right way to treat players.

It had been agreed with Newcastle that the Shackletons could stay on in Gosforth while they were house-hunting in the Sunderland area, but Len claimed that his former club nagged him so constantly about when he was going to move that he could not stand it any longer. So, after a week or two, they moved to a friend's house in Newcastle until they found somewhere to live in Sunderland. Pointing out that the club had had 18 months' service from him before selling him at a profit of £7,050, Shack considered Newcastle's insistence on reclaiming their house petty in the extreme.

There is little doubt that Newcastle were not the most considerate of employers at the time Len Shackleton was one of their players. Yet the uncomfortable fact remains that, almost as soon as he had gone, they entered perhaps the most successful period in their history. At the end of that season, 1947-48, they won promotion back to the First Division, where they stayed for 13 years. Then, with the dashing Jackie Milburn switching from the right wing to centre-forward, Chilean international George Robledo replacing Shack at inside-left and another gifted new signing, Bobby Mitchell, taking over from Tommy Pearson on the left wing, they recorded the remarkable hat-trick of FA Cup triumphs in 1951, 1952 and 1955 that practically defines the club to this day. As Shackleton joked in that Sky Sports interview by Brian Moore: 'They won the Cup three times – despite not having me!'

It is not necessarily the case that Newcastle were a better team without Shackleton. They may well have enjoyed the same amount of success, or even more, had he stayed: we shall never know. What is not in contention is that both Milburn and Joe Harvey had their doubts about his usefulness to the team. For all their admiration of his skill, they worried about his commitment. 'Shack was unbelievable!' Milburn was quoted as saying in the 1990 biography of him by Mike Kirkup, *Jackie Milburn In Black And White*. 'If he had had the guts or the will to want to do well, instead of joking and carrying on, he was untouchable as a footballer... He was absolutely the tops in ball control.

'He was doing these things all the time in training, making mugs of goalkeepers. I've seen Jack Fairbrother dive at his feet in training, and Shack would just let him come, then just ease the ball away. Why, the ball was only inches from Jack's fingers, and Jack was wild-eyed. He would have killed him if he'd got him. Him (Shackleton) and Tommy Pearson gave an exhibition one day at Newcastle against Cardiff, when they kept the ball between them with six or seven defenders around them, frightened to death to tackle. And this happened for 90 minutes, before we beat them 4-1.

'It was sheer entertainment with Shack. He admitted later on that he had no interest, but he just wanted to feel that he'd entertained the public. Oh, he was unbelievable – but hopeless! Joe Harvey says to George Martin: 'We'll *never* win anything with Shackleton in the team. We've got to get rid of him.' And it was true! I've nothing against Len, he was a smashing fella, but he had no interest other than entertaining the crowd. He would rather beat three men than lay on a winning goal. And we got rid of him! He signed for Sunderland.'

There was an extraordinary postscript to Shackleton's two-year spell with Newcastle, and Milburn was directly involved in it. Three years after Shack had left St James' Park, the Magpies reached the first of those three FA Cup finals they became famous for winning. And while they were preparing to go out to face Blackpool in 1951, Shackleton somehow wangled his way into their Wembley dressing-room. There, in all seriousness, he tried to persuade his former team-mates to refuse to play in English football's world-famous, end-of-season showpiece unless they were paid properly for entertaining a crowd of 100,000. In other words, he tried to get Newcastle to go on strike an hour or two before the start of the FA Cup final.

Milburn related the story in Mike Kirkup's book. 'That's why I came to admire Shack more than anybody,' said the Newcastle centre-forward. 'He insisted that we were playing for buttons. He insisted on this, way back to the war years. Aye! In fact, he came over just before the '51 Final – he was playing for Sunderland at the time – and spoke to the lads. 'Hey, you want to refuse to go on the bloody pitch,' he says, 'because they're making nearly £40,000 on the gate.' It was three and a tanner for a ticket then, and about a couple of quid for a seat. And he went through the whole routine of what they were clicking, the FA, and how much they were making, and what we were getting.'

Shackleton's outrageous intervention was confirmed by another member of the Newcastle team that day, left-half Charlie Crowe. 'He came down to the '51 Final when we were there,' Crowe told me. 'How the hell he got in I don't know, but he came into our dressing-room and said to Jackie, 'Jackie, this is about the best time. What you want to do is say that you don't feel like playing: then you'll start to get some money!' As is plain from the fact that Newcastle beat Blackpool 2-0 that day, with Milburn scoring both goals, they did not act on Shack's advice. Seemingly, the team decided that, if they refused to play, the board would soon draft in another 11 players only too willing to take their places in an FA Cup final.

From what Milburn said about the incident, it is clear that Shackleton was simply repeating something he had always believed: namely, that English professional footballers were seriously underpaid in terms of the income they generated at the gate. Four years later, in his autobiography, Shack spelled out his complaints about the FA Cup final in particular. Why, he argued, should the players on the winning side get restricted bonuses of only £20 each – and the broken-hearted losers nothing at all – when a normal Wembley attendance for the game's showpiece normally produced takings of £50,000? He underlined his objection to this imbalance graphically by pointing out that, at a recent final, the massed bands that had played before the game and at the interval had received £320 – or £80 more in total than the players who had provided the main event.

However, the fact that Shackleton tried to get the Newcastle players to take the sort of direct action that would have endangered their participation in the club's first FA Cup final for 19 years does suggest some malice aforethought towards a board of directors he never liked. It is perhaps relevant here that he complained bitterly about not having received any sort of bonus from Newcastle for having played 25 games for them in their promotion season, 1947-48, before his transfer to Sunderland. In fact, it seems just as likely that he was acting out of mischievousness as on a point of principle when he bowled into that Wembley dressing room to try to stir up unrest.

Curiously, there is not a mention of that little drama in Shack's own autobiography. His only reference to that particular final concerned the pre-match row there was the night before the game over the tickets allocated to the Newcastle players' wives. Apparently, the wives were understandably furious when they discovered that, instead of sitting together close to the Royal Box, as had been promised, so they could see their husbands shaking hands with the monarch at the time, King George VI, and perhaps lifting the cup, they would be scattered all over the stadium, some of them not even under cover (in those days, only the two sides of Wembley were roofed).

According to Shackleton, when Ida Harvey informed her husband, Joe, about the shabby way the wives had been treated and demanded something be done about it, 'the balloon went up'. The angry players told the Newcastle directors they would refuse to play unless the situation were corrected, an ultimatum that quickly persuaded the board to back down and give the wives seats nearer the Royal Box. Even then, Shack insisted, Mrs Harvey was not close enough to see her husband lift the FA Cup after Newcastle had beaten Blackpool.

Given the rapid results that threat of strike action produced, it is perhaps a little surprising the players did not respond more readily to Shackleton's subversive suggestion about match fees shortly before kick-off. Maybe the ticket business was what prompted him to make it in the first place. But the Newcastle players' refusal to hold the club to ransom over money was entirely understandable: when you are that close to playing in an FA Cup final, you don't want to do anything to endanger it. Clearly, though, Shack had a point when he argued that the Newcastle of those days was not a happy or well-run club.

'I knew what the Newcastle fans were like because of the wartime football between Bradford (Park Avenue) and Newcastle,' Shackleton told Brian Moore, 'but the club, as a club – those people upstairs, and whatnot – I never hit it off with. Fortunately, when I left, I went to Sunderland, which is 12 miles down the road. So, in effect, you are playing amongst the same kind of people. I loved the Geordies – though the Sunderland people would stone me if they heard me call them Geordies: the local name is Mackem.

'The fans are so brilliant at Newcastle that I feel guilty when I call them (names). But I'm not calling the fans, I'm calling the club. Just because I played 11 years (actually, it was nine and a half) for Sunderland and only 18 months for Newcastle, I've no bias against Newcastle – I don't care who beats them!'

CHAPTER FOUR
BREAKING THE BANK

What Len Shackleton did not realise, perhaps, when he joined
Sunderland as English football's first £20,000 footballer, was
that the 'grandest club in soccer' as he called them proudly and
prophetically, were launching one of the most ambitious attempts to
buy success the game had seen. Between 1948 and 1955, they scoured
the British Isles, and beyond, for talented new players and bought 15
or 16 of them for a total outlay of about £250,000 – very big money
half a century ago, big enough certainly for Sunderland to be labelled
the 'Bank of England' club and pre-date Roman Abramovich's
Chelsea by quite some time.

At £20,050, Shack was one of the more expensive acquisitions.
Others were Wales international centre-forward Trevor Ford
(£30,000), Wales international centre-half Ray Daniel (£27,500),
England international outside-left Billy Elliott (£26,000) and
England international inside-forward Ivor Broadis (£18,000).
Shackleton recalled pulling Ted Purdon's leg when the South
African striker was signed for just £12,000. 'You mustn't
mix with us,' he said to the newcomer, while chatting to Daniel, his
best friend at the club, and Elliott. 'Go and talk to the other serfs
and peasants.'

Sunderland could afford to splash the cash because they were playing in front of 60-70,000 crowds at their old ground, Roker Park, every other week and attracting big attendances away from home in the good old days when the visitors could still claim a portion of the gate money. Not only that, but their wage bill, in common with all the other Football League clubs, was negligible by comparison. With players earning only £10 a week during the season, and just £8 in the close season (this increased gradually over the years, but the top rate of pay did not exceed £20 until 1961), the iron hand of the maximum wage saw to it that the clubs were comfortably in profit. In fact, this serious financial imbalance was to become a real bee in Shackleton's bonnet, as we shall see in due course.

For the time being, however, he was happy enough to mount a defence of his new club's expansive approach to team building. Sunderland, he argued in his 1955 autobiography, had always had progressive ideas. In common with clubs such as Arsenal, Newcastle United and Aston Villa, they worked on the assumption that only the best was good enough, and they were prepared to make front page news to get the best. Shack also reminded his readers that the Wearside club had frequently been condemned and ridiculed by lesser rivals for being among the most active participants in the transfer market.

'From Plainmoor to Pittodrie, football's Land's End and John O'Groats,' he said, 'the Sunderland manager Billy Murray and his free-spending directors were abused; they were accused of attempting to buy the honours of the game with a cheque book.' He could also have pointed out that Sunderland were not the only club trying to buy success at that time. There was a good example close at hand, since Newcastle spent something like £110,000 on just 11 players, Shackleton included, between 1945 and 1950.

The guiding hand behind Sunderland's lavish outlay belonged to the Sunderland chairman, Bill Ditchburn. A self-made furniture tycoon, Ditchburn had only one passion in life, and that was his home-town football club. 'He had red and white eyes,' said fellow director and close friend Bill Martin. Urged on by Ditchburn, Sunderland were keen to recapture the prominence in English football they had enjoyed at the turn of the century, and then briefly during the years leading up to the Second World War. The latter period had seen them win the League Championship in 1935-36 and, the following season, the FA Cup. Sadly, however, it was all to end in tears.

It nearly started that way, too. In contrast to Shackleton's six-goal debut for Newcastle, his first First Division game for Sunderland was a 5-1 hammering by Derby County at the Baseball Ground; and, at the end of his first season at Roker Park, 1947-48, Sunderland finished third from bottom of the table, only four points clear of relegation. To have gone down would have been a particularly severe blow because it was Sunderland's proud boast at the time that they were the only club to have maintained unbroken membership of the old First Division since being elected to it in 1890. It was all a bit of a shock for Shack, and he confessed that he thought he had dropped the biggest clanger of his life by joining the Wearsiders. Indeed, he told his wife not only that he thought Sunderland had bought him just to try to keep them up, but that there was no way he could save them.

Later, with the benefit of hindsight, Shackleton was a lot more upbeat – though not entirely uncritical. Recalling how the criticism of Sunderland's buying policy had turned to amusement as the 'Bank of England' club sank towards the bottom of the First Division, he applauded the Roker Park directors for ignoring the wiseacres who delighted in reminding them of the adage that you can't buy success. 'As if determined to demonstrate their contempt for public opinion,' he said, 'the Sunderland board bought bigger and bigger, until only one first-team player – right-half Stan Anderson – had been signed without payment of a colossal fee.'

At the same time, the realist in Shackleton compelled him to admit that Sunderland had been guilty of some indiscriminate buying and had made some regrettable signings through a failure to research the players properly. In the dressing room, he said, they were well aware that the 'wheat would have to be sorted from the chaff' before Sunderland started winning matches. In fact, he even admitted that they were not a team in the true sense of the word. 'When 11 famous footballers, each an individual star in his own right, are suddenly thrown together and expected to fit in as a machine,' he reasoned, 'there is bound to be some discord. It takes time to harness and control a team of thoroughbreds. It took time to achieve the blend at Roker Park.'

Discord there certainly was in the team Sunderland were purchasing off the shelf, and nowhere more than in the prickly relationship between inside-forward Len Shackleton and centre forward Trevor Ford. It was crucial, in terms of creating and taking goal-scoring chances, that these two players should be on the same wavelength, but they simply could not get on with each other. In his own 1962 book, *Soccer with the Stars*, Billy Bingham, the Northern Ireland international winger Sunderland bought from Glentoran for £10,000, also defended his new club's buying policy up to a point. But then he added: 'The flaw in their thinking, however, was the assumption that every star player must be potentially a good player for Sunderland, irrespective of his style or of his known limitations. They were not to know, of course, that two such outstanding players as Len Shackleton and Trevor Ford would never be able to fit in with each other.'

Bravely, Shack addressed the problem head-on in *Return of the*

Clown Prince, his follow-up in 2000 to the more famous *Clown Prince of Soccer*. He certainly did not spare his own feelings by quoting directly from Ford's 1957 autobiography, *I Lead the Attack*. Acknowledging that the two of them had taken an instant dislike to each other, he reproduced the following passage from Ford's book: 'Since the war more centre-forwards have "bit the dust" playing for Sunderland than any club I know… Sunderland had started the 1948-49 season with their new inside-right signing from Newcastle – Len Shackleton – and straight away his dazzling dribbles and individual ball jugglery became the hub of nearly every attacking move.

'From this moment on, Sunderland centre-forwards wore a worried look on their brow. What could they do? Here was a style of inside-forward play completely foreign to them – and few of them found the answer… You can't blame Shack for the type of game he plays. For him clowning seems just as much a part of the game as scoring goals. But you can blame the club for permitting it…Shackleton is amongst the immortals as a ball-player. His dazzling dribbles, his weaving and bobbing with the ball at his feet, is a heartbreak to opponents and a joy to watch, but what a pity his clowning has been allowed to nullify much of the co-ordination of the forward line…

'Twenty-one other players on the field were transfixed as Shack did tricks with the ball the like of which I'd never seen before. The crowd loved it. This was the clowning Shack at his best, but where did it get us? Precisely nowhere. The result was that when he did make a move, the opposing defence was in position and the attack broke down. Time and again when I thought Shack was going to slip a goalscoring pass to me he would veer off.'

Seeking an objective view of a problematic relationship that, quite obviously, left Ford unsure whether to laugh or cry, Shackleton quoted from Billy Bingham's autobiography. 'The situation between Shackleton and Ford had never been a happy one and now it deteriorated,' wrote Bingham. 'They appeared to dislike each other off the field and never seemed to strike up an understanding on it. Each blamed the other for this state of affairs and I suppose there were faults on both sides. Trevor, supported by most of the press, claimed that Shack wouldn't play to him.

'I remember that after one spate of criticism on this subject, we went out to Holland to play the Dutch "B" team and won 7-3. Len made one of the goals by going right through the Dutch defence with an amazing dribble, finally sending the goalkeeper the wrong way with a feint. Then, when he had only to tap the ball in, he instead rolled it back to Ford, somewhere near the 18-yard line. "Here you are Fordy," he shouted, "don't say I never give you a pass." Trevor Ford controlled himself well enough to be able to crash the ball into the back of the net.

'Considering what a great footballer he was, it can hardly be denied that Shack should have been able to give any centre-forward a reasonable service. "Fordy", of course, wasn't just any centre-forward, he was the most dynamic spearhead in the game at that time. Yet he had his shortcomings, too. When Trevor complained that he never knew what Shackleton was going to do next he wasn't telling us anything new, because most of us thought that half the time. Shack didn't know what he was going to do next himself. But you didn't have to play with him long to realise that one of his favourite moves was the reverse pass.

'Thus, if I saw Len set off on a diagonal run carrying the ball towards me on the right wing I could be fairly sure that his final pass wouldn't be to me, in front of him, but somewhere to his left and behind him. Poor "Fordy", who wasn't a great positional player at the best of times, never seemed to cotton on to this, and consequently if he was in the right place at the right time it was more by accident than design.'

At this point in the argument, it is probably worth mentioning that one of the greatest attacking players British football has seen never had any trouble combining with Len Shackleton. Sir Tom Finney, who first played alongside Shack for the Football League towards the end of the war and partnered him several times afterwards in representative football, says he invariably enjoyed the experience. 'I always found him very simple to play with,' Sir Tom insisted 'It was a question of reading the play, really. I think that accounted for a lot of the players he played with – reading the game and how they wanted to give you the ball; but I just felt he was a very skilful player and great to play with.'

Ford defended himself against charges of not being able to read Shackleton's intentions by pointing to the service he got from Sunderland's other inside-forward. 'Ivor Broadis may not have reached Shack's heights as a ball-player,' argued the big Welshman, 'but he was a prince to centre-forwards, for he would invariably draw his man and then send a pin-point pass to the advancing leader. As inside-forwards, Shack and Broadis were devastating in the way they could bamboozle the defence and if we had been able to combine in the orthodox way, I'm sure Sunderland would have set up goal-scoring records. Perhaps we might have helped the club to their most elusive target, the championship of Division One...'

Clearly, this destructive personal relationship was not helping the team and could not be allowed to continue. Matters came to a head following a game at Aston Villa, when Ford refused to play the following week. He told manager Billy Murray that, in effect, he had to choose between Shackleton and himself, because he would not play if Shack were in the team. Murray tried to broker a peace deal between the two of them, but Ford refused to accede to the manager's request that they should shake hands and make up.

'Shack and I were as different as chalk and cheese,' wrote Ford. 'We had developed our own styles of play – Shack as the ball-playing clown; myself as the tearaway centre-forward. Shack preferred to toy with the ball and the opposition; I preferred to steamroller the defences and blast for the net. It was impossible for Shack to change his style to suit me, and impossible for me to change mine to suit him. In that, and that only, we came out of the same melting pot, and to me, at any rate, there never seemed any chance of us hitting it off as part of a team. I never played with Shackleton again…'

In the end, Sunderland decided to cut their losses. Significantly, however, it was Ford they decided to sell, and not Shackleton. In all probability, they calculated that Shack was the greater crowd-puller and that it was easier to replace Ford than him. Bingham summed up the end of the affair nicely: 'Eventually, the only remaining remedy, short of transferring one or the other, was to play them in alternate matches. This ridiculous state of affairs clearly couldn't last for long and one Saturday evening in November [1953], Ford was quietly transferred to Cardiff City. The consolation for the shattered dream of the Sunderland board was that at least they got back the £30,000 they had paid for him three years earlier...'

So far as Ivor Broadis is concerned, there was no need for Sunderland to buy Ford in the first place. Living in retirement in Carlisle, he told me that he thought the forward line was working perfectly well as it was. 'When I went to Sunderland,' he said, 'Shack and I were lined up with Dickie Davis, who was the centre-forward, and the first season there we scored I don't know how many goals between us. Then, for some reason, they bought Trevor Ford. I'm not suggesting Trevor wasn't a great player, but Dickie Davis had scored something like 19 or 20 goals that season, and I could never understand why they wanted to change that trio.'

As for Ford's assertion that he received a much better service from him than from Shackleton, Broadis said: 'Yes, well, I don't know about that,' before quickly changing the subject. Touchingly, in view of the fact that both of his former team-mates are now dead, he also asked not to be quoted on what he told me about the sort of passes Shackleton would give Ford. But is pretty clear that Shack had the capacity and the mischievous nature, as we shall see from subsequent examples, to make other players look bad if he so wished. 'I wouldn't say they were the best of friends, let's put it that way!' said Broadis in a pithy summation of the relationship.

As the 'baby' of that so-called Bank of England team, wing-half and local boy Stan Anderson arrived on the scene too late to witness the Shackleton-Ford feud at first hand. Even so, he is able to offer some interesting observations on the matter. 'That was just before my time,' he said, 'but I heard all about it. They said Shack used to play the ball just in front of Trevor, so he couldn't get to it; and he was probably clever enough to have done that. But the opposite was true of him in the first match I played when I got into the team. Dickie Davis had replaced Ford at centre-forward and, thinking about it later on, Shack tried his damnedest to make Dickie a better player. He was knocking every ball through to Dickie, who scored two or three goals against Wolves that day. To be honest, I think Shack was trying to secure Dickie's place in the team.'

Billy Bingham describes Ford as 'a typical Welsh boy with jet black hair in a widow's peak at the front and sturdy shoulders. Not a big six-footer, but five-ten or eleven.' And judging by Anderson's other comments on the uneasy relationship between Shackleton and Ford, it is conceivable that there was an element of physical jealousy in it so far as Shack was concerned. 'When we used to see him in the dressing room, Trevor was always combing his hair in the mirror, and Shack probably took umbrage at him over that,' added Anderson. 'He was always a very smartly dressed lad was Trevor, good-looking as well, and Shack probably thought, "Well, I'm a better player than him. I'll show him!" '

Another slant on the issue comes from Johnny McSeveney, the Scot who was Shackleton's left-wing partner at Sunderland. He suggests that Shack may have resented Ford's closeness to the club's directors. 'Fordy was a one-off and he was more or less doing his own thing,' said McSeveney, 'but if Len could avoid giving him the ball, I don't think he gave him it. He'd find somebody else. I wouldn't say they were enemies or anything like that – I wouldn't go that far – but I think they were different personalities. And Fordy was in with the directors, as well. He was always around Billy Martin and that crowd. In those days, the directors used to come into the dressing room and they always went to the same people. You really had to get yourself established for it to happen to you. Bingham and I used to sit by ourselves.'

Despite the Shackleton-Ford problem, results began to improve pretty quickly for Sunderland after the 1947-48 season, when they had finished the season close to the relegation positions. The following season brought the humiliation of that famous FA Cup fourth-round defeat at Yeovil, but they moved up to eighth in the First Division. Then, in 1949-50, they came within an ace of winning the title. They finished third, just one point behind the top two, Portsmouth and Wolves, Portsmouth taking the honours for a second successive season, this time by virtue of a better goal average, as it was then. Ironically, Jimmy Stephen, Shackleton's old mate from his Park Avenue and Bevin Boy days, had moved to Pompey by then and was a member of the side that won the League Championship twice on the trot.

Not that there was ever any jealousy on Shack's part, as Stephen recalls. 'Len was a great guy,' he said. 'A story I often tell about him concerns my first game for Portsmouth in 1949. I was in the RAF then and couldn't always get away to play for them; but on this occasion I did. I got a weekend pass – 48 hours' leave – and the game, strangely enough, was against Sunderland at Fratton Park. Len, of course, had been transferred from Newcastle to Sunderland by then. So it was old mates joined up again, but on opposite sides. And, during the game, there was an incident that typified him. It was over a 50-50 ball that either of us could have got to; but Len, knowing it was my first game for Portsmouth, shouted: "Yours, Jimmy!" and let me have the ball. And I thought: "My God, our friendship comes before club loyalty!" That was terrific. What a thing to do!'

What was really galling for Shack and Sunderland that season was the fact that they had been in pole position for most of the campaign, then threw it away towards the last.

What cost them the title, Shackleton felt, was losing at home to Manchester City on 15 April 1950. It was a nightmarish defeat for Sunderland because victory had looked a formality. They had not lost at home all season, while City had not won away. In fact, City's form had been so poor, they ended up being relegated. But it was a day when nothing went right for Shackleton's team. They twice missed a penalty and lost 2-1. When the referee ordered the first penalty to be retaken because the goalkeeper had moved, Jackie Stelling again failed to score from the spot.

Since City's goalkeeper that day was the magnificent former German POW, Bert Trautmann, there was not too much shame in not putting the ball past him. 'Bert Trautmann had one of his games where he stopped everything,' recalled Broadis of that heartbreaking game. 'For some reason, I was played at centre-forward, where I'd never played before. That was two or three games before the end of the season, and we finished third, I think. But we should have won the First Division; and it was that, I think, that probably led to Dickie Davis being replaced by Trevor Ford.'

It was as close as Shack was ever going to get to a League Championship medal. Despite losing fewer games than anybody else in 1954-55, Sunderland were the lowest of three clubs who all finished four points behind the champions, Chelsea; but they were never really title contenders otherwise. Twice in succession, though, it looked as though they might win the FA Cup. In 1955 and 1956, they reached the semi-final of the competition without getting to Wembley, which must have been hard to bear. First, they lost to 1-0 Manchester City at Villa Park, then they went down 3-0 to Birmingham City at Hillsborough.

Understandably, Shackleton did not disguise the fact that being denied an FA Cup final appearance two years running was a bitter experience. Regretting that, in 1955, Sunderland had missed out on a North-Eastern final against Newcastle, he claimed that the semi-final against their bogey side, Manchester City, ought not to have been played because the pitch was unfit. He said there was so much water on the surface, the players had difficulty moving the ball more than a few yards and the contest was a complete farce. Not only that, but Sunderland had had the better of the game.

The sickening defeat at Villa Park completed a thoroughly miserable season for Shackleton. It had not started that way, his England recall towards the end of 1954 and Sunderland's lead at the top of the First Division suggesting great things were in store for him and his club. There was even some speculation that he could be voted 'Footballer of the Year'. But then came rejection again by England and Sunderland's sudden collapse in March and April of 1955. Shackleton's own form deteriorated to such an extent that he was dropped for the first time in his career following the dreadful performance he gave in an FA Cup fifth round replay against Swansea Town at Roker Park on 23 February. Sunderland won 1-0, but Shack confessed that they did so in spite of him rather than because of him.

His lethargic display could be traced to the illness – it sounds like influenza or a viral infection of some sort – he woke up with on the day, 12 February, that Sunderland lost at home for the first time against Charlton Athletic. However, an examination by the club doctor suggested he was imagining his illness and, foolishly, he played. He also played in the original cup tie at Swansea the following Saturday, a 2-2 draw, despite having spent most of the intervening week in bed. As he was feeling terrible and had done only one hour's training in the 11 days preceding the replay, it was hardly surprising that, in his own words, he played like 'a man in a dream' against Swansea at Roker Park.

'A man in a nightmare' might have been a better way of describing his state of mind because, for what must have been the first time in his Sunderland career, he was given the bird mercilessly by the fans. As his state of health was not common knowledge, many of them thought their idol guilty of not trying and let him know in no uncertain terms what they thought of him. Fully aware of how poor he had been, Shack went to see manager Billy Murray, apologised for his performance and asked to be left out of the first team. Murray complied, but then recalled Shackleton after one outing with the reserves. On his return to the first team, however, he picked up an ankle injury and missed three games because of it, one of them the 2-0 sixth round victory over Wolverhampton Wanderers at Roker Park.

While out of action, Shackleton was immensely heartened by the angry reaction of his fans to vicious criticism in one newspaper and suggestions that there might not be a place for him in the Sunderland side when he reported fit again. That moment came a week before the semi-final, and he was immediately reinstated at the expense of one of his best friends, Ken Chisholm, following an unimpressive display by the Sunderland forward line against Arsenal in the

League. Obviously a bit embarrassed about taking Chisholm's place, Shack swore that, despite the 1-0 defeat by Manchester City, he had played in that semi-final as well as he was ever likely to play.

For personal reasons, he saw the semi-final loss to Birmingham the following season as an even greater disappointment. Seemingly, he had promised his eldest son, Graham, then just a schoolboy, that he could go to Wembley and see the Queen if Sunderland reached the final. The boy had become very excited about that prospect, so it was not only his own disappointment Shack had to deal with when Sunderland lost at Hillsborough. He argued that, by teaching Graham how to lose, and lose properly, the experience had given the youngster a very important lesson in life. But that moralizing sounded more like making the best of a bad job than anything else.

At least one of the other Sunderland players thought Shackleton and the club might have been more successful had he not insisted on taking a one-track approach to winning things. Stan Anderson says: 'Lenny always used to say that it was impossible to win the Double. One year, when we were flying high in the League – I think we were second or third most of the time – and got to the semi-final of the FA Cup, there was a players' meeting. And I remember Lenny standing up and saying: 'You can't win them both, you know! You've got to decide – one or the other.' And we got beaten in the semi-final and finished fourth in the League, so we didn't win any of them.

'It was a shame, really, because the team that was at Sunderland when Lenny was in his heyday was good enough to win the Championship and probably good enough to win the FA Cup as well. We were probably the best side in the League at that particular time, but it just didn't happen for us. We lost games after Easter we should never have lost and finished up four points behind Chelsea. I think that if you go out and play each game as it comes, anything's possible. That's the attitude players have got today, but it probably wasn't there back then.'

It was not long after Sunderland's second successive FA Cup disappointment that the club, and English football, was rocked by the scandal that was to end an era at Roker Park. In January 1957, an informant signing himself only 'Mr Smith' wrote to the Football League giving them details of illegal payments he alleged the Wearsiders had made to players. These payments were regarded as illegal because they were in excess of the iniquitous maximum wage, enforced ruthlessly by the League from 1901 until 1961, and of the derisory £10 signing-on fee.

But the maximum wage, subscribed to by the majority of clubs because it supposedly ensured the poorer clubs were not priced out of the market, had the effect of leaving the better-supported clubs with plenty of money. That being the case, it was common knowledge that the financial rules were being flouted by many. As Simon Inglis pointed out in *Soccer in the Dock – A History of British Football Scandals, 1900-1965*: 'Primarily, because of the need to keep extra payments out of club accounts, "illegal" wages and bonuses usually changed hands in a variety of ways, often more subtle than the simple brown envelope full of bank-notes slipped into the jacket pocket.

'For example, the payments might be presented to the player's wife in the form of jewellery, which she could never wear in public because players were not supposed to earn enough to afford such luxuries. Instead the player would resell the jewellery for his "bonus". Occasionally extra money would be handed over by the conclusion of quite ridiculous transactions, such as in a couple of apocryphal cases from the 1950s when two players were "rewarded" by the sale of a worthless old car for over £1,000 and a mongrel dog for £500.

'Cheap or even free accommodation was another hidden benefit which allowed the club to keep officially to the maximum wage. One player after the Second World War was reputed to have rented his semi-detached house for one shilling (5p) a year. Another ploy was to let the player buy his club house for a pittance, then a few years later he would sell it at the true market value for an enormous profit. That way none of the bonus entered the club's books...The essential point, however, as both Jimmy Guthrie and Jimmy Hill each stressed as chairmen of the Players' Union, was that it was degrading for players to have to earn their due in such an underhand, unsavoury manner. Players' wages were already slipping behind the general rise in wage levels during the 1950s and it was humiliating for them to have to maintain and improve their standard of living by accepting "illegal" extras.'

The Players' Union were foremost among a growing body of radicals who wanted to blow the lid off the whole issue. They included Trevor Ford, who had been fined £100 when reported by the Chelsea chairman after asking him about the chances of a part-time job should he agree to join the London club instead of Sunderland in 1950. Six years later, Ford tried to expose the game's hypocrisy over illegal payments in his frank autobiography. He claimed that, when he signed for the club in 1950, manager Billy Murray had promised him a part-time job worth £1,000, plus the house of his choice to be decorated to his satisfaction at Sunderland's expense. But the Welsh international refused to give the authorities further proof without some guarantee of immunity. As a result, Ford, then 31 and playing in Cardiff City's reserve team, was suspended *sine die* by the League until he appealed successfully against the ban a couple of months later.

Content previously to sweep allegations of illegal payments under the carpet, the Football Association and the Football League were forced to act by the letter to the League from 'Mr Smith'. The information he provided about Sunderland's financial dealings was so detailed and accurate that it was strongly suspected that he was either one of the directors himself or being fed information by one of them. Why a club director would wish to inform on his colleagues is a question that has never really been answered, although the suggestion is that there was some sort of power struggle going on in the boardroom. So 'Mr Smith' could have been intent on punishing certain individuals rather than attempting to clean up the game.

When the FA and the League examined Sunderland's books, though, they could find nothing incriminating. It was not until Alan Hardaker, who had only just taken over as secretary of the League, queried the sum of £3,000 for the purchase of straw to protect the pitch from snow and frost that the case was cracked. When Hardaker checked with his brother Ernest, the chairman of Hull Rugby League Club, he was told £3,000 would buy straw for twenty-five seasons, never mind one. The entry in Sunderland's books would not have been irregular in itself; however, it was accompanied by the lightly pencilled and incriminating question, "Where do I post this?"

What a joint FA and League commission eventually uncovered was that Sunderland had placed orders with two contractors – one for straw, the other for tarmac – far in excess of requirements. When the suppliers delivered just the smaller, required amounts, Sunderland were given credit notes. These notes were then cashed at a later date and the extra money, which never appeared in the accounts, was paid over to the players. Although this had been going on for five years, the total sum involved – £5,427 14s 2d – was quite small. Once this had been divided among a number of players it hardly represented a windfall for any individual.

Sunderland chairman Bill Ditchburn, the eccentric little local businessman who had tried so hard to make his beloved club the foremost in the land through liberal use of the cheque-book and other, less straightforward financial processes, took full responsibility for the scam. Mistakenly, he thought only he and Bill Martin, of the eight-strong board, knew about the irregularities. He said he had always told the board to let him do the worrying, then added revealingly: 'But I didn't worry, because I knew every other club was doing the same.' What he should have worried about, clearly, was his relationship with some members of the board and what they had found out about the way he was running the club. 'His bluntness has upset everyone, including his fellow directors,' wrote Bob Pennington, the *Daily Express* football reporter, prophetically of Ditchburn at the time.

Yet the Sunderland chairman was extremely popular with both the workmen at his furniture factory and the players at Roker Park. No wonder, really, in the latter case because every new player he signed was immediately fixed up with a part-time job or commercial interest to secure his future. As Inglis pointed out: 'Rules or no rules, it was almost inconceivable to pay nearly £30,000 for a player to perform in front of packed grounds and yet compensate him for his move to the tune of only £10, a figure which had been agreed upon in 1891.' 'He is the kindest-hearted man I have ever met,' said one of the directors of Ditchburn's furniture business. He also had the common touch. Len Shackleton recalled how the Sunderland chairman, bow-tied and wing-collared, used to go out in his distinctive pink and mauve Rolls-Royce to buy fish and chips.

But none of this was protection against the wrath of the FA and the League. Ditchburn and Martin were banned permanently from football and *sine die* suspensions were imposed on two other members of the board, vice-chairman Stanley Ritson and Lawrence Evans, while the remaining board members, Colonel John Turnbull, John Reed, Jack Parker and Sydney Collings, were severely censured for failing to report their suspicions to the FA. In addition,

Sunderland received a fine of £5,000, by far the heaviest ever imposed on a club by the FA: previously, the record sum had been the £750 Newcastle United had to pay for fielding weakened teams before their appearance in the 1924 FA Cup final. However, manager Billy Murray and club secretary George Crow were exonerated for the time being.

Five of Sunderland's players, past and present, were not so fortunate. On 25 April 1957, Ray Daniel, Billy Elliott, Ken Chisholm (then with Workington), Willie Fraser and Johnny Hannigan were called before another joint FA-Football League commission at the Midland Hotel, Manchester. All were accused of having received illegal signing-on fees from Murray, who, under pressure at the earlier commission, had named names. When the five players then refused to incriminate themselves, they were suspended *sine die*. But thanks to the assiduity of a young articled clerk at George Davies & Co, the solicitors handling the players' defence, a serious flaw was discovered in the prosecution case. Going through the rule books of the FA and League with a fine toothcomb, the clerk discovered that the governing bodies had contravened their own regulations.

What he found was that the FA and the League – and therefore any commission wholly or partly appointed by them – did not possess the power to suspend a player or official *sine die*. Only member clubs could do that. In addition, as the commission was appointed only to inquire into the allegations against Sunderland, it had no powers to adjudicate. FA rules stated that judgment had to be the responsibility of a new commission composed of different individuals. 'Thus,' says Inglis, 'perhaps in its panic, perhaps through lack of knowledge or planning, the commission had broken the rules of the very bodies which set it up.' No change there, then.

As a consequence of those blunders, the members of the joint

FA-League commission ended up in court themselves as defendants five years later and lost the case. The punishments meted out to the Sunderland directors, manager and players were rescinded, but in some instances it was too late to matter. Billy Murray, for instance, resigned a month after receiving his £200 fine in May 1957 and died a couple of years later. Bill Ditchburn and Bill Martin not only had their lifetime bans lifted, but received compensation of £650 from the FA in an out-of-court settlement. Ditchburn, who had been broken by his suspension, vowed to regain his seat on the Sunderland board; but the balance of power there had shifted in his absence and, at 74, he found himself no longer wanted at the club that had been his life. Two years later he, too, was dead.

You may be wondering what all this has to do with Len Shackleton. Well, when the commission discovered that Sunderland had paid all their first team illegal bonuses during the runs to the semi-finals of the FA Cup in 1954-55 and 1955-56, Shack was among another eight current and former players who were found guilty. The others were George Aitken, Stan Anderson, Billy Bingham, Joe McDonald, Bill Holden (then with Stockport County), Sam Kemp (Sheffield United) and Ted Purdon (Workington). Their obscure punishment was to be docked six months' qualification for accrued share of benefit, the payment due to a professional footballer then after the completion of a certain number of years' service.

This slap on the wrist, which is what it amounted to, was in line with the reduced punishments imposed on the five players who had been charged initially with receiving illegal payments and banned *sine die*. The commission had opted for a surprising degree of leniency after the players, on the advice of the Players' Union, decided to break their silence and confess all. The leniency was surprising because the union's solicitors, for a number of sound, practical reasons, had decided not to let the FA and League know for the time being that they had found a fatal flaw in their opponents' case. So the commission was not acting under direct duress of any kind.

In the background, however, the campaign for the abolition of the maximum wage was gathering strength precisely because of the Sunderland case, or cases. All along, Cliff Lloyd, secretary of the Players' Union, and Jimmy Hill, its new chairman, saw their firm support for the accused players as a step nearer the union's ultimate goal; and the experience they gained from intense and protracted negotiations with the FA and League was to stand them in good stead when it came to the crunch over the bigger issue four years later. However, it was only the threat of strike action that did the trick in the end, and that is where Len Shackleton comes in again.

Having called on the FA and League to hold an inquiry into the whole question of improper payments, Jimmy Hill proposed that no action should be taken against players 'on evidence freely provided': in other words, he wanted an amnesty for those who owned up to having received money under the counter. To that end, he drove up and down the country trying to persuade as many footballers as he could to sign a document admitting to the misdemeanour. He aimed to get 100 of the union's 2,500-strong membership to sign, but finished up with no more than 40. 'Sometimes,' wrote Maurice Smith, football correspondent of *The People*, sadly, 'I feel professional footballers are their own worst enemy.'

One of those who had refused to put pen to paper, it transpired, was Shack. Needless to say, this revelation attracted a great deal of publicity, coming as it did from the dressing room of the club at the centre of the controversy. 'This player will have to go,' one of the 18 Roker Park signatories was quoted anonymously as saying. 'The boys just don't want him in the ground after his refusal to sign the union's confession.' Then aged 35 and within a couple of months of retirement, Shackleton, the 'scab', defended himself by arguing that the best way to change the wage and bonus structure was not to sign confessions, but to strike. 'I am a union member, but I still have the right to form my own opinion,' he said defiantly.

It is tempting, like those aggrieved Sunderland players, to see Shack's unilateral approach to the problem as selfishness or the sheer cussedness for which he was famous. Examples abound of his daring to be different, but all the evidence here suggests he simply weighed up the options and decided not to follow the crowd. He was certainly intelligent enough to have done that, and history argues that he reached the right conclusion. As Simon Inglis put it: 'In 1961, as a direct result of Hill and Lloyd's skilful negotiations and a threatened players' strike, the maximum wage was also deleted from the rule book, after 60 years (the £10 signing-on bonus had been abolished in 1958). In some ways Len Shackleton was right – a strike threat had been the best ploy.'

Curiously, Shack had little to say about this episode, or the illegal payments business as a whole, in *Return of the Clown Prince*. The only comment he made was uncharacteristically bland. All he said was that he remembered the Football League holding a commission which resulted in Bill Ditchburn, the Sunderland chairman, and the players involved being banned from the game *sine die*. He was not involved personally, he added, because the investigation did not go back as far as the time when he joined the club. Nor, he insisted, was the team affected too much by all the disruption, since most of the players involved had already moved on to other clubs. Then, as he pointed out, the lifting of the bans enabled the banned players to resume their careers soon afterwards. But, in his only sign of real emotion, he did regret that Bill Ditchburn had been unable to regain power, Syd Collings having taken over as chairman of the club in the little man's absence.

Typically, Billy Elliott remembers that disturbing episode rather more tartly. 'Five of us were banned,' he said, 'but if there was anybody that should have gone, the lot of us should have: it's as simple as that. Just to pick on five didn't make any sense. I think the authorities goofed up all round. They were probably trying to make an example of us, but what kind of an example? That's the thing.' But Elliott does challenge the story about Shackleton being unpopular with the other Sunderland players for becoming a dressing-room 'scab' by refusing to sign Jimmy Hill's 'confession'. 'Coming from the same town as him, being brought up together and playing for Bradford Park Avenue, I think I would have been the first to know about something like that, don't you?' he said dismissively.

By the time – 1961 – footballers were free to earn whatever they could negotiate with their clubs, Shack was a journalist. He had been fortunate with injuries for most of his career, but a persistent problem with his ankle had forced him to call a halt to his playing days four years earlier. After giving him trouble for five years, the ankle finally 'went' during the first half of Sunderland's opening game of the 1957-58 season at Roker Park. Significantly, some thought, it was the first under new manager Alan Brown and against Arsenal, of all teams. Knowing he had been getting by just on natural ability, he guessed it was all over for him. In fact, he admitted as much the following day in the weekly column he did for the now defunct Sunday paper, the *Empire News*.

After the match, Johnny Watters, the Sunderland physiotherapist, assessed the damage and recommended that Shackleton should see a specialist in Barnsley the following Monday. But as soon as he returned home that night, he called his family doctor, Dr Rodger George, who was also a personal friend, and asked his opinion. Worried that Barnsley seemed a strange location for a so-called expert and, knowing his career was on the line, he wanted to make absolutely certain he was getting the best advice. But the GP pointed out that not even the finest Harley Street specialist could tell them anything they didn't already know. He also suggested that if Shack did not follow the club's advice and see their specialist, it could be misconstrued as a way out of the game of his own making.

On the Monday, therefore, he kept the appointment in Barnsley, where the specialist decided that he should come back on the Wednesday for a manipulative operation under anaesthetic. He received the results of that operation on the Thursday and was not surprised to be told he must quit the game immediately. If he did not, the specialist warned, he'd almost certainly end his days as a cripple. Trying to be philosophical about the situation, Shackleton consoled himself with the thought that, at 35, he had lasted for a long time and had enjoyed a marvellous career.

Journalist Doug Weatherall was with Shack when he travelled down to Barnsley to see the specialist. 'I remember he had a Humber Hawk car,' he said. 'Then he came out and told me his playing days were over. He played only 45 minutes for Alan Brown, Sunderland's new manager, then retired at half-time and never played professionally again. In those days, I was working for the *Daily Herald* and lots of us thought he had no intention of putting up with Alan Brown.'

The appointment of Brown certainly seems to have played a part in Shackleton's decision to retire. To say that Shack did not rate the tough taskmaster who replaced the popular Billy Murray is putting it mildly. Later, he went on record as saying that he thought Brown was a 'terrible' manager and supported his argument by pointing out that Sunderland were relegated from the First Division not only in Brown's first season, but again after he had returned as manager 12 years later.

This was not a simple clash of personalities between ageing star player and gung-ho, new, young manager. Shackleton was far from being the only Sunderland player who could not stand Brown. The easy-going Billy Bingham was another. 'I'd love to have seen him (Brown) with Shack,' chortled the Irishman. 'That would have been a beauty! I think Shack retired when he knew Alan Brown was coming. He was muck or nettles, Alan Brown; that's all he was. He wasn't truly sophisticated. Shack wouldn't have stayed with him. Shack said: "Bye, bye" just as he was coming, then I said: "Bye, bye" myself because I found it difficult to work with him. I was quite easy – I wasn't a rebel or anything – but I really did find him difficult.

'There are certain managers who suit your personality, and Bill Murray suited mine. He was like a father-figure, Murray. Not that he praised me all the time, but his attitude was balanced. Brown was strange. He would ignore you for weeks and not talk to you. You never felt part of his team, and I was so glad to go I even went to Luton. I could have gone to Manchester City and other places, but I went to Luton because they had five or six internationals then and weren't a bad team. It wasn't a bad decision, either, because next thing I was in the FA Cup final!'

Brown did not endear himself to Shackleton by seeming to turn a deaf ear to the player's perfectly reasonable request for some sort of pay-off after giving Sunderland nearly ten years' outstanding and money-generating service. In those days, players did not qualify for a testimonial match automatically as they do today: it was very much at the discretion of the club whether one was granted. But the approaches Shack made to Brown and then one of the directors, Jack Parker, whom he believed to be a 'decent sort', yielded nothing but empty promises.

So, Shack resorted to animal cunning – you might even call it blackmail – in a way that caused an echo of the illegal payments scandal to ring loud and clear. Becoming a little desperate, he decided to approach the chairman, Syd Collings, over something that

Collings, then just a new director, had said to him when he had been transferred from Newcastle to Sunderland in 1948. According to Shackleton, Collings had told him he would be paid a fee and that if he did not get it, he was to go and see him about it. Until then, there had been no need to put Collings' offer of help to the test; but now, Shack decided, the moment had come to do so.

Deliberately confronting the chairman in the dressing room in front of one or two of the players, he stated his case. Then, almost as an afterthought, he remarked how fortunate it was that the Football League inquiry had not gone back as far as when they had both joined the club. Seeing Collings beginning to get hot under the collar at this uncomfortable reminder of past misdeeds, Shackleton seized the moment and asked for a benefit match. The ploy worked so well that the board granted him one within a week.

And so, the finest and happiest period of Len Shackleton's playing career – the nine and a half years he spent with Sunderland – came to an end on a rather painful and discordant note. He was leaving the game, too, without a single medal to show for the outstanding artistry and entertainment he had brought to English football. All he could look back on were a few near things in the League and the FA Cup, just five England caps and exactly 100 goals in 348 League and FA Cup appearances for his club.

'Like the Manchester United of today,' reflected Shack many years later about the so-called 'Bank of England' club, 'Sunderland had the right idea; but they didn't carry it out properly. Just because you get the best players that are playing, it doesn't mean to say you're going to have a good team. You've got to find the right players, you've got to have the right blend. But we didn't: we bought all these players, left, right and centre.

'It was successful in the sense that we got to two FA Cup semi-finals and we got beat in the last game of the season when we should have beat Man. City to win the League. So I suppose if we'd have won the League and, perhaps, one of the cup finals, we'd have been classed as successful. But it wouldn't have been successful enough.'

Roman Abramovich and Chelsea, please note.

CHAPTER FIVE
ENGLAND

WHEN, at the age of 14, Len Shackleton became the first lad from Bradford to play for England schoolboys, it looked as though a long and glittering international career lay ahead of him. Three successive and impressive appearances at that junior age level served only to strengthen the perception that here was a gifted young player destined to win a string of senior caps for his country. The interruption of his career by the Second World War did nothing to alter that view, either. The torrent of goals he scored for Bradford Park Avenue between 1940 and 1946 demanded national recognition.

Everything seemed to be going according to expectations when, towards the end of the war, Shack experienced the 'great thrill' of being chosen to play for the Football League against the Army's Northern Command at York. His first senior honour in representative football was made all the more memorable for him by the fact that, playing at inside-right, he was partnered at outside-right by a small, wiry 'unknown' called Tom Finney. Describing Finney enthusiastically as 'a winger in a million', Shackleton could not resist observing that his youthful partner went on to win more than 50 England caps – 'despite his brilliance'.

The sarcastic final remark reflected the contempt Shackleton eventually came to feel for England selectors who, he believed with some justification, were not qualified to assess a player's ability and had denied him his fair share of international caps through their ignorance. But, for the time being, all was still set fair for Shack. The press continued to be very supportive, nominating him time after time for important matches; and the selectors responded by giving him plenty of opportunities to prove his worth.

He finally reached the brink of the senior England team when he was picked to play for an FA XI against the Army PT side at Wembley. It was, in effect, an international trial match; but those playing in it must have wondered what was going on when the selectors watched only the first half before retiring to choose the England team for the Victory International against Scotland at Hampden Park in April 1946. Shackleton need not have worried, if worry he ever did about football. When the players returned to the dressing rooms after the match, they were informed of the selectors' deliberations and he discovered that he had been picked to represent his country at the highest level for the first time.

Sadly and unfairly, those Victory Internationals, played in the transitional season – 1945-46 – between wartime and peacetime football, were not accorded full international status. There is no mistaking, though, the pride and delight Shackleton, still with Bradford Park Avenue at that point, felt at being selected to play for England's senior side. Even better, it gave him a heaven-sent opportunity for a gloat at close quarters over Arsenal's decision to reject him when he was a diminutive teenager. Staying at a hotel in Glasgow before the game, circumstances brought Shack face to face with George Allison for the first time since the Arsenal manager had given him his marching orders from Highbury.

They encountered each other in a hotel lift as Shackleton was going up to his room. Allison was the only other occupant, and the player was sorely tempted to say to him: 'I shall be playing for England against Scotland in a few hours' time. Do you still think I'll never make the grade as a footballer?' Instead, Shack held his tongue for once and contented himself with wondering if the Arsenal manager would recognise his fellow lift-traveller. In the end, Allison smiled and said: 'You're Shackleton, aren't you?' And that was it: not another word was spoken. However, knowing Allison had recognised him and would be a spectator at the big match, Shack felt he had even more reason to do well at Hampden Park.

Revenge for Shack was to be no sweeter than that, though. England lost 1-0, he played poorly on his senior international debut and was promptly dropped for the first of many times at that level. Then a month short of his 24th birthday, he was replaced by the recalled, 32-year-old Raich Carter for England's two remaining matches during that strange hiatus between war and peacetime normality: a 4-1 win against Switzerland at Stamford Bridge and a 2-1 defeat by France in Paris. Given Carter's immensely greater reputation and experience, being dropped in those circumstances was no disgrace and no reason to feel too aggrieved.

Even so, Shackleton took it hard. So hard, in fact, that he even began to wonder whether George Allison's poor opinion of his ability might have been right all along. But he consoled himself with the thought that much more famous players had been 'ground into the dust of the wind-swept, bumpy bowl of Hampden Park', as he put it. Neither Denis Compton nor Joe Mercer played for their country again after that defeat by the old enemy ended England's run of victories in 1946. 'It was a sad day for England, as well as for the Shackletons, Comptons and Mercers,' concluded Shack, 'the all-conquering war-time international XI was no longer invincible, and selectors had a great time chopping and changing before the next game.'

Use of the word 'invincible' about that wartime England team was something of an exaggeration. Of the 32 matches they played, mostly against the other Home Countries, prior to the game at Hampden Park in 1946, they lost six and drew six. The notion of an 'all-conquering' XI was probably fostered by the massive victories (8-0, 6-2 and 6-1 against Scotland and 8-3 against Wales) they ran up between 1943 and 1945. Not only that, but Scotland's 1946 victory at Hampden was the first time they had beaten England in nine matches.

Worse still for Shackleton, he had conceded the free-kick just outside the penalty area from which Manchester United's Jimmy Delaney scored Scotland's winner. Given the fickleness of the FA selection committee, which had been re-established in 1946 after being disbanded during the war, it was hardly surprising that it was to be some time before Shack was chosen again to play for England. 'I was out, and not until the game against Denmark three [it was two, in fact] years later was it decided I had paid the appropriate penance for my soccer sins,' he reflected rather petulantly.

Unfortunately, in Copenhagen in September 1948, England could only draw 0-0 with a team of Danish amateurs, who had finished third in the Olympic Games two months earlier and were playing their first game against professional opposition. In his authorized biography of Sir Stanley Matthews, David Miller quotes Tommy Lawton as saying, after that result: 'Denmark was my last game, I had a stinker. Len Shackleton missed about four, and so did I.'

Billy Wright, who played at right-half in that match, recalled Shack's contribution even more vividly. In *A Hero For All Seasons*, the authorized biography of the former Wolverhampton Wanderers and England captain by Norman Giller, Wright is quoted as saying: 'I recall that Shack made his debut wearing a pair of rugby boots. "They're more comfortable," he explained, "and they give better grip in muddy conditions." That certainly seemed the case when in the fifth minute he waltzed round the Danish goalkeeper and side-footed the ball towards goal. Shack turned ready to receive the congratulations of his team-mates, not realising that the ball had stuck in a mound of mud on the goal line...

'The Danish game was an embarrassment to us all, because we were expected to beat them with ease. To use that old football cliché, the mud really was a great leveller. At the after-match banquet, the Danish captain said we had given them a football lesson but had forgotten to shoot. That just about summed it up.'

As a result of the failure to beat Denmark, Shack was out on his ear again for the next international, away to Northern Ireland in Belfast a month later. England won that one 6-2, with Shackleton's replacement, Manchester United's Stan Pearson, scoring one of the goals. So it was a bit of a surprise when Shack was restored to the side for the following game, a 1-0 win against Wales at Villa Park in November 1948. But out he went again until October 1949, when England beat Wales 4-1 in Cardiff in a World Cup qualifier – the first in which either country had taken part.

That meant Shackleton had missed six internationals, in the course of which the selectors had tried four other inside-lefts: Jack Haines of West Bromwich Albion, Pearson and Jack Rowley of Manchester United and Middlesbrough's Wilf Mannion. In international terms, Haines was even unluckier than Shackleton: making his debut, he scored twice in a 6-0 trouncing of Switzerland, yet never got the chance again to appear for England because of an injury sustained playing for his club. If nothing else, that sad little tale illustrates just how fierce the competition was at the time for the inside-forward berths.

At least Shack had to wait only five years before being recalled. Not surprisingly, he could scarcely believe it when he, then in his 33rd year and nearing the end of his career, was picked to play for the

Football League against the Irish League at Liverpool. He was sorely tempted to tell the selectors where to go, because he had made up his mind that he was finished with international football and would refuse to play if chosen again. 'I had lost the taste for international football,' he confessed, 'such things do happen, just as a hungry man, eager for the feast, loses his appetite if kept waiting too long. The taste, the appetite, the eagerness, had died during those five years.'

At the same time, Shackleton knew the Football League game was effectively a trial match for the full internationals against Wales and West Germany that were to follow. And, while not too happy about having to audition for another England cap or too fussed about playing against Wales once more, the prospect of taking on West Germany, winners of the 1954 World Cup, had really captured his imagination.

In a quandary, Shack struggled to reach a decision. On the one hand, he was determined to stick to his resolution that England, having managed without his services for so long, could carry on without him. On the other hand, he was desperately keen to have a crack at the World Champions. 'I wanted to meet the Germans at Wembley,' he said, 'to try and prove in my own small way that it was not the prerogative of every footballing nation to rub the Englishman's nose in the dirt.'

During Shackleton's five-year 'exile' from international football, of course, the England team had experienced a succession of shocks and embarrassments that called into question their right to be regarded still as masters of the game. First, there was the fiasco of the ill-prepared and ill-fated sortie to the 1950 World Cup finals in Brazil, during which – unbelievably – England lost 1-0 to a scratch side from the USA; then, in November 1953 and May 1954, came successive thrashings by that marvellous Hungarian team of Puskas, Kocsis and company, who won 6-3 at Wembley – thus becoming the first foreign side to triumph there – and 7-1 in Budapest. After being humiliated like that, England did reasonably well to reach the quarter-finals of the 1954 World Cup, where they went out to the defending champions, Uruguay. Even so, English pride was hurt; and – despite all the recent evidence that other countries had not only caught the inventors of the game up, but overtaken them – the feeling persisted that England could still show the rest of the world a thing or two about playing the game.

Shackleton personified that hurt and that feeling. Forced to watch helplessly from the sidelines as England had been humiliated at home and abroad during his five years out of international football, Shack was desperate to test himself against the 'alleged supermen' of world football and see for himself just how good they were. These, of course, were the feelings of a supremely gifted, and extremely frustrated, footballer who considered himself at least the equal of any player on the planet. 'It was like watching a house burn down and being denied the right to contribute the bucket of water in my hand,' he lamented. 'I did not flatter myself I could extinguish the flames – the Football Association had spread the paraffin too widely – but I wanted to have the opportunity of helping.'

It must have been excruciating for him, feted and adored by the Sunderland fans at Roker Park and a crowd-puller wherever he played in the country, to sit there for five years hoping in vain his name would appear in the next England team (no substitutes, so no squads in those days). What hurt more than anything was being passed over in favour of players he regarded as being less talented. He said he would not have minded so much if all his rivals had been as gifted at Raich Carter and Wilf Mannion; but there was so much chopping and changing that he felt at times as though the selectors were picking the names out of a hat.

It is interesting to study the long list of inside-forwards the

England selectors preferred to Shackleton during his five years in the international wilderness: Jackie Sewell, Redfern Froggatt and Albert Quixall (Sheffield Wednesday), Len Phillips (Portsmouth), Tommy Thompson (Aston Villa), Eddie Baily (Spurs), Stan Mortensen and Ernie Taylor (Blackpool), Don Revie (Manchester City), Wilf Mannion (Middlesbrough), Roy Bentley (Chelsea), Johnny Morris (Derby County), Stan Pearson (Manchester United), Harold Hassall (Bolton), Johnny Nicholls (West Bromwich Albion), Johnny Haynes (Fulham). The selectors even picked wing-half/centre-half Billy Wright as an inside-forward for the match against Austria at Wembley in 1951, although injury prevented him from playing.

While not everybody would agree that all of those players were less deserving than Shackleton of a place in the England team, it is easy to picture the agonies he went through as each team was announced and his name was missing once again. Shack said that he and his wife, Marjorie, used to sit there with fingers crossed waiting for the team to be named. Indeed, it became her custom to ask: 'Which pair of inside-forwards are they trying on for size this time?'

As the years went by, so the Shackletons' hopes of an international recall dwindled. It got to the stage where they did not care much whether they heard the England team announcements or not. Breaking point was reached when Shack was not included in the 1954 World Cup squad following the 7-1 thrashing by Hungary in Budapest. 'If selectors call on me after this lot is over,' an angry and disillusioned Shack told his wife, 'I won't bother to play.'

But when the call finally did come in the autumn of 1954, Shackleton found he just could not resist it. What prompted the selectors to turn back at last to Shack is a mystery. England had just won 2-0 against Northern Ireland in Belfast, with the two inside-forwards, Don Revie and Johnny Haynes, scoring the goals. There was some heavy press criticism of the performance, but it was still a gross over-reaction to drop both Revie and Haynes and six other players for the match against Wales at Wembley the following month.

Vacillation on that scale, of course, was at the root of England's problems in those days of an international selection committee. As Billy Wright said of those wholesale changes: 'This was at a time when the selectors seemed to be acting like headless chickens, and it was difficult to get any continuity or rhythm. It was a particularly frustrating period for our manager Walter Winterbottom, whose plans were continually sabotaged by the juggling of the selectors.'

In the meantime, Shackleton was still agonising over the invitation to play for the Football League against the Irish League, a fixture that came after the England game in Belfast. In the end, he talked it over with George Childs, his partner in the business he had set up in Sunderland, and it is rather disappointing to discover that commercial considerations played a part in his final decision to take part in the game. Childs gave him the sound advice that he would have to play for the Football League if he wanted to be in contention for the games against Wales and West Germany. He also pointed out that Shack's new hairdressing salon was due to open around the same time as the West Germans were coming to Wembley, and the publicity would give the business a wonderful send-off.

Needless to say, Shack's fancy was tickled by the idea of the selectors helping to launch his new business after ignoring him for all those years. But, even now, when commercialism is rampant in English professional football and, sometimes, it seems money is the only thing that counts, Shackleton's brazenness in that instance does grate a little. Maybe it was just a touch of bravado, an attempt to show that the selectors could not make him dance to their tune and that he was coming back into international football on his terms not theirs, but it still struck a discordant, unflattering note.

In the event, Shackleton need not have bothered to agonise. A groin injury sustained in Sunderland's First Division game at Everton ruled him out of the inter-League match scheduled for the following Wednesday. He was disappointed because, knowing the Irish opposition would not be of the highest quality, he had been looking forward to displaying the full range of his talent to the selectors. But the injury proved to be a stroke of luck. Marjorie, Shack's wife, reported back to him that the inter-League game at Anfield had been a shambles and that he had been fortunate to miss it.

As planned before the groin injury had taken Shack back to Sunderland for treatment, Mrs Shackleton had stayed on in Lancashire with friends after the Everton game. Shack was pleased to find her verdict was endorsed by the press, who decided almost unanimously that West Ham United outside-right Harry Hooper was the only League forward to show anything approaching international form at Liverpool. Eddie Baily and Harold Hassall, the League inside pair, were less impressive, and Shackleton readily acknowledged that he had played himself into the team to face Wales by *not* playing for the Football League.

He was doing a spot of gardening when he learned from a neighbour that he had been picked for the game against the Welsh. At least it made a change from being informed of your selection by a newspaperman, which was often the case. But Shack refused to believe it until he saw it written down in the *Newcastle Journal* the following morning. His version of the team was: Wood (Manchester United); Staniforth (Huddersfield), Byrne (Manchester United); Phillips (Portsmouth), Wright, Slater (both Wolverhampton Wanderers); Matthews (Blackpool), Bentley (Chelsea), Lofthouse (Bolton), Shackleton (Sunderland), Mien (whoever he might have been!). The official, FA version, on the other hand, reads: Wood; Staniforth, Byrne; Phillips, Wright, Slater; Matthews, Bentley, Allen

(West Bromwich Albion), Shackleton, Blunstone (Chelsea) because Nat Lofthouse withdrew before the game.

The strange thing about Shackleton's two mistakes is that they involved members of the forward line in which he made his long-delayed and long-awaited return to the England team. So you would think all the names would have been seared on his memory, particularly as *Clown Prince of Soccer* was published only the following year. The kindest thing one can say is that the identity of the left-winger in Shackleton's team must have been lost in some kind of horrendous misprint; but it is difficult to understand how he could not have remembered it was Ronnie Allen, an entirely different kind of centre-forward, and not winger Frank Blunstone as Shack claimed, who replaced the rampaging Lofthouse.

In the event, neither Shackleton, Allen nor Blunstone scored in England's 3-2 victory over Wales at Wembley on 10 November 1954. All the goals were claimed by Roy Bentley, who, having been cold-shouldered by the selectors after the World Cup humiliation by the USA four years earlier, celebrated his own recall with a notable hat-trick. It was sorely needed to overcome a Welsh team whose attack was led dynamically by the peerless John Charles. In a thrilling match on a rain-soaked surface, Charles scored twice to bring the scores level before Bentley got his third goal.

For one of the few times in his life, Shack had obeyed orders. Tipped off that it was his individualism that had been responsible for his long absence from the England team (one selector, when asked why Shackleton had been consistently left out of the England team, replied: 'Because we play at Wembley Stadium, not the London Palladium!'), he decided reluctantly to conform to the selectors' apparent desire for players who would part with the ball quickly. 'With Germany still on my mind,' he revealed, 'I decided just before the Welsh game that if that was the way the FA wanted me to play, I would string along with them and follow their strange ideas – even though I had been picked on my club games as an individualist.'

Clearly uncomfortable at having modified his style of play so drastically, Shackleton consoled himself with the thought that it was just a means to a much-desired end – selection to play against world champions West Germany. The selectors were delighted, one of them asking: 'Why can't Shackleton always play that way?', but those who knew him well were nonplussed by his conformity, especially the uncharacteristic readiness he had shown to get rid of the ball quickly. Some friends in Sunderland even thought he had 'sold out' just to get more caps. At the time, Shack did not feel he could explain his reasons to anyone; that applied even to David Jack, the football writer and close friend who collaborated with him on his autobiography. He did drop Jack a strong hint, however, that things might be entirely different against the West Germans.

No more than three weeks separated England's international matches against Wales and West Germany, but the selectors still felt they had to tinker with the team. Ray Wood was replaced in goal by Wolves' Bert Williams and Blunstone gave way on the left wing to the great Tom Finney; Shack, though, was one of those who kept his place. 'I well remember Len getting his cap against West Germany,' said Stan Anderson. 'They [the selectors] could not ignore him. He was playing out of his skin at the time, absolutely out of his skin. In fact, for Lenny to get only five caps was bloody disgraceful! When you think of some of the other people who were picked in his position, he should have got 20 at least.'

As for the Germans, they came to Wembley on 1 December in some disarray and in the process of rebuilding. Badly hit by injuries and illness, they fielded a side that was nothing like as strong as the one that had shocked favourites Hungary in the final of the World

Cup a few months earlier. In fact, England were faced by only three members of the team that had beaten the Hungarians 3-2 in Berne. Even so, West Germany were still strong enough to make a game of it in front of an expectant crowd of 100,000, who broke the existing Wembley receipts record by paying a total of £51,716 to watch the new world champions in action.

The spectators' reward was to be treated to a magical display of the attacking arts by Matthews and Shackleton, whose virtuosity proved central to England's 3-1 victory. Matthews supplied the centre from which Bentley headed England into the lead in the 27th minute; then Shackleton combined neatly with Finney to provide the chance from which Allen made it 2-0 three minutes into the second half. But when the Germans clawed back a goal through a breakaway, a comfortable win looked like becoming rather more problematic until Shack conjured up perhaps the finest single moment of his chequered career.

Having refused to heed either Sepp Herberger, the manager of the West German team, who said he thought his team had no chance of winning, or the English press, who had predicted a walk-over for England, Shackleton played much of the game in the conformist mode he had adopted so pragmatically for the previous match against Wales. Imagining that the Germans were trying some 'kidology', he had made up his mind to 'treat the game with all the respect due to a meeting with the world champions.' So he decided that, until he had really got the feel of the opposition, there would be no room for clowning.

Calculating that, if West Germany were actually as weak as they claimed, England might build up a healthy lead, Shack decided that would be the moment 'to pull a few tricks out of the bag', as he put it. The change came after half an hour, by which time he had become fed up with the pretence. Such was England's superiority, he played his normal game from then on. Shackleton, typically, thought West Germany were so poor a side that England would have had the game won by half-time had it not been for the heroics of their goalkeeper, Fritz Herkenrath. But he did not agree with those who claimed Herkenrath blocked shot after shot more by good fortune than good judgment. The goalkeeper's uncanny anticipation and skill at narrowing the angle, Shack decided, meant the only ways to score were by dribbling the ball round him or chipping it over his head.

An opportunity to test that theory came ten minutes from the end of the game. Shackleton had already failed narrowly to score sensationally when he ran the ball out of play after beating three men and rounding Herkenrath, and he was determined not to be so profligate when a similar opening presented itself a few minutes later. Let Shack take up the story of his most famous goal: 'This time, I thought, the second method of beating goalkeeper Herkenrath must be employed. True to type, he ran out to meet me but, just as he was about to pounce, I produced my right-foot "mashie niblick" and was relieved to see the ball float over his head into the untenanted goal.

'That goal was, perhaps, my most memorable scoring effort in a lifetime of soccer. It is not easy to explain, but I felt a keen satisfaction – not because the goal made our victory over Germany certain, but because I had decided exactly how to go about scoring it long before the chance presented itself. Anticipation and fulfilment.' And there you have Len Shackleton, the footballer, in a nutshell: the ultimate individualist, he got more pleasure from planning and doing something difficult well than from knowing it ensured his team would win.

Among the spectators that day at Wembley was Wilf McGuinness, then just a young player with Manchester United but, later, Sir Matt

Busby's immediate successor as manager of the club. He was there on a day out with the United squad. 'They sent all the professionals to watch that game, just to see Shack,' McGuinness recalled. 'I'll always remember it for his brilliant dribble that didn't lead to a goal. He went past a lot of players and, if he'd scored, it would have been just *the* goal. Never mind your Peles – this would have been the one! Unfortunately, he ran it past the post.'

The reaction to the victory over the World Cup winners, and to the key performances by Matthews and Shackleton, was little short of rapturous. Matthews, then 39 and heavily criticised by some previously, was christened 'Scintillating Stanley'; and the press, conveniently overlooking the fact that West Germany had been very much below strength, even hailed 'a great England team' as *de facto* world champions – a claim no less spurious than the one made by the Scots when they beat England at Wembley in 1967.

Nevertheless, the Germans themselves had been deeply impressed by both Matthews and Shackleton. 'It was amazing that Matthews could play so well at his age, a tribute to his fitness,' recalled Jupp Derwall, who was at inside-left for West Germany that day and who went on to succeed the great Helmut Schoen, Herberger's successor, as manager of the national team. 'He gave our full-back Kohlmeyer a match like he'd never had before, one he'd never forget. But we all knew about Matthews. He was famous from before the war. Shackleton came as a surprise. *He did things with the ball we did not associate with English footballers.* His goal came from exceptional skill and confidence. When we discovered that Shackleton was past 30 years old it made us wonder why he had not made a much bigger impact as an international player. From what Herberger told us, it was because Shackleton normally played to suit himself. Later on in Germany, we had a similar problem with Gunther Netzer.'

Being compared to Netzer, another clever footballer with big feet, was quite a compliment in itself. Netzer was at his peak in 1972, when West Germany beat England 3-1 at Wembley before going on to win the European Nations Cup. That success was the springboard for their triumph in the World Cup on home soil two years later; but Netzer lost out then to Wolfgang Overath, whom Schoen felt was a more reliable, though less gifted, presence in midfield.

As with Netzer, rejection awaited Shackleton. It did not look that way at first, though. Because there had been such widespread approval of England's performance against West Germany, the FA were even moved to suggest that the team might be kept together, assembling at various times, in preparation for the next match, which was against Scotland four months later. But Shack had been dropped too many times to take such constructive thinking at face value. When a friend insisted that the selectors would not dare disturb such a good international team, he predicted that six or seven members of it would be dropped before the next match.

Ultimately, it was seven, with Shackleton, of course, being one of those to suffer. The others were Staniforth, Phillips, Slater, Bentley, Allen and Finney, whose places were taken by Johnny Meadows (Manchester City), Ken Armstrong (Chelsea), Duncan Edwards (Manchester United), Don Revie (Manchester City), Nat Lofthouse (Bolton Wanderers), Dennis Wilshaw (Wolves) and Frank Blunstone (Chelsea). The selectors could justify their return to wholesale chopping and changing by pointing to the bulging scoreline – 7-2 in England's favour. Not only that, but it was the first time England had beaten Scotland at Wembley for 21 years, Wilshaw scored four goals and Duncan Edwards, then only 18, celebrated his international debut at left-half with a performance that alerted the world to the immense power and talent of this exceptional, but doomed, young player.

So, Len Shackleton's short, sporadic England career was over; but at least it ended on a high note. He could take some comfort, too, from the fact that even the incomparable Tom Finney was considered surplus to requirements at the same time. There was a particularly poignant moment immediately following the game against West Germany. Shackleton revealed it during that illuminating Sky Sports interview by Brian Moore in 2000. Resurrecting the old argument about who was the better player, Matthews or Finney, and making it clear he thought the more versatile Finney was without peer, Shack recalled: 'After the England-Germany game, Tom came to sit with me on the bus. "Why can't he [Matthews] play outside-left?" he said. "Why is it always me?" Tom was such a nice guy, that's the nearest I ever heard him come to saying anything untoward about anybody, never mind a colleague; but he was seething.

'Tom Finney is the best winger I've seen, left or right. He is also the best centre-forward I've seen, and he could play inside-forward as well! He was brave, he was quick, he was fast – he'd got everything. He got what he deserved eventually, which was a knighthood. Tom's a good mate of mine, and nobody was more pleased than me to see him get that.'

The only real consolation for Shackleton himself was that he had succeeded in proving a point. As his son, Roger, said, 'The 1954 England v Germany match must have been somewhat cathartic for him, because he was able to prove to himself that he could perform proficiently and entertainingly at the highest level. One cannot prove a negative of this sort, but the blindness and prejudice of the selectors of that time must have been extremely frustrating to live through first-hand – especially if one is able to accurately identify the position for what it was at the time, but still not be afforded a proper opportunity to acquit oneself fully. He must have been hurt by his exclusion from the England team in the sense that an adverse selection decision is inescapably personal. He was aware of his natural ability and also put a lot of time and effort into practising his skills.'

Nor was it only rejection that soured Shackleton's experience of playing for England. The Football Association's penny-pinching over travel costs was something else that infuriated him. Quite rightly, he felt it was scandalous that players selected to play for their country should be compelled to undertake long train journeys in crowded, third-class compartments. Billy Wright and Bill Slater had to do that on their return to Wolverhampton following England's historic 3-1 victory over West Germany in 1954, and he himself had to take matters into his own hands to get a more comfortable berth on the night sleeper back to Sunderland.

Promised a first-class ticket, he was handed a third-class one after the match and told there were no first-class sleepers available. At King's Cross, however, Shackleton – unrecognised by the ticket clerk – found it no problem at all to upgrade to a first-class compartment. As he pointed out, after helping to beat the world champions at Wembley, he returned home with the princely sum of £20, his match fee of £50 being halved by income tax and further reduced by the cost of the upgrade on the night sleeper. He was also £5 out of pocket on trips to and from training sessions in preparation for the game, having chosen to travel first class in those cases as well.

The pain of being rejected yet again by his country was hardly alleviated for Shackleton by the severe disappointments he was having to contend with at his club as well. That same season, if you recall, Sunderland, after threatening to do the coveted League and FA Cup double, fell short in the closing stages of both competitions. Not only that but, having being feted as the forgotten man who had become England's hero – and who had even been touted as a possible Footballer of the Year – he found himself dropped by Sunderland for the first time in his career. So a further snub by England must have been harder than ever to take.

There is no doubt whatsoever that having a selection committee who picked players just on current form – or, worse still, out of favouritism – and could overrule the manager was no way to run a national team. 'When Syd Collings [the Sunderland chairman] was chairman of the FA selection committee,' said Stan Anderson, who was eventually capped twice by England, 'I remember him telling me once: "Keep playing the way you are and I'll get you into the side." I thought that was wrong. The manager should be able to say: "These are the people I want," and pick his own team. But it didn't happen like that in those days, I'm afraid. People got international caps because they had somebody on the selection committee, which is a bit of a tragedy.'

But while it is easy to castigate the selectors for failing to recognise and reward the genius of Len Shackleton often enough, it is difficult to imagine how such an obdurate, unrepentant individualist could have been accommodated for long by a manager, Walter Winterbottom, who was just beginning to lay down the foundations of the country's first coaching scheme and trying to get England to play to some sort of recognisable tactical plan. As Sir Stanley Matthews, a Shackleton fan, observed: 'The difficulty of fitting such an individual and inconsistent genius into a team's playing system was Len's Achilles heel, certainly at international level.'

As it happens, Winterbottom would have loved to have had Shackleton in his team all the time – provided the player had been willing to compromise to some extent on his addiction to individualism and showmanship. 'If only Len had been prepared to meet us halfway there wouldn't have been many better inside-forwards in the game,' the first England manager told Ken Jones in his fascinating, insightful history of England's attempts to win the World Cup, *Jules Rimet Still Gleaming?*. 'With his touch, his brain, his marvellous anticipation, he should have been one of the greats. Trouble was that Len only wanted to play the game his way, purely for fun.'

Winterbottom expanded on those thoughts on Jimmy Armfield's Radio Five Live programme. What he said, in effect, was that, because Shackleton was so much of an individualist, he could not always combine easily with other players. The example he gave was of Stanley Matthews' liking for the ball to feet, whereas Shack preferred to supply team-mates with passes to run on to. Winterbottom obviously felt it was just Shack's bad luck that, while he was clearly talented enough to play for England, other inside-forwards fitted in more readily with totemic figures like Matthews.

'He could link up all right,' said Winterbottom, 'but he would do a lot of personal skills which were purely isolated from the game. He'd trick a player and then he'd turn around and beat him again: there's no need to do it! And he would try fancy tricks when a good, straight through-pass was on. But it was clever and the crowd loved it, too, let's be fair. When he played against [West] Germany, I do remember the crowd just rising to him almost like the feat of Gazza [that, for the benefit of those who have spent the last 20 years in an underground cave, is Paul Gascoigne to whom he is referring] when Gazza scored against Scotland in the European Championship. He could produce tricks of that order and that giftedness, which is exceptional.'

Even Billy Bingham, Shackleton's former Sunderland team-mate and close friend, is forced to admit that there were serious flaws in Shack's mindset as a player. 'The entertainer, the clown – call him whatever you want – he had talent in abundance,' said Bingham of Shack. 'But maybe he hadn't the resolution that some people have to

Bradford Park Avenue's modest current ground.

The wall of Shackleton memorabilia in Bradford Park Avenue's clubhouse.

The kind of powerful shooting that once dislodged a crossbar.

A collector's item – Shack actually heading the ball,
and in front of empty terraces!

This is how you cross the ball, Derek Tapscott!

Shack meets The Duke of Gloucester before the game against Wales at Wembley in 1954 that saw his recall to the England team after a five-year absence.

Shackleton celebrates as Roy Bentley (number 8) scores one of the three goals that formed a match-winning hat-trick in the 1954 international against Wales.

© Empics

Shack poses for a portrait before one of the games he loved most –
Arsenal v Sunderland at Highbury. Hence the white, change strip.

fight even though you're losing. Maybe he didn't care as much as I did. You understand what I mean? I'm trying to paint the right picture rather than just say he didn't want to win. It wasn't that: football was just a game to him. I lived through that period with him and I knew his talent; and if he'd had that edge, that demanding thing to win, he'd have had 100 England caps.'

It did not help, of course, that Shack had almost as little time for Winterbottom as he did for the selectors. He despised the latter as businessmen who knew nothing at all about football and he did not think much of Winterbottom, either. A former teacher who had played just 25 games at wing-half for Manchester United before a spinal injury ended his career, the England manager had not done enough in the game to earn Shackleton's respect: that much was obvious.

'I don't think he got on too well with Walter,' reflected Stan Anderson in something of an understatement. 'He probably thought Walter didn't know enough about the game to be able to tell him what to do. That was his attitude in general. He wouldn't even talk to people who wanted to praise him. When we went out to presentations, and that kind of thing, he used to hate people coming up to him and saying: "Oh, I saw you playing wherever, and doing this or that!" He'd say: "What's the bloody point? They don't know what they're talking about!" So I can well imagine him being a bit uppity with Walter, because he was a stickler for laying everything down the way he wanted it to be played; and I don't think Len would have taken too kindly to that.'

Tom Finney is another contemporary who could not understand why Shackleton did not play more often for England. 'I recall one game when we played [West] Germany,' he said at his Preston home, 'and he had an excellent game. Yet he was not selected for the next game. That's the way it was it was in those days with England. You were picked one game and left out of the next with no explanation or anything. The more you thought about it, the more you understood that Walter Winterbottom wasn't picking the team. He was picking it – well, suggesting it – and then it was discussed [by the selection committee].

'Personally, I always admired Len: I thought he was a tremendous player. He had tremendous ball skills and was the sort of player who appeals to spectators. I think the selectors recognised that he was very skilful, but he didn't get anywhere near the number of caps he should have had. I think they looked on him as a bit of a maverick. But the average sort of person you talked to admired him, and so did his team-mates. He was looked upon as a valuable asset in a side. He was the sort of player who could win you games out of nothing.'

Shackleton himself believed until his dying day that his skilful individualism could have been integrated into the England team had he only been given a proper chance to prove it. 'If you're picked to play for your country, you must be good enough,' he argued only a few years ago. 'But different players need different ways to get into a side. In my case, what I needed was three or four games on the trot for England, to get into it, get accustomed to it. If I wasn't good enough to play, I shouldn't have been picked in the first place.'

At times, Shackleton's attitude to Winterbottom was almost friendly. In one dissertation on coaching, Shack described the England manager as a popular figure who had the knack of being able to make friends with everyone, 'even odd characters like me'. He also complimented him on 'his wonderful gift for passing on verbally all the things that matter in football' and acknowledged that he was 'a soccer student whose life is dedicated to the game'. In the next breath, though, Shackleton was complaining about Winterbottom's inability to 'demonstrate perfect control of the ball in the manner of, for instance, Peter Doherty or Wilf Mannion.'

The perfect coach, he concluded, would have the communication skills of Winterbottom and the practical skills of a competent professional footballer. Where one was missing, he insisted, the coaching suffered.

That was Shack trying hard in 1955 to be objective and diplomatic about Winterbottom, and succeeding. But his true feelings came out elsewhere. In an interview conducted much later by Brian Leng, of the Sunderland fanzine, *The Wearside Roar*, he described the England set-up as a complete shambles and Winterbottom as absolutely useless. 'I remember he always wore a tracksuit with "WW" on the front,' he said contemptuously. 'I used to call him "Washer-Woman"!'

Shackleton then went on to repeat a funny and famous story that illustrates perfectly his lack of respect for the well-meaning academic who was England's first manager. 'We were playing the League of Ireland in Dublin,' said Shack, 'and on the morning of the match Walter proceeded to give us his tactical talk. Starting with our keeper, big Frank Swift, he said: "Frank, when you get the ball, throw it out to Eric Westwood... Eric, you pass it to Harry Johnston, Harry move it up to Peter Harris..." He went through the entire team, mimicking all the playing actions as he spoke, until finally the ball ends up in the box. "And you Shack," he nodded to me, "You kick it in!" Can you credit it, at such a level, "You kick it in!" – he couldn't even say shoot! Apart from that he'd ignored one minor detail – the opposition. Where were they in all this? So I couldn't resist it and replied: "Which corner would you like it in, Walter?" '

Shackleton was even more dismissive of the selectors. He went through them scathingly in his autobiography as he belittled their qualifications for England selection duty. Arthur Drewry, he pointed out, had connections with the fishing industry in Grimsby, Harold Shentall was a wholesale provision merchant from Chesterfield,

Harry French a wholesale greengrocer from Middlesbrough, Sir Amos Brookhirst a Huddersfield solicitor, Arthur Oakley a retired Wolverhampton businessman and Joe Mears a London transport contractor. All of them had one thing in common, Shackleton observed, and that was a 'striking absence of any soccer-playing background of any note'.

Continuing in the same vein, and growing more sarcastic all the time, he rightly deplored the fact that England teams were being selected by businessmen who did not know the first thing about the game, while men who had been successful as players had not been given any opportunity to use their knowledge of the game as international selectors. 'When in two minds about buying a certain type of motor car, I call in a motoring expert to help me in my selection,' he finished by saying. 'That seems the correct thing to do, although, working on the FA selection system, perhaps I should ask the advice of a deep-sea diver, or a veterinary surgeon.'

Although, as we have seen, Shackleton's international career was over, to all intents and purposes, by the time *Clown Prince of Soccer* was published in 1955, it is most unlikely, after that diatribe, he would have been considered for selection again even if he had been 23 and not 10 years older. It was, in effect, a burning of the boats by a footballer who knew his playing career was nearing its end. It was also one last major effort by a frustrated patriot to get the FA to bring some sanity and consistency to their selection policy. Since Alf Ramsey was appointed to succeed Winterbottom seven years later as England's first autonomous manager – and went on to win the World Cup – Shackleton was entitled to feel he had played some small part in bringing about much-needed change in the running of the national team.

CHAPTER SIX
REBEL

Len Shackleton rather resented being called a rebel. As far as he was concerned, he was simply obeying the wishes of his conscience or using simple common sense when he protested about something or someone. He set out his feelings on the matter in the preface to *Return of the Clown Prince*. 'In the past,' he said, 'I have often been accused of being controversial but this has always been out of general conviction and I have never, deliberately, set out to be sensational. I do not regard myself as a rebel although, because of the set-up of the professional game in my time, I certainly believe that I had a cause.'

Very early in Shack's playing career, though, it was quite clear that he was a proud, intelligent being with a mind of his own and not someone willing to accept the status quo blindly or bow to the dictates of authority if he felt them to be unreasonable or plain wrong. His blunt refusal at Highbury, as a humble Yorkshire ground-staff boy a long way from home, to tie the shoelaces of George Allison when ordered to do so by the self-important Arsenal manager, was the first recorded example of a rebelliousness, genuine or perceived, that was to define Shackleton's life and reputation almost as much as his ability to entrance football crowds with dazzling tricks and daring showmanship.

The confirmation of this contrariness, if you like, came with the publication 20 years later of his famous autobiography, *Clown Prince of Soccer*. Even football followers who never saw Shackleton play, or who are not entirely familiar with the details of his career, know about that chapter in the book. It was chapter nine and entitled 'The Average Director's Knowledge of Football': underneath, to the fury of the football establishment and the delight of players and most fans, was nothing but a blank page. It was a masterstroke that said so much about what Shack thought of the game's rulers in the 1950s by saying nothing at all.

Like many good ideas, the blank page was almost an accidental creation. When asked how it came about, Shackleton explained that it occurred during one of his Friday night writing sessions at his Seaburn home with David Jack, his collaborator on the book and a football writer on the now defunct Sunday newspaper, the *Empire News*. Jack would stay with the Shackletons over the weekend so that author and collaborator could complete another few pages.

One weekend, after they had been beavering away for a few weeks, Shack decided they should have a break. He proposed that they take the day off and go out somewhere. At that point, Shackleton threw a blank sheet of paper on the table; and when Jack asked him what it was, he replied facetiously that it was 'the average director's knowledge of football'. The journalist thought that was a great idea and, trusting in the instincts of his trade, insisted they use it in the book.

Clown Prince of Soccer was an instant success. When it went on sale in Sunderland in September 1955, the public clamoured to buy copies of their hero's life story and read his controversial views on the game. 'The queue for it was amazing,' says Doug Weatherall, for many years the *Daily Mail*'s respected representative in the North-East and the doyen of football writers in that area. A lifelong

Sunderland supporter, he adds: 'There's a booksellers in the town called Arrowsmiths, and the queue to buy the book was an amazing length before the shop even opened. It looked like a queue at a football match!' Sales were so brisk that the publishers struggled to keep up with demand and were into a fifth edition by Christmas.

Shackleton himself did not think it was just the blank page that created all the interest. He sensed that his autobiography was popular because it was the first written by a footballer who was 'playing hell about the game'. And play hell, he did. As the blank page indicated – and as we have seen already in this narrative – football club directors were a major target for his anger and contempt, especially those who doubled as England selectors. But Shack took up many other contentious issues as well. They included the poor rates of pay footballers were receiving and the savagely unfair nature of their contracts of employment.

He utterly condemned the professional footballer's contract of those days, calling it 'an evil document' that was hopelessly one-sided. What he could not understand was how the retain and transfer system had managed to survive all the criticism it had attracted. Public indignation had been voiced and questions asked in the House of Commons, he lamented, yet the 'canker', as he called it, remained in the system of the game, spreading unrest and dissatisfaction everywhere.

Explaining the one-sidedness of the contract, he pointed out that, once a player had signed for a League club, it tied him to them for life if they wished to retain his services. But if the club no longer wanted to keep the player, the contract could be terminated on the spot without notice. It meant, he argued in typically colourful language, that footballers were nothing but puppets dancing on the end of a piece of elastic held by their lords and masters, the directors of the club.

Years ahead of his time, he argued that, in its place, there was a need for a new form of agreement that would allow players freedom of movement once they had fulfilled their contractual obligations to any particular club. He was not optimistic about the chances of such an agreement being implemented, however. Regretting that the Players' Union had been rebuffed at every turn in their attempts to improve their members' lot, he said it was difficult to envisage any change until 'the staid gentry of Preston [where the Football League have their headquarters again now] and Lancaster Gate are superseded by younger, more realistically-minded men.'

To underline the restrictive nature of the English footballer's terms of employment, Shackleton pointed out that he and two of the domestic game's other outstanding players, Tom Finney and Wilf Mannion, had been unable to consider extremely lucrative offers from clubs in Italy and Turkey because they knew their existing employers, Sunderland, Preston North End and Middlesbrough, were simply not prepared to consider transferring them; and, in those feudal days of 'soccer serfdom', that was the end of the matter regardless of whether the player's contract had ended or not.

As for footballers' pay, Shack was particularly vexed by the enormous discrepancy between what the players earned and what the clubs received through the gate as a result of the massive post-war boom in attendances. Starting at 35.6million in the first season proper after the war, 1946-47, they peaked at 41.2million in 1948-49. By 1955, they had fallen back to 34.1million, but gates of 60-70,000 for First Division matches were still common. Compare this with the situation today, when attendances are again increasing: the aggregate for the Premier League and Football League in 2002-03 was 28.3million, and only Manchester United can accommodate a crowd of more than 60,000.

Admission prices were much lower then, of course; but as Terry Venables once said to me with regard to this very subject: 'Sixty or seventy thousand of anything is a lot of money!' A lot of money, certainly, when you are paying your players just £15 a week, the maximum permitted in 1955. In *Clown Prince of Soccer*, Shackleton used the most glamorous fixtures to drive home his point. Complaining that the fee received by an England player for representing his country was then only £50, while the gate money for an international match was in the region of £50,000, he calculated that the 22 players who generated that kind of income were paid little more than 2 per cent of it.

To drive home his point, he made telling comparisons with the entertainment industry. Would Tommy Trinder (then a famous stand-up comedian), he asked, feel adequately recompensed with a fee of £1,100 if he attracted a £50,000 audience? If Don Cockell (then the British heavyweight champion) and Rocky Marciano fought before a crowd that had paid £50,000 to watch them, would they consider they were overpaid at £550 each? Yet footballers were so used to accepting paltry payments for playing football, the international match fee of £50 was actually regarded as excessive.

'I recall playing at Highbury Stadium, on Cup Final eve in 1954, as a representative of "Old" England against Young England in a match which produced not less than £6,000 in receipts,' he said. 'My fee that night was £6. Further comment seems unnecessary, except to state that it was nothing less than an insult to pay a talented artist like Stanley Matthews that sum for the performance he put on for the benefit of 43,000 spectators at Highbury.'

Football's refusal to pay its players what they were worth, in terms of the gate money they generated, the entertainment they provided and their value to the team, clearly irritated Shackleton beyond measure. 'He'd actually thought about it, and the old "cloth cap" image was alien to him,' said Malcolm Macdonald, now a football broadcaster and pundit. 'The "being grateful for what you get" attitude just didn't work with him. He was a man who knew he was an artist and felt that, as such, he had rights which the rules of the game and the behaviour of the people who ran it were never going to afford him.'

Johnny McSeveney experienced his left-wing partner's financial irritation at first hand and recalled it in a way that illustrates just how blunt and visionary Shack could be in the same breath: 'The thing he always used to say when he was talking about money – like, it was always money, money, money: Yorkshireman, you know – was: "I should be paid more than you!" And when I asked Len how he made that out, he'd say: "Because I'm a better player than you!"

'And so it went on, and we'd argue the point. He used to go on and on about it. He always had the conception that star players should earn star money. It wasn't a case of: "I should get £100 a week", or anything like that: he just felt that the star player should earn more than somebody else, like the stage people. When you looked at the Palladium and places like that, the star performers got the big money and, at the lower level, they were paid accordingly. And that was his conception of the whole thing. But I always used to argue that it was a team game and that it took one sort of player to make another: that we were all important. So if the pay was all the same, as it was then, it was brilliant.'

Shackleton's suggested solution to what he saw as the pay problem was, in addition to a major loosening of the FA's purse-strings, the abolition of the maximum wage. 'Why not run a football club like any other business, with each player coming to his own agreement with his club about wages, length of contract, benefit payments and any other relevant items?' he reasoned. 'If Stanley Matthews is worth £50 a week to Blackpool, let the club pay him that figure.' The abolition of the maximum wage would bring many benefits, he contended. They would include the elimination of illegal payments, signing-on presents and 'back-door bargaining', all of which the FA and Football League were keen to stamp out.

This may sound old hat now, but it was sensational, subversive stuff back then. Shack really was the first active footballer to put his head above the parapet in such a provocative manner. He was merely giving voice to what most of the country's other professional footballers were thinking, but they were afraid to speak up individually in case their clubs or the ruling bodies took action against them. Naturally outspoken, Shackleton had also reached that late stage in his career when he no longer gave a damn what anybody thought about him. In his 34th year, and dropped again after playing so well against West Germany, he knew he had no chance of getting back into the England team and could not see how else the authorities might hurt him.

'If you had an original thought in those days, you were a rebel,' reflected Ivor Broadis, the former Sunderland player and England international who also became a football writer in retirement. 'While we weren't exactly the "soccer slaves" people talked about, everybody knew we were grossly underpaid: well, those who thought about it knew. Shack certainly knew it and he spoke out against it. There weren't very many who did that.

'I used to write in the *Evening News* when I was in Manchester [playing for Manchester City], and I'd talk about the footballer's contract, which was diabolical, really. And, you know, the tendency was that if you spoke out or expressed views contrary to theirs [the football authorities'], the quicker you were out of the way, the better. If you did speak out against them, as Len did, and they weren't too happy about it, then I imagine they might get their knife into you. Certainly, it was ridiculous that he didn't get more England caps, wasn't it?'

The sweep of Shackleton's criticism was so wide, and its intent so serious, as to make the title of his autobiography extremely ironic: in reality, *Clown Prince of Soccer* should have had a question mark appended. Here we had an intelligent footballer who had thought long and hard about the state of the game he loved and was voicing his discontent in the hope of getting the authorities to right perceived wrongs. As we have seen already, Shack's criticism was of the constructive variety. Another example was the remedy he proposed for that vexed issue, the infuriating and unsettling habit the unqualified England selectors had of making wholesale changes from game to game.

His suggestion was that the amateurish selection committee, consisting of several club directors, should be replaced by a professional one containing only three members, all of them successful club managers. The men he named as suitable candidates were: Arthur Rowe, whose 'push-and-run' tactics won the old First Division title for Tottenham Hotspur in 1950-51; Jimmy Seed, under whose guidance Charlton Athletic had won the FA Cup in 1947; Joe Smith, who was the long-serving manager of Blackpool when they won the FA Cup in the famous 1953 'Matthews Final'; Cliff Britton, the former England international who had taken Everton back into the First Division after one of their rare demotions; Ted Drake, the man in charge when Chelsea won their only League Championship to date in 1954-55; Stan Cullis, whose 16-year reign at Molineux saw Wolverhampton Wanderers win the First Division title three times and the FA Cup twice; and Tom Whittaker, who, as George Allison's successor, steered Arsenal to two League Championships and one FA Cup triumph.

Shackleton envisaged their jobs as being full-time, too. He proposed that the FA should pay each of the three selectors £50 a week, a tidy sum then, but one that he felt could be easily met from the funds in the ruling body's coffers. Relieved of their club responsibilities, Shack's three wise men would spend their time talent-spotting with an expert, unbiased eye. Half the trouble with the existing selection system, he rightly felt, was that consistency and impartiality were impossible when selectors would naturally try to push the claims of players at their own clubs.

Any spare time the three new selectors might have, Shackleton suggested, could be utilised by letting them make unbiased assessments of referees. This, of course, was at time when referees' assessors were unheard of and the only evaluation of the officials' performances came from the two clubs concerned: inevitably, these flawed reports were often determined by the result.

Furthermore, Shackleton argued, the expert knowledge and experience of the three selectors could be put to other uses. He had in mind the fresh ideas they might inject into pre-match training sessions or international get-togethers, although he did not hold out much hope for the latter. It might have been simpler, of course, if Shack had just advocated the appointment of an all-powerful England manager to replace Winterbottom. But that seems to have been a step too far, even for him, in the mid-1950s.

Younger readers may be surprised to learn that the club v country issue was becoming a major obstacle to England's progress as long ago as 1955. Even then, international get-togethers had to be kept to a minimum because of the clubs' reluctance to release players. Yet, as Shack observed with quiet anger, England were already beginning to suffer in competition with the continental countries because they were quite prepared to adjust their domestic programmes so that their national teams had maximum time to prepare for international matches.

The over-committed English could afford to be at such a disadvantage before the war, Shackleton pointed out, because they were so obviously superior to the continentals as individuals and teams. But the opposition had improved so markedly in the decade since the war that England now needed all the pre-match preparation they could get. One prime example of unpreparedness he gave was of his left-wing partner in an England 'B' game against Holland, Wolves' Jimmy Mullen, having to ask the team manager when he could expect Len Shackleton to pass the ball to him. Shack being Shack, he joked that the answer would have been: 'When you least expect it – probably when Len's facing the other way.' But he was making a very serious and valid point.

Coaching, then a new-fangled concept being promoted by England manager Winterbottom, who doubled as the FA's director of coaching, was another controversial topic to which Shackleton directed his thoughts. Given the lack of respect he often displayed for Winterbottom, it is tempting to believe Shack was anti-coaching, *per se*. That, though, is far from the truth. Like other players of his age, Shackleton came from a generation that had been largely self-taught. Before the war, organised coaching had been practically non-existent: managers did little more than choose the players a club wanted to buy or sell, make sure they were kept fit and pick the team. So it was hard for those kind of footballers to adjust to the new 'fetish' that coaching could improve players and, fundamentally, they remained suspicious of the new methods being imposed upon the game.

Shack even made the point that few products of the post-war coaching schemes could hold a candle to self-made artists such as Stanley Matthews, Tommy Lawton, Wilf Mannion and – one of his favourite players – Jimmy Hagan, all of whom had been denied the benefits of coaching during their younger days. In fact, he went so far as to claim football in Britain between 1948 and 1955 had reached an all-time low, in that players between the ages of 30 and 40 had been able to see off the competition for places from younger, coached men. However, he made it absolutely clear he was not condemning coaching *per se*. His feeling was that coaches had a valuable contribution to make, provided they did the job properly and did not try to teach old dogs new tricks, so to speak.

Shack could scarcely credit it that a coach had tried to teach Newcastle United's players – many of them seasoned internationals – to kick the ball correctly at one session in the 1954-55 season. 'I can just picture my old team-mate Jackie Milburn being told how to shoot... after scoring more goals than his instructor had probably ever dreamed of,' he reflected in total disbelief. As mentioned earlier, Shackleton was firmly of the opinion that only coaches who had been first-class players should be allowed to instruct others, especially those at the top of the profession. An ability to convey ideas clearly and effectively was another, more reasonable, qualification he demanded.

The weakness in this argument, as Shack had the good grace to acknowledge, was that some of the most successful British coaches working on the continent at that time had been only moderate footballers during their own playing careers. George Raynor and Duggie Livingstone, who had flourished in Sweden and Belgium respectively, were two cases in point. But Shackleton brushed aside this counter-evidence on the grounds that Raynor and Livingstone had played at a time when everyone had to be of a very high standard to hold down a first-team place. Besides, he added contentiously, young continental footballers were more eager to learn than their British counterparts.

Perversely, Shack had no hesitation in lionising Jimmy Hogan, the gifted English coach who taught most of Europe – Austria and Hungary in particular – to play football. The praise he heaped on the great soccer evangelist is perfectly justified ('My ideal, and I had to do a lot of searching, would be Jimmy Hogan…'); the only problem being that Hogan had been an unremarkable footballer with various clubs including Burnley and Fulham and, as such, did not appear to possess the demanding qualifications for coaching Shackleton thought necessary. Yet Shack laments the fact that this 'great football sage' was in demand everywhere in the world but his own country while still arguing, in effect, that only great players could make great coaches. That theory has been disproved so often since then, all one can do is make allowances for the fact that Shackleton was pontificating at a time when coaching was in its infancy in Britain. Clearly, too, he could bend the facts to suit his argument when necessary.

The authorities were decidedly nervous about Shackleton's autobiography from the start. Even before it was published, he had been taken aside by Sunderland manager Billy Murray, who wanted reassurance that it wasn't going to be 'too naughty'. Murray, it transpired, had been leaned on by Alan Hardaker, the formidable secretary of the Football League, who had warned him of dire consequences if the book turned out to be 'over the top'.

Indeed, there was some newspaper talk of Shack being banned from the game as a result of that insulting blank page about the average football director's knowledge of football. But, in reality, he met with little hostility at clubs up and down the country. What tickled him most was when a Portsmouth director told him how brilliant he thought the book was. 'At first that surprised me,' Shackleton said, 'but then it suddenly dawned on me what was happening. He obviously didn't think of himself as the average director – none of them did. They obviously thought: "Oh, he's not talking about me, it's the other lot." '

On the whole, the autobiography was well received. Most newspapers, certainly, reviewed it favourably. 'No-one has ever played football quite like Len Shackleton, and no footballer has ever written a book quite like this,' said Newcastle's *Evening Chronicle*. 'In print, as so often on the field, he has produced something at once unorthodox, sensational and controversial.' To which the *Sunday Sun* added sagely: 'All the critics seem to have forgotten one thing, that in his book Len really tried to do something for Britain's national game. He reveals abuses and neglect which show just why Britain's reputation is now so low among the football nations.'

There were plenty of dissenting voices, however. The *Daily Mail* reviewer, for instance, snarled: 'Len Shackleton, erstwhile England inside-forward – he never wants to play for England again – has written the most bitter attack on Soccer [sic] I have ever read.' Many of his readers seemed to agree too. 'Shackleton's book insults ordinary intelligence,' fumed 'Disgusted' of Bradford. 'Most directors are very interested in football and therefore set out to acquire knowledge of it. What does Shackleton know of hairdressing [He owned a hairdresser's at the time]? Yet, I imagine he's the boss.' Bravely, Shack included this and other hostile views in *Return of the Clown Prince*. His only complaint about them was that they were written in reaction to the *Mail* review and not to *Clown Prince of Soccer* itself, which his critics did not appear to have read.

Whatever the general public thought about the book, it is beyond dispute that Shackleton's constructive criticism was part of the growing discontent that helped to bring about major reforms in English football during the following eight years. The changes started with the scrapping of the pathetic £10 signing-on fee in 1958, continued with the abolition of the maximum wage three years later and culminated in the destruction of the retain and transfer system in 1963. He saw himself as more frustrated by the many injustices in the game than as a rebel trying to upset the status quo; nonetheless, he was proud to say that nobody had fought harder than he to get the maximum wage lifted.

There is unqualified support for that claim from players' union quarters, past and present. Jimmy Hill, the articulate, charismatic and hard-working chairman of the union when the bitterly-fought campaign for the abolition of the maximum wage was conducted successfully in the late 1950s and early 1960s, and Gordon Taylor, chief executive of the Professional Footballers' Association, which is what the union is called today, both agree that Shackleton and his autobiography played an important part in wearing down the resistance of the football establishment to much-needed reforms.

'Len was a rebel,' said Hill, 'and the game needed rebels in those days to get it straightened out. I'm sure he played his part. It was unfortunate that he wasn't one of those who benefited when the maximum wage finally went, because he'd done his bit to get rid of it. He was a lone voice with the nerve to start the argument, draw attention to it. He had the nerve to do that, just as he had the nerve to dribble the ball up his own goal line. His extraordinary ability was worth more than twenty quid a week, or whatever, and it was probably not even £20 when he was playing – more like £12 or £14. His capacity to entertain was worth a hell of a lot more than that, and you can understand him feeling strongly about it.

'Shack was daring to say the things he did say publicly, because most of us wouldn't have dreamed of opposing those above us, as it were – directors and everybody else. It was unheard of because there were very few players who had the sense of grievance and the outrageousness to do it – and who were important enough for journalists to be prepared to quote them. Len, of course, was a good enough player to be in that category. The public believed what their heroes had to say, and he was one of the early ones who were prepared to voice an opinion and stand up and be counted.

'That blank page of his was such an accurate page. When I was on the FA Council, I was the only one of the 90 or so members who could be guaranteed to hit the goal from the penalty spot! Nobody else could have played football at the professional level. And since I've been off it, there hasn't been anybody [from the professional game]. I mean, it's unbelievable! I'm not saying there should be 89 former professional footballers on the council, I'm just saying it might help a little bit if somebody has done it out there in the middle, providing the FA with its income. Admittedly, they appear to be using Trevor Brooking now at last, so at least there is one guy there who can be relied upon to do that. But it's certainly still a strange old scene in some directions.'

Taylor, whose considerable clout in football's current corridors of power is due in no small part to the battles fought and won by Hill and that redoubtable union secretary, Cliff Lloyd, nearly half a century ago, agrees entirely with his distinguished predecessor about Shackleton. 'Definitely, without any shadow of a doubt, yes,' he answers to the question of whether the so-called Clown Prince made a serious contribution to the lifting of the maximum wage and the ending of the retain and transfer system. 'All the players then hated the restrictions on them. Even the great Tom Finney admits these days that he felt a sense of frustration when a big Italian club came in for him, and the Preston chairman said: "Well, there's no way you're leaving this club!" They just didn't have the freedom to capitalise on their ability.

'We're talking now of the mid-1950s, when the campaign was building up. We had people like Jimmy Guthrie, who was chairman of the Players' Union then, people like Len Shackleton, people like Wilf Mannion, who made his own particular stand. Then it all got motivated. Jimmy Hill was elected chairman to succeed Jimmy Guthrie and it went on apace. Everybody cried doom and gloom. I can remember being a youngster with Bolton on twelve quid a week and the manager, Bill Ridding, said: "That'll be the end of the game!" when the maximum wage was abolished. Five years later, we won the World Cup!'

Ironically, Shackleton had mixed feelings in later life about the consequences of the major reforms for which he and his fellow union members had fought so hard. A chapter in *Return of the Clown Prince*, for example, was entitled clumsily but revealingly: 'Commercially a full circle – from a game with a business in it to a business with a game in it'. While glad that footballers were now being paid, and treated, in accordance with their capacity to entertain large crowds, he could not help wondering whether it had all gone too far. He certainly admitted that his wife, Marjorie, thought so. 'At least arrangements these days are on a commercial footing for players,' he said, 'though whether overall this is for the good of the game, I don't know, only time will tell. I talk with my wife, as a football fan of long-standing herself, quite often about this. She is absolutely against what she feels are the "obscene" wages commanded by top players today.'

Shack, though, could not bring himself to be quite so condemnatory of the £60,000-£100,000 per week being earned by the modern game's outstanding crowd-pullers. Remembering that he and his contemporaries had fought against the maximum wage and for freedom of contract because the clubs and the FA used to trade on the popularity of the players, he could hardly complain too loudly about where it had all led. Only slightly miffed at having missed out on the pay bonanza, and stressing that his wife did not think current wages 'obscene' because he had been denied them, he simply wished today's players good luck. 'I'm certainly not aggrieved about what the lads get today,' he insisted, 'because it's simply the commercial outcome of a long-fought and now past struggle.'

Shackleton was also a touch ambivalent about the consequences of the George Eastham and Jean-Marc Bosman cases, which between them blew away the restrictions on players' freedom of movement between clubs. In *Return of the Clown Prince* Shack went into great historical detail about Eastham's successful challenge to the English retain and transfer system in 1963 and Bosman's equally successful litigation, some thirty years later, against restraint of trade in European football; but he did so without committing himself overmuch on their ramifications. Though clearly a supporter of Eastham (as a journalist, he actually introduced the player to the wealthy businessman, Ernie Clay, whose financial backing enabled him to persist with his bid to be transferred from Newcastle United to Arsenal) and the principle that a footballer should be able to change jobs as freely as a motor mechanic, say, at the end of his contract, Shackleton was manifestly less enthusiastic about Bosman.

Of course, the ruling in the Belgian's favour by the European Court of Justice also removed most of the restrictions on the number of foreign nationals who could play for European clubs. So Shack obviously shared the PFA's concern that an unrestricted influx of foreign footballers could seriously affect the development of young English players, a fear that has proved far from groundless. He was also worried, with good reason, that transfer fees which might normally have been ploughed back into English football at a lower level would now be diverted abroad, or into the pockets of players and their agents.

Yet none of these misgivings is expressed with any real force: with none of the conviction or sardonic wit, certainly, that Shackleton brought to his diatribes against the maximum wage and the retain and transfer system in *Clown Prince of Soccer*. 'It will be interesting to see just how things develop from here,' he said, with disappointing meekness, in the updated version of his classic. 'If nothing else, it also emphasises one long-standing aspect of the game, that without such controversy fans and enthusiasts would soon find things rather dull. Football has always been a game of opinion and it will continue to be the case!' No doubt that uncharacteristic note of surrender was just a simple example of how age can mellow a fellow. After all, the joking firebrand of yesteryear was 78 by the time *Return of the Clown Prince* was published.

It was not just on the major football issues of the day that Len Shackleton turned his searching gaze in 1955. He also offered his twopenn'orth about directors – that blank page notwithstanding – managers, referees, football pools, the welfare of down-at-heel former players and even the distribution of FA Cup final tickets. His comments on directors and managers were directly linked, in that he raged against the refusal of many boards to let their managers manage and against the compliance of the managers who allowed this to happen. 'Glorified office-boys,' he called them contemptuously.

Making it clear that the prospect of becoming a manager himself appalled him, Shackleton argued that it would be better to have no managers at all than just 'nominal' managers. At the same time, he feared for the future of English football if matters were left in the hands of directors entirely ignorant of the game. He talked of the 'unbelievable lack of knowledge in the board room' and confessed that he and his team-mates would have a good laugh in the dressing room when they compared stories about the ignorance of the nincompoops in charge of the club.

One director, claimed Shack, had asked him if his 'spikes' were comfortable and, as it was a windy day, told him to keep the ball up in the air. Another, in the Midlands, was said to have instructed his coach to tell the players to kick not with their insteps, but with their toes because that would make the ball travel further. Then there was the classic about the time Arsenal were trailing at half-time against Manchester United at Old Trafford. One Arsenal director, not realising the Gunners were playing in their change strip because of the colour clash with United's red shirts, is reported to have said he hoped his team could keep up their good form in the second half!

It was not a total condemnation of football club directors that Shackleton issued, though he thought 90 per cent of them knew nothing about football and, in the case of the other 10 per cent, a little knowledge was a dangerous thing. He did have a good word for 'the progressive approach' of the Sunderland board and singled out the chairman, Bill Ditchburn, and his staunch supporter, Bill Martin, for special praise. This, however, was questionable on two counts: it sounded as though he was just sucking up to his current employers and, when the illegal payments scandal broke over Roker Park a couple of years later, Shack's claim that the board went 'out of their way to investigate the rights and wrongs of soccer' had rather a hollow ring.

As for the managers, Shackleton urged clubs to allow them complete control over the selection of teams and their backroom staff. He also insisted that they ought to have the last word on which players were to be bought and sold. Clerical work should be left to the club secretaries, he added, and business matters to the directors. Even now, those lines of demarcation are not clear, but they must have been extremely blurred then for Shack to have spoken out so strongly on the subject. He also railed against the precariousness of a football manager's employment, the tendency of clubs to sack their man on a whim; but nothing has changed so far as that aspect of the job is concerned and it never will.

Referees, by and large, got a sympathetic hearing. Although Shackleton complained about the 'homers', the pompous, the over-zealous and the cowards in their ranks, he did acknowledge the difficulties of the 'thankless task' they were expected to carry out. Typically, he also proposed certain reforms, some of which were before their time. They included scrapping the compulsory retirement age of 47, the fast-tracking of retired footballers as trainee referees, the employment of permanent refereeing 'teams' of a referee and two linesmen and, last but not least, a doubling of the match fee.

Shack could barely contain himself, though, over the continued refusal of the FA and the Football League to accept money from the football pools companies: Littlewoods, Vernons, Copes, Shermans, *et al*, who had first offered the game £50,000 a year in 1936, then double that figure in 1945. Reminding everyone that, even after the biggest boom in attendances English football had ever seen, some clubs were struggling to survive, he found it incredible that the game's ruling bodies clung to the haughty, puritanical belief that pools money was devil's gold.

To make matters worse, as Shackleton pointed out, sport elsewhere in Europe was profiting from the English League programme, which provided the fixtures for several foreign football pools as well as our own. That was certainly true of Sweden and Switzerland. A share of the profits was then returned to sport in those countries. In Norway, £300,000 a year was granted to sport from the state pools. Yet the patrician view persisted in boardrooms up and down England that the pools could bring only corruption to football and hardship to a populace that would be tempted to spend more on gambling than it could afford.

It is all a far cry from today, when professional football grabs at every conceivable source of income and would be in serious danger of collapse without the vast sums it receives from television, sponsors and the National Lottery as well as the pools companies. Here again, too, it looks as though the forthright, visionary opinions Shackleton expressed in 1955 may well have helped to create a climate, at the very least, in which the authorities could be made to see commercial sense.

The man who actually did the trick was another hard-headed

Yorkshireman: Football League secretary Alan Hardaker. A couple of years after taking over in 1957, Hardaker persuaded his management committee to claim copyright over the fixtures in a test case against Littlewoods, which the League won. As a result, the Pools Promoters Association, which represented most of the pools companies, agreed to pay a total of £250,000 a year to the Football League and the Scottish League. That figure had risen to £2million by 1977 and eventually peaked at about £12million.

Shackleton was also incensed at the failure of the Football League to use its Jubilee Benefit Fund to help football's needy, as had been intended when the fund was set up in the late summer of 1938. Though frozen during the six years of the Second World War, it had earned considerable interest during the hostilities and was, in Shack's opinion, the ideal means of helping those players who had been aged between 27 and 31 when the war began. Lucky enough – in football terms – to have been only 17 himself when the war started, he pointed out that many players had returned to their clubs in 1946 as veterans or has-beens and were facing a life of hardship and re-training. Yet, he contended, the League were reluctant to put the money to good use and were deaf to pleas from the Players' Union to let them administer the fund. In October 1947, Shackleton recalled grimly, the fund stood at £65,000; but only eight footballers had received benefits from it, the largest individual grant having been just £300.

He was equally critical of the way FA Cup final tickets were distributed. Shack accused the system of being 'out of date, full of loopholes for the spiv, and aimed, so it seems, at ensuring that genuine supporters of the two clubs concerned are the last to be considered.' He suggested that, instead of receiving 15,000 tickets each, the finalists should be allocated 75 per cent of their average home attendance. Calculating that that would account for something like 52,000 tickets, Shackleton added cuttingly that this would leave 'the very considerable number of 48,000 for the titled ladies, film stars, friends of the FA, and even a few followers of football'.

Sensible and practical as many of Shackleton's proposals were, the insistently critical tone of his book did not endear him to the powers-that-be. During the season in which *Clown Prince of Soccer* was published, 1955-56, Shack was invited by the Football Association of Kenya to play some exhibition matches there, and in the neighbouring Tanganyaka (now Tanzania), during the close season that followed. The invitation looked to have been prompted by the publication of his autobiography, since the secretary of the Kenyan FA, JH Whittingham, referred to it in glowing terms and praised the author for his 'outspokenness'. Sunderland had no objection to his going, but not so the English FA. Something of a furore ensued when, in a letter to Whittingham, the secretary of the FA, Sir Stanley Rous, intimated that permission might not be granted for Shackleton to go to Kenya because of 'his attitude to governing bodies'.

In the end, a rash of unfavourable newspaper headlines about the FA 'banning' Shack from going to East Africa persuaded them to think again; and they eventually gave up that particular attempt to punish him for having had the effrontery to criticise them in his book. Even then, though, Rous could not resist adding a snooty postscript to his letter of approval for the trip. 'The Football Association has not publicised this matter,' he warned Shackleton, 'and I would suggest that you keep the matter confidential and leave the publicity to this Association after the matter has been finalised. You will remember that it was the publicity which was given prematurely to your previous invitation which caused complications and embarrassment.'

No doubt Shack, scourge of football's establishment and a man with a keen sense of humour, had a good laugh about that.

CHAPTER SEVEN
ESSENCE OF SHACK

A straightforward account of the highs and lows of Len Shackleton's playing career with Arsenal, Bradford Park Avenue, Newcastle United, Sunderland and England tells only half the story. Rejection by Arsenal, goalscoring on a record-breaking scale with Park Avenue, disaffection with Newcastle after a sensational start, contentment with Sunderland, frustration with England, contempt for authority and campaigns for reform are just the bare bones of the tale. What made Shack a legend, and keeps his reputation burning bright even today, half a century on, was an extraordinary ability to manipulate a football more cleverly, arguably, than any Englishman who has ever played the game. That, coupled with an irrepressible desire to entertain and a gift for outrageous showmanship, is what sets him apart from other footballers, past and present. There have been more complete players than Shack, but none quite like him.

Gifted, extrovert ball-players such as Jim Baxter, Paul Gascoigne, Alan Hudson, Tony Currie, Rodney Marsh and Frank Worthington were all heirs to the maverick tradition established by Shackleton in the 1940s and 1950s. Many of the contemporaries I interviewed for this book compared Shack to George Best; but that seems to me a false comparison, though a deservedly flattering one. While every bit as clever as Best at manipulating a football, if not more so, Shackleton was never as consistent or hard working as the wiry Northern Irishman. Like Shack, Best loved to take the mickey out of opponents – especially those who tried to kick him into Row Z; but he was also prepared to tackle back like a defender and get up to head the ball if a scoring chance presented itself, two things Shackleton rarely bothered to do. Nor would Best play to the gallery just for the sake of it: all of his wonderful technique was focused on scoring or making goals and beating the opposition.

Wilf McGuinness, the former Busby Babe and Manchester United manager, put it this way: 'Shack did the same sort of things that Bestie did, but nowhere as quick or as good. Like Bestie, Shack had good balance, but the end product wasn't always there, as it was with George. He was the George Best of his time, if you like, but he wasn't, in my opinion, of the same quality. He was certainly a brilliant dribbler, but I never saw him tackle and I did see George tackle. Remember, though, that I was only 18 at the time.' Remember, too, that McGuinness had to be naturally biased towards Best because of the United connection.

It is worth taking into consideration, however, that George Best was playing at a time, the 1960s and early 1970s, when, largely as a result of the introduction of European football to the English fixture list by his club, the competition for honours and league placings was starting to get serious. As a result, individualism was increasingly subordinated to teamwork. It would be wrong to suggest the exact opposite was true of Len Shackleton's playing days, but the fact that there were only two trophies to be won – the League Championship and the FA Cup – meant an awful lot of teams did not have much to play for come the second half of the season and the individual could flourish in a relatively uncompetitive setting.

'In those days,' recalls Stan Anderson, the outstanding local boy in Sunderland's 'Bank of England' team, 'there wasn't as much emphasis on winning. It's life and death now, but back then there was more emphasis on the FA Cup than there was on the League. Len always said: "Now we're in the semi-final, you know, we should take it easy next week [in the League] so nobody's injured." I used to think it must be great to win the championship, but Len, he wasn't bothered. Getting to Wembley was the important thing. I suppose the whole structure of football has changed now, with European cups and whatnot. It's the League that's important now – if you can finish on top, or second, third or fourth, you're in the European Cup.

'I remember when I took over as manager of Middlesbrough in 1966 [Anderson is the only player to have captained all three of the North-East's leading clubs] and was looking through some old books that had been left on the desk. There were results like Middlesbrough v Blackburn Rovers – 4-0 at home, 5-0 away. There were lots of results like that, and I can understand why. If you get a really good team now, like Chelsea or Arsenal or Man U, they get beaten on the odd occasion, but only 2-1 or 1-0: they don't get stuffed five, like they used to in those days. The attitude then was: "If we go two down, what the hell!" They thought they might as well get beaten four or five.'

Without question, then, there was much more scope in the ten years after the war for the talented individual to express himself, should he so wish. Not only that, but with few recreational alternatives available to them, football fans wanted desperately to be entertained in those austere years following the war when most things pleasurable were still rationed. Whether any of this registered consciously with Shack is difficult to tell; but one should like to think someone as intelligent as he was would have been aware of the situation. In any case, he was such a natural show-off that the managers and coaches of any era would have found it difficult to control his histrionic tendencies. This part of his game could probably be traced back to the fact that he learned his trade in the comparatively easy-going atmosphere of wartime football: so he came into the resumption of structured competition at the end of the war as a fully-formed free spirit.

On top of everything else, of course, he was one of the most fantastic ball-players the game has witnessed. The tricks he was capable of performing with that old leather ball, which weighed a ton when wet, almost defy belief. They may not sound so exceptional now, when we are used to seeing players like Zinedine Zidane and Thierry Henry make today's lighter, waterproof job do all manner of extraordinary things; but Shack could bend it like Beckham before David's father was born, never mind old 'Goldenballs' himself, and he could put so much backspin on it that it would return to his beckoning finger from 12 or 15 yards away.

Jack Rollin remembers seeing him doing just that before that big England game against West Germany in 1954. 'The referee was the well-known Italian, Concetto Lo Bello, and he called to Shackleton for the match ball, which Shack had got hold of,' recalled Rollin, the man who made *Rothmans Football Yearbook* the 'bible' of English football, and the author of many other useful books on the game. 'So Shackleton hit it towards the referee; but he'd put backspin on it, and the ball came back to him as Lo Bello went to pick it up.' Shades of clowns in the circus.

Not only that, but he was cracking jokes as the teams lined up to meet the VIP of the day before the kick-off. Interviewed for Sky Sports by Brian Moore shortly before he died in 2000, Shack was asked what the most memorable moment of his career had been. There were goals and passes galore he could have talked about, but he plumped instead for humour. 'When the VIP – I think it might have been Anthony Eden – had shaken hands with us in the England team,' he said, 'he turned to go down the German line. And I looked across at the lad opposite me. Now Wembley's a beautiful ground, as you know, the surface is absolutely magnificent. So I said to the lad opposite: "Hey, Fritz, if we win the toss, we're going to bat. It's a bit green, but we're going to bat." That was in front of 90,000 people, but you've got to have a bit of fun, Brian.'

That was typical Shack: full of mischief and absolutely nerveless just before one of the most important matches of his career. Typical, too, in that he relished the memory of a joke ahead of a goal. Earlier in that same interview he had explained why that was his usual order of priority. Emphasising how he had always tried to enjoy his football, he said: 'I'm not talking about money as such, but we had the maximum wage in those days, and we could get the same money at Arsenal or Wolves or Man. United as you did at Sunderland. So you had to have something more than money to motivate you, and that was enjoyment for me. I used to enjoy the game – that's the point. If I wanted to make the ball go through somebody's legs, I'd do it. Whether it was the right thing to do for the team or not was just hard luck.'

One way he often demonstrated that love of enjoyment was by playing one-twos off corner flags, which must have been of more robust construction then than they are today to make that possible. Not all of them were, clearly, because he complained that Chelsea should install stronger poles after breaking one with a pass at Stamford Bridge.

Retired journalist Doug Weatherall was actually the beneficiary of one of those geometrical tricks. 'We were playing on the same side in a charity match at North Shields,' he explained. 'I was still young enough to play in those days, and this was after Shack's career was over; but he was still amazing on the ball. Anyway, he was near the corner flag and I was behind him calling for a pass. So he aimed the ball at the corner flag and it came back out directly to my feet. It was absolutely brilliant! Shack was not the best player I've ever seen, but he was easily the best ball-master. You can have your George Bests, or anybody, but nobody was better with the ball than Shack.'

No doubt Shackleton was aided in these astonishing feats of dexterity by the rugby boots he wore because this softer footwear gave him a better 'feel' for the ball than the regulation issue with rigid, bulbous toecaps. The latter had to be 'broken in' before they became wearable and anything like comfortable. When my father was a professional footballer before and during the war, he used to order his boots a size too small and then sit with them on in a bowl of water until they stretched and were moulded to the shape of his feet. After that, the softening-up process was completed with liberal coatings of Dubbin.

Shack, however, went for the rugby boots – perhaps after seeing the soft, custom-made football boots Stanley Matthews, another ball artist, favoured. Incidentally, when rooming with Matthews on England duty, Shackleton was surprised to discover that the great man and supreme professional used to have his everyday shoes weighted so that his football boots felt like 'dancing pumps' when he put them on. His eyes were also opened by Matthews' practice of sandpapering his boots to get the maximum out of them.

Many believe one of the secrets of Shackleton's magical ball control was the unusual length of his feet. They were long and thin enough to set him apart: certainly, it was rare to see a man of Shack's medium height standing in a pair of size tens. He could use them like hands, too. Roy Bentley, the England inside-forward who played alongside Shackleton at Newcastle before moving on to Chelsea, confirms the fact. 'He was an amazing character,' Bentley recalled. 'For his size, he had the longest feet I've ever seen. The toes were like long fingers and they enabled him to virtually catch a football with his feet – even a goal kick coming down from God knows what height. You see them doing it today, but it is a different ball to what we had. You know how you've seen tennis players kill a ball by sort of catching it on the back of their racket? Len could do that with his football boots and a football. I think he wore rugby boots, actually, because rugby boots in those days had a sort of pointed toe: more pointed than the football boot, anyway.'

Billy Bingham, too, used to marvel at the way his Sunderland team-mate would casually pull down, out of the air, balls that other footballers would have struggled to make use of with head or chest. 'What was so remarkable about him,' said Bingham, 'was he wasn't a big chap. He was no more than five eight or nine, at most, but he had big feet. He used to play football-tennis in the gymnasium in Sunderland and he would catch the ball as it was coming through the air. You and I would get it on our thigh, or perhaps volley it over the net; but he used to catch it on his foot! I've seen him do it in games, too. Where other people would be heading balls that were coming down, or chesting them, he would be putting his foot up and bringing them down – dead! Terrific control! And those big feet and a low centre of gravity gave him that utter confidence he had, which was undeniable in everything he did.'

Bingham reckoned it was those games of football-tennis that enabled Shackleton to keep his skills honed. 'As a footballer,' said the Irishman in his autobiography, 'he was a genius, a master of ball-control, the most wonderful dribbler I have ever seen – and that includes Stanley Matthews. Naturally gifted with agility and balance… he nevertheless worked at his game with an intensity that might have surprised those who sometimes accused him of shirking his inside-forward duties.

'One thing that I am quite sure developed his extraordinary

talents was the game of football-tennis, which was a regular feature of our training in the Roker Park gymnasium. In this game, the ball could be played over the net with any part of the anatomy except the hands and arms, and as a rebound off the walls still counted as a good return, you had to be really adept at ball-control. If you've seen Shack pull down a shoulder-high ball using an outstretched foot as if it were a hand, you can imagine what it was like trying to beat him at football-tennis.'

Johnny McSeveney also marvelled at his left-wing partner's skill at those games of football-tennis. 'The ball would come across and he would flick it on to the wall with his head and, without him even turning round, the ball would come back over his head and he'd catch it with his foot! Then he would catch it with his knee, roll it down his leg, flick it up again and knock it back over the net. It never went straight back over the net: he always had to do a couple of tricks. He'd catch the ball anywhere on his torso, he was so good at it. You could use any part of your anatomy in those games. It was down in the gym there at Roker. We played head tennis a lot and had wee competitions. It was good for skills, and there were snooker tables for those who were waiting to take part.'

Head tennis, Sunderland-style, was clearly not for the faint-hearted. 'Shack loved anything competitive,' reports Stan Anderson. 'He played football-tennis a lot with Ray Daniel and one or two others and they used to spend a lot of time at it. Well, that was their training routine, you know; it probably kept them fit. He was very competitive, very fierce and very athletic was Lenny.'

Shackleton agreed that those games of head/football-tennis – sometimes substituted for afternoon training – helped to improve his ball control. Shrewdly, he always chose Ken Chisholm as his partner and they would usually play Daniel and Ted Purdon. Shack realised that although Chisholm was not particularly fast and could not shoot brilliantly, he was skilful and could head the ball well. In fact, the partnership was so good, they would win five games out of seven on average. Shackleton boasted that they could have won every time if they had wanted but, as they were playing for five 'bob' (25p) a time, were reluctant to clean Daniel and Purdon out.

Stan Anderson is another former team-mate who was fascinated by Shackleton's feet. 'He had the funniest feet I've ever seen on a football field,' he said. 'He had great long toes and very thin feet. I don't know what size boot he was, but for a smallie – he was only about five foot six or seven – his feet must have been nines or tens. Huge, curly feet, I used to call them. But he was a wonderful striker of the ball and there was none of this one-footed play: he could play equally well with both feet.'

Whatever the reasons for Shack's urge to entertain and his capacity to do it, nobody thrilled, delighted or amused a crowd more easily or more often than he did when in the mood. Lifelong Sunderland fan Doug Weatherall says he and thousands of others used to make sure they got to Roker Park early on match days just to see the tricks Shackleton performed while giving his usual one-man show during the kick-in.

Weatherall adds that his elder brother, Jack, worshipped Shack to such an extent that he would not go and watch the team play if the great entertainer was not in the side. 'This applied to so many of his fan club,' Weatherall said in the stirring obituary he wrote for the *Daily Mail* on the occasion of Shackleton's death in 2000, 'that Sunderland would try to suppress news that he might miss a match through injury and once estimated that his absence could knock 10,000 off the attendance.'

Shackleton was always one to respond to a challenge, too. On one occasion, he went out of his way to give the fans a treat after seeing the ball-juggling performed by a centre-forward called Amalfi before a friendly against his club, Racing Club of Paris, that Sunderland, one of the first clubs in England to install floodlights, played one evening at Roker Park. Grabbing a ball, Shack proceeded to demonstrate that anything Amalfi could do, he could do better. But he was not another David Burnside, a young West Bromwich Albion player of the 1960s, who could dazzle the crowd with his 'keepy-uppy' routine as half-time entertainment, yet looked quite ordinary under pressure in a match. Shack was eminently capable of bamboozling opponents with his tricks anywhere, at any time and under any kind of conditions.

Johnny McSeveney recalls that Shack's ball-juggling act was not the only time he gave in to his exhibitionist urges during that friendly against Racing Club. 'He had a name all over the bloody place, you know, and when he picked the ball up nobody in their team would tackle him. So, juggling with it in front of the dug-out, he pulls his shorts up, pats down his hair, lifts up his wrist and says to Bert Johnston, the trainer: "How's time, Bert?" All this with three bloody players around him!'

Not all of his peers enjoyed the sight of Shack taking the mickey out of other players. Although Stanley Matthews was clearly a great admirer of his skill, there was an unmistakable note of disapproval in the account Matthews gave in his autobiography of Shackleton tormenting an opponent. 'He even made fun of fellow professionals not blessed with his considerable talents,' wrote Sir Stan. 'In one game for Sunderland, having beaten a full-back, he put his foot on the ball and pulled the cuff of his shirt sleeve back, implying he was checking his wristwatch and not taking any notice of events on the field. Then, as the full-back came roaring in for a second bite of the cherry, he dragged the ball back with the sole of his foot, to the delight of the Roker Park crowd but to the great annoyance of the opposing full-back, who rightly felt he had been made a fool of. The full-back in question tackled fresh air, Len slipped away with the ball at his feet and rubbed salt in the wound by arrogantly gesturing with his hands that he was taking a cup from its saucer and sipping tea.'

Penalties were one of Shackleton's specialities and provided him with endless opportunities to act the goat. Billy Elliott, who played alongside him at Bradford Park Avenue and Sunderland and was anything but a ballet dancer, recalls him backheeling one into the net at Park Avenue. The late Brian Redhead, the former Radio Four presenter and interviewer, treasured a similar memory. Redhead's recorded recollections were played back in the 1996 programme on Shack that formed part of the *Football Legends* series Jimmy Armfield, the former Blackpool and England full-back and present-day broadcaster, hosted for Radio Five Live.

Revealing that Shackleton, 'a man of immense wit', had been his favourite footballer when he was a teenager, Redhead said: 'I once saw him take a penalty against Manchester City, when Frank Swift was still alive. He put the ball on the spot and then he walked almost to the halfway line and he ran like a train at the ball and took a tremendous kick, and Swifty dived, but the ball was still on the spot! He hadn't actually touched it, and he turned round and he back-heeled it into the net and the crowd went raving mad! And old Swifty walked out and he took Len Shackleton's head in between those great hands and he kissed him!'

Sometimes, he tried something other than the backheel. There was one such variation during that controversial trip to Kenya and Tanzania in 1956. Taking a penalty in a match at Dar-Es-Salaam, he went on one of his long run-ups and made as though he was going to shoot really hard to the left. Then, at the last minute, he just pushed the ball into the other corner with the inside of his foot while the goalkeeper dived the wrong way. Again the crowd went wild: so wild, in fact, that some of the spectators who had climbed tall coconut palms to get a view from outside the packed ground actually fell off their perches. The way he told that story, with perhaps just a little exaggeration about people falling out of trees, showed just how much he loved to get that kind of response to his tricks.

As the example above illustrates, Shack's reputation as a magical entertainer was certainly not confined just to Britain. Johnny McSeveney recalls the enthusiastic reception his friend and left-wing partner got when Sunderland toured Denmark and Sweden during the Scot's first year at the club. 'We went by ferry from Harwich,' he said, 'and when we got to Esbjerg, in Denmark, there were people waiting there by the boat shouting: "Mr. Shack, Mr. Shack!" Our first match was in Copenhagen, and Len said to me: "We've got to win these matches! We've got to put a show on!" When he said that, you knew he was on song. We won that first match 3-1 and then, in the second one, he scored a hat-trick. It was the first he'd got all season, and the Danes were raving about him. "I love these games, I love these games!" he kept on saying.'

Shackleton also seemed to love performing one trick more than any other. It was the chip shot that brought him his famous goal for England against West Germany. Bingham claimed it almost became an obsession with Shack – to the exasperation of his team-mates when it did not come off and he could easily have scored with a more straightforward effort. When he did make it work, though, Bingham conceded, it was 'brilliantly spectacular'.

A goal of that type he remembered clearly was one Shackleton scored against Aston Villa in a League game: 'Len, who had been slacking a bit in his usual inside-forward role, was having a spell at outside-left at the time. I can see him now moving down the touchline, beating the full-back, drawing the centre-half, then beating him and another defender, too, until he was right on the by-line approaching the near post. The goalkeeper, Keith Jones, started to come out, and when he was about five yards away, Shack figuratively drew out his No.9 iron and delicately chipped the ball over the goalkeeper's head and into the net from a ridiculously narrow angle.'

It looks like Villa were Shackleton's 'bunnies' when it came to the chip shot, because Bingham recalled another example of the great man's boldness and finesse at Villa Park when he spoke to me more recently. 'I usually took the corners on the left side to put in an inswinger,' he said, 'but Shack shooed me away on this occasion. "We'll play a one-two," he said. So I said: "Okay", and gave him a short ball at the corner. He took it and dribbled into the box, beating two men in the space of about two feet. The goalkeeper then came to the near post, to stop him crossing the ball or scoring, and was as close to the post as one foot. Shack was about three feet away from him and he chipped it over his head like a mashie niblick shot: he just went at it like a golfer. He went "bumph" and the ball went up in the air and dropped inside the side-netting on the far side of the goal. I'll never forget it! It was unique. You could try it maybe 50 times and you wouldn't do it; but he tried it and scored!'

The opponents for whom Shackleton reserved the full range of his stunning talent were Arsenal. He insisted that his habit of playing outstandingly well against them was not a question of his exacting revenge for their hurtful rejection of him as a teenager: his explanation was that he always turned it on at Highbury because the game's top brass, England selectors included, were always likely to be present there. That was important, he argued, because the North-East's remoteness from London meant it was harder for players up there to be noticed by the powers-that-be. The fact that Newcastle's Jackie Milburn won only 13 England caps, he felt, was a glaring example of that neglect. Shack's theory, of course, did not explain why he also did his damnedest to bring about the Gunners' downfall when Sunderland played them at Roker Park. In short, nobody really believed that it was a question of anything other than Shack showing Arsenal what they had missed by letting him go as a kid.

The most outrageous of many such acts by him while playing against the London club occurred at Highbury. Again, Billy Bingham is a valuable source of information. He recalls that Shackleton was having his usual 'blinder' against Arsenal. He had scored and was playing so confidently that he had performed one of his favourite tricks. This was to run the ball down the touchline and tempt the linesman to flag it out of play while keeping it just in play all the time. Then, to general astonishment, he stopped in the middle of the game to instruct Derek Tapscott, Arsenal's Wales international winger, how to cross the ball.

'Tapscott was having a bad time,' said Bingham. 'He was running down the wing and sending the ball behind the net all the time when he tried to centre it. So, Shack was on his side of the field, got the ball, looked up and hit it away to me. Then he turned round, grabbed Tapscott by the shoulders and said: "Derek, look!" and he started giving him a demonstration. "When you get the ball, hook your foot back," he told him. And he's done this in front of the whole crowd! He's actually shown him how to do it on the field! That epitomised Shack – that's exactly what he was like. Maybe he didn't care too much about winning and losing, and things like that. Maybe he did care underneath that jokey façade, I don't know. Maybe I'm short-changing him. But he was certainly an exhibitionist and he had the attributes to put on an exhibition, let me put it that way.'

Judging by Shackleton's opening remark in that Radio Five Live programme, *Football Legends*, he would have agreed wholeheartedly with Bingham. 'I probably got the name of the Clown Prince because I used to go out and enjoy the game,' he told the host, Jimmy Armfield. 'That's what it was – I used to enjoy myself just like clowns do to provide the entertainment. I wasn't as good a competitor as I might have been or should have been, but results weren't too important. I used to enjoy the game, and that was what it was all about to me – enjoying it.'

Bingham recalls another example of the arrogance Shackleton used to display against Arsenal. 'Another day, when we were playing at Roker, the ball was crossed in from the left. I was very lively then and I was quite good at heading at the far post. But when I got my head to this centre, I clashed with the goalkeeper, George Swindin. So Shack trapped the loose ball on the goal line and beckoned me to get up off the ground before the 'keeper. Being quite nippy, I got there first and put the ball in the net. Oh, the crowd loved that! Every time we played the Arsenal, he'd take the piss out of them. He used to love that game. I think we beat them 7-1 in a fun game at Roker in the 1950s [it was in September 1953]. Can you imagine Arsenal getting beaten 7-1 now? But even then they had some very good players. Their left-back, I remember, was the England international, Lionel Smith. They were a strong team, but Shack always turned up trumps against them.'

George Swindin, certainly, must have hated the sight of Shackleton and Bingham. In one game against Arsenal at Roker Park – it may even have been during that 7-1 drubbing – Bingham broke through the Gunners' defence and fired in a shot that Swindin could only parry. The ball broke to Shack, who just needed to put it into an empty net. Instead, seeing Swindin on all fours and scrambling towards him in the mud, he took the ball to the goal-line and beckoned the goalkeeper towards him, saying: 'Come on George, it's not in yet!' Then, as Swindin lunged for the ball, Shackleton rolled it over the line.

Strangely, his justification for such cruel humour was that, the previous week, a linesman had made him look foolish in front of

30,000 spectators at Charlton by flagging for a throw-in when Shack had been indulging himself with one of those teasing runs down the touchline and just keeping the ball in play. He had nearly been too clever by half against Arsenal, though. As Sunderland manager Billy Murray pointed out to him angrily at half-time, the correct decision should have been a bounce-up (i.e. a dropped ball), not a goal, because the referee had blown his whistle for a goal before Shackleton had actually put the ball over the line. Therefore, the ball had become dead without the referee noticing.

It was also against Arsenal, at Highbury, that Shackleton famously stopped and sat on the ball in the middle of a First Division match. He had a more logical explanation for that bout of iconoclastic behaviour. 'I used to love entertaining the fans, certainly,' he told Brian Leng of *The Wearside Roar*, 'but more often than not it was a time-wasting tactic. For example, when I sat on the ball at Arsenal, it was my way of saying to the home fans: "We've got the ball, we're winning and if we've got the ball, your lot are not going to score!" So it was a tactical thing, not just playing to the crowd.'

Nevertheless, Shack played to the crowd at Highbury often enough and entertainingly enough to bring at least one Arsenal supporter under his spell. Ken Goldman, a London solicitor who used to be Arsenal's ClubCall man and also contributed to their match programme, goes so far as to describe him as 'my favourite ever player'. Goldman, an FA coach, former secretary of the London Coaches' Association and current president of the North Middlesex Referees' Association, adds: 'He was unbelievable, the best ball manipulator I've ever seen.

'The example that stands out for me was when he was playing against Arsenal at Highbury. During the course of the game, the referee blew up for a foul and Shackleton was about 20 yards from the touchline, two or three yards outside the penalty area on the right-hand side. And when he kicked the ball towards the crowd, they all started to boo, thinking he had kicked the ball away. It bounced three times towards them and then, suddenly, it changed direction and bounced three times back to him. At once, the boos turned to cheers – gasps, even.

'I was there to see it with my own eyes, and I know it wasn't a fluke because I saw him do something similar at Chelsea. He played at Sunderland with this guy, Charlie "Cannonball" Fleming, and they used to have this routine during the warm-up where Shackleton would stand on the 18-yard line and Fleming on the D. Then Shack would kick the ball towards the penalty spot, it would spin back towards the edge of the area and Fleming would crash it into the net.

'There were other things as well. I'm not sure whether he scored with this one, but he once did a prodigious, double-footed, side-footed kick, so that he was well off the ground when he hit the ball sideways on the volley. I think he did score with that, but I know he did with another fantastic effort. In fact, I've still got a newspaper photograph of it: it was during a midweek game at Highbury. What happened was that Arsenal had a reserve goalkeeper called Con Sullivan, and he came and punched the ball in a parabola so that it went up in the air and then down to the edge of the penalty area, where Shackleton hit it on the volley. He sent it straight back on the same parabola, and it went into the net in the small space between the crossbar and the head of one of the full-backs, Dennis Evans.

'The only other ball manipulators I've seen in English football who compare with Shackleton are Tommy Harmer and Glenn Hoddle [both of Tottenham Hotspur, if you please!], who were also quite outstanding. The only current player in English football who reminds me of Shack is Bolton's Nigerian international midfielder, Jay-Jay Okocha. It's wrong to compare Shackleton with George Best because they were two entirely different players. Best was dynamic, played at speed and, although he enjoyed beating players, he invariably went towards goal. Shackleton, on the other hand, was a total entertainer. The game for him was about attitude and arrogance. If he could take the piss out of a player, he'd love it. Best, of course, has confessed to getting a "hard-on" by doing the same thing; but that apart, they were two entirely different players.'

As we have seen already, Shackleton was unlike most of the other mavericks who followed him in English football in the sense that he was a thinker about the game, a player who used his brain as well as his feet to fox opposing teams. Take what he did with corner kicks when Sunderland were leading by one goal and it was late in the game. Instead of crossing the ball into the middle or playing it short to a team-mate, he would roll it down the touchline and back towards his own goal. The ball would then run out of play and the bemused opposition would be awarded a throw-in in their own half. Shack's reasoning was that winning a corner in the dying minutes was not an advantage because it meant you had one man out of the game, the taker of the corner kick, and that made it easier for the other team to counter-attack. What is more, the opposition would be so stunned by the unexpectedness of the manoeuvre, they would be slow to take the throw-in, thus using up valuable time.

In fact, he thought many of the unusual things he did – what other people looked upon as 'tricks' or showboating – were perfectly logical means of gaining an advantage over the opposition. In that *Football Legends* radio programme about him on Five Live, Shackleton talked about the time he was hemmed in against a corner flag by big Peter Sillett, the Chelsea full-back. 'Well, we get the ball into the corner flag there, about a yard off the corner flag,' he said, 'Peter with me, kick it on the corner flag and if you hit it in the centre it comes out. It did and I'm nearly in the penalty box. Peter is wondering what's happening. But that to me is a plain tactic. Not difficult to do, really, but it gets misconstrued as "showmanship".'

That same ploy was something that stuck in Brian Clough's mind from seeing Shackleton in action. 'I only watched him play a few times,' he said, 'but I remember he went to a corner flag with the ball and they were kicking him and hacking him so much that he made a gesture like, "If you want the ball, here, I'll give you it." Now, of course, everybody takes the bloody ball to the corner flags and bores the arse off you. They don't know what do with it when they get there.

'Len was years ahead of his time. Don't forget, either, that he was in competition with people like Middlesbrough's Wilf Mannion. Wilf was so much of an idol, my dad used to stand to attention when he saw him. But he was into Shackleton, too. Of course I would have had him in one of my teams. I had various rules when I was in management, but one main rule was: "If they've got talent, no matter where it is and how they use it, it was my job to get the best out of them." And Len had so much talent it was incredible. They say he was a bit of a luxury, but that's a load of bloody rubbish! I wish everybody on the field, in all positions, had had his talent.'

Shackleton himself was puzzled by the fact that not everybody could put enough 'bottom' on the ball to make it come back to them from 12 or 15 yards; but this sounds very much like a genius not being able to understand the inability of mere mortals to perform godlike feats. Newcastle team-mate Bob Stokoe was one of those who attempted to copy the back-spin trick and failed miserably. 'Many is the time,' he confessed, 'that I, as a young lad after I had seen him do this sort of thing, used to go on the training ground on my own with a few balls to try and do it. It was such an embarrassment, because the ball went further the other way!'

Shackleton's tricks were not confined to the football pitch. Off the field, he became famous for his uncanny ability to toss a coin high in the air, catch it on his instep, flick it back up in the air, then drop it neatly in the top pocket of his jacket. His footballing contemporaries insist he was putting on that little show throughout his career. Shack, however, says that he did not start doing it until Don Revie arrived at Sunderland from Manchester City. Since Revie, who had made his name by replicating the innovative, deep-lying centre-forward role Nandor Hidegkuti had introduced with the brilliant Hungarian national side of the 1950s, played for City in the 1956 FA Cup final, it means he joined Sunderland not long before Shackleton retired in 1957.

According to Shack, who does not seem to have liked him very much, Revie challenged him to repeat the trick after he had bragged about it, and provided a demonstration using a sixpence, in the Sunderland dressing room. But, having seen the impetuous Ray Daniel try and fail, Shackleton refused to rise to the challenge at that point. Realising practice was called for, he went away and spent a few days perfecting the trick with a half-crown, which was about the size of today's fifty pence coin and considerably larger than a sixpence.

Then, returning to the Sunderland dressing room, he went one better than Revie by flicking the coin right up to the ceiling before catching it on his foot and lobbing it into his blazer pocket. Revie, apparently, had been flicking his coin only 18 inches into the air at the start of the trick, so Shackleton felt he had put the newcomer firmly in his place. 'That was great – stealing the thunder from Revie, "the show-off",' he said, with evident satisfaction.

It takes one to know one, I suppose, and that little story does convey something of the self-confidence, competitiveness and perfectionism that were integral parts of Shackleton's personality. Without them, he could not have been the kind of footballer he was. He also had a wicked sense of humour, as he showed when asked to repeat the trick during a live interview on Tyne Tees Television. The interviewer was worried sick because Shack, having a bit of fun, had deliberately failed two or three times to pull the trick off in rehearsals. But, when it came to the real thing, the half-crown went straight in the pocket, no messing.

The downside of Shackleton's brilliance was a lack of consistency, a tendency to drift out of matches and an unfortunate habit of going missing when his own team were under pressure. As we have seen in a previous chapter with Ron Greenwood and Bradford Park Avenue, it was the wing-half playing immediately behind Shack who felt the pinch when he did not come back to help man the barricades. Stan Anderson went through the experience very early in his career at Roker Park. 'I was only 18 or 19 at the time,' he said. 'I'd only played a handful of games and I was playing right-half at Huddersfield with Len in front of me. Len Quested was at left-half for Huddersfield, and Tommy Kavanagh, their inside-left, was playing against me.

'In the first half they were coming through in droves: the left-back was coming up, the left-half was coming up and Kavanagh was going through. I was getting run ragged; and when I came in at half-time the manager gets on to me about it, saying that my job was defending. "My bloody job?" I said. "They're coming through in droves!' Then, pointing at Len, I added: "Anyway, what about him?" Shack was there straight in front of me, and I always remember hearing him say to a bloke next to him: "God, we're getting played hell with by blokes who haven't been in the game five minutes!" And that was his attitude. He didn't take it to heart, or anything like that. I always used to relate that story to him whenever I saw him and we'd have a laugh. He never held grudges and we always got on well. He was a lovely fellow, Len, an absolute comedian.

'But it was quite true when people would say: "Oh, he's not bothered today." There were certain games where Lenny gave it up as a bad job. That was especially true when the ground was muddy and he couldn't do what he wanted to do. I think he felt that his first duty was to entertain the spectators, and this was the reason for the difference between most of his performances home and away. His attitude was: "Right, this is the crowd who pay my wages, so I'm going out to entertain them!" Then away from home, he probably thought: "Well, there aren't many spectators from Sunderland today," and he just used to go and do a moody.

'That's the way Shack was, and the way it was generally in those days. You tried your best to win your home games and, if you won most of them, you'd be in the top half of the League. You didn't have to win many away games to win the League, either. I remember the year we finished fourth, 1954-55, Chelsea won the Championship with 52 points! That would be unknown today. All right, it was only two points for a win then, but that total's still not equivalent to winning the Championship now. It would be about 15 points behind today's champions.'

For the most part, Anderson subscribes to the majority view in the Sunderland team that Shackleton's formidable strengths more than made up for his weaknesses. 'To be fair,' he said, 'you just had to give him the ball. If you won it in defence, you gave him the ball and followed in behind him. If he wanted to use you, he'd use you. If he thought he could go through two or three people, he would. He took all the free kicks, both on the left and the right. He got involved and was always trying things. He was an experimenter on the football field and wonderful to play with. When he was on his game, he just took over. You gave him the ball and he would create something. I'd see some of the stuff he used to play through defences for people to run on to and I'd think: "God, I wish I could do that!" He was a class act, there's no doubt about it.'

Bingham endorses that view and takes it on a stage. 'His control was tight,' says the former manager of Northern Ireland. 'He could come out of tight situations, and he could do a double shuffle over the ball as well. He had all sorts of tricks. The only thing that you could say about him that was negative was that he wasn't a good header of the ball – and he didn't need to bother. He didn't get into the rough and tumble of heading in the goalmouth, and things like that. Confidence – he oozed it! He had the sort of confidence in himself as a player that you don't often see. His attitude was: "Give me the ball and I'll show you what I'm capable of: give it me anywhere, even with three men around me, and I can do something with it!"

'I'd bracket him with Stanley Matthews in terms of skill and as a great individualist, in that you could give the ball to Stanley and he made things happen. Nowadays, we have a passing game where we pass it around a lot and keep possession; but when you got the ball out to the wings in our day, you used to run at the full-back straightaway, one-on-one. You were supposed to try and beat him and either get in a centre or a shot. And Shack was wonderful at transferring the ball from the left side of the field to me on the right. He'd get possession at inside left and pretend to put the ball down the left; but then he'd whip round and – whack – he'd put it on a plate for me with a crossfield pass every bit as good as David Beckham can manage.

'There was nobody better than Shack at beating a man when he got the ball in that dangerous position in front of the box, either. He'd pretend to hit it, then drag it back. Pretend to hit it with his left foot, then pull it on to his right: pretend to hit it with his right foot and pull it on to his left. Sometimes, I've seen him dribble the ball right into the goalmouth in matches!'

Willie Watson, who, until his death in 2004, was the lone surviving member of the 1949 Sunderland side beaten by Yeovil in one of the FA Cup's biggest upsets, was another former team-mate who believed that Shack's creative ability outweighed his occasional laziness or indifference. Watson, one of the wing-halves who had to put up with Shackleton's irritating tendency to go missing when the opposition were attacking, said, 'I would certainly have him in my side despite the annoying moments you got from him. At the height of his game, he was excellent when he was "on", but he could be bad when he was "off". When he comes to mind, though, I think of his good points without thinking too much of the other side. He was a brilliant individualist.'

Generally speaking, in fact, other players seem to have been remarkably indulgent towards Shackleton. Team-mates, as we have just seen, realised that his ability to win a game out of nothing was much more important than his occasional disappearing acts, while not as many opponents as might have been expected tried to kick him out of a game or exact revenge for having had the mickey taken out of them. He does seem to have been protected to some extent by the aura of greatness he carried with him. That, certainly, is the impression one gets from Wilf McGuinness's recollection of playing against Shackleton in the game in which the then young wing-half scored his first goal for Manchester United.

'It was in April 1956, at Sunderland,' said the former United man. 'I was playing because I was the understudy to Duncan Edwards and he was away with England for the game against Scotland. In those days, of course, you couldn't cancel League games when international matches were taking place. I'd played a couple of games for the first team when I was 17, and now I was 18. We drew 2-2 and it was a great thrill for me, scoring that first goal. It was a pretty good result, too, considering Roger Byrne and Tommy Taylor were also away with England.

'I was not directly up against Shack. The man I was marking was Charlie Fleming, but I always remember Shack taking the ball and doing his tricks in the corner, spinning it towards the corner flag and nutmegging the full-back, Ian Greaves. We were all in awe of him because we knew so much about him. Well, maybe not in awe exactly, but we did look up to him. We'd heard all about him, and he did do all those tricks and was very, very skilful. He was something exceptional: he was a thrill. His dribbling and his control were fantastic. He didn't just knock it and run: it was one foot to the other. In fact, it was as though the ball was actually tied to his boots. It didn't always come off and, when it didn't, his team-mates would be furious. Most of the time, though, it did come off.'

Players more experienced and hard-bitten than the Busby Babes, however, were not prepared to be so respectful towards Shackleton. Roy Paul, Manchester City's tough Welsh international wing-half, was one of them. 'Len played in a position where they used to get some terrible stick from people like Roy Paul,' said Stan Anderson. 'His only idea was to stop Lenny playing, knock him about, and it was terrible. You can quite understand that, when the maximum wage was still on, Len thought that, for £20 a week, he wasn't going to get kicked up the backside! I suppose it was an attitude that was prevalent in those days.

'There was no doubt about it – people used to set out their stall for him. They probably thought that if they could stop Shack playing, they could stop the whole thing. And, since he was the playmaker, that was probably true. But he used to wander around, so he was difficult to mark. Sometimes he'd finish on the left wing; then he would drop back in defence a bit and start picking up the ball from there.'

Even a dedicated destroyer like Roy Paul found it difficult to nail Shackleton completely. He was too quick and clever for most of the hard men in the game then, a fact borne out by the relatively small number of injuries he sustained during his career. 'Some tried to have a go at him,' says Ivor Broadis, 'but he wasn't injured much, Shack. That is indicative of the fact that opponents found it very, very difficult to pin him down. He could certainly look after himself as well; and he had a bit of contempt for people who tried to put other people out of the game.'

Billy Elliott put it another, less flattering way. Elliott, whom Shackleton rated the hardest of the hard and compared more than favourably to Roy Keane, Norman Hunter and Billy Bremner and who played for England as many times as Shack, said laconically and revealingly of his old pal and former team-mate at Bradford Park Avenue and Sunderland: 'Most people used to get at him because he was a little bit of a jumper.'

That unflinching assessment of Shackleton's taste for the physical side of the game is given some credence by a story Doug Weatherall tells about a derby game between Sunderland and Newcastle in front of a Roker Park full house of 68,002 – the biggest League crowd there had ever been in the North-East. 'Joe Harvey had played with Shack at Newcastle, of course: he'd been his captain there. Anyway, Joe says to him: "Don't you come anywhere near me because you know what you're going to get!" Shack played well in that game, but he didn't go particularly near to Joe.'

Charlie Crowe, the other wing-half in one of those superb Newcastle teams, remembers with a chuckle the time Shackleton tried to arrange a non-aggression pact with him before one Sunderland v Newcastle match at Roker Park. 'We were kicking in,' said Crowe, 'when Len came over to me and said: "Charlie, I've got a hell of a good idea. When I get the ball, you leave me alone; and when you get the ball, I'll leave you alone." I told him that was impossible, that I couldn't do it, and went over to Joe Harvey to have a few words because I was supposed to be tight marking Shack. Joe just set his teeth and said: "Oh, it's going to be one of those days!"

From another story Crowe tells, he clearly did not comply with Shackleton's wishes on that occasion, and others. 'My daughter, Lesley, was once going across to Tenerife with her husband when Shack got on the 'plane and put his briefcase down next to her. Seeing "L. Shackleton" on it, she said to him: "I think you know my dad." So Shack said: "Your dad? What do they call him?" And when she told him, he lifted his trouser leg up just over the knee and said to her: "That's what your dad did!" You can imagine the effect this had: the whole 'plane was aghast!'

Yet, in fairness to Shackleton, it should be pointed out that Johnny McSeveney recalls him fighting on behalf of another player in one game. 'It was at Manchester United and my debut,' he said. 'I'm not sure what had happened exactly, but one of their wingers had a go at one of our players and Len took up the cudgels on his behalf. It got so heated that the referee had to intervene. There were no yellow cards then; it was just a caution. Shack, as I discovered, was not normally like that; but as it was my first game, I thought: "Oh, what's happening here?" '

Other former team-mates insist, too, that Shackleton was strongly built enough, and courageous enough, to 'look after himself' on the football field, if necessary. 'He was strong in the upper body,' recalls Ivor Broadis. 'He had a good breadth of chest and was a sort of square-shouldered chap. The muscles in his legs weren't as well defined as in his body, but he did have this square-shouldered, strong look about him.'

Confirmation of Shackleton's strength and courage came, too, from Professional Footballers' Association chief executive Gordon Taylor. Taylor, who played for Bolton Wanderers and several other clubs before becoming head of the players' union, said: 'He was quite reasonably built and made, and he could look after himself. He was quite a brave player and he wasn't one who was always on the floor.

The Bolton defence then (just the names of the full-backs, Roy Hartle and Tommy Banks, used to strike fear into opposing forwards), were the hardest in the League; but they'd probably intimidate the great Sir Stanley [Matthews] more than they'd ever intimidate Len.'

Elliott, a typically blunt, down-to-earth Yorkshireman, who served with the Royal Navy on the harrowing north Atlantic convoy run during the latter part of the war, made another uncomfortable point about Shack and their time together at Park Avenue. 'In those days,' he recalled, 'sometimes there were a certain number of players who were not fit. They were not really gifted like he was, either, and he used to take the mickey out of them.' But, for all his obvious reservations about Shackleton – 'He was in and out' – Elliott shares the general admiration for his outstanding individual ability. 'He could play, there's no doubt about that. Skill-wise, he was unbelievable. In fact, his skill factor was probably amongst the best that's ever been,' says a man whose own career was devoted mostly to stopping other players playing.

Coming from Elliott, that assessment of Shackleton's ability is quite a tribute. This, it is said by those who saw him play for Bradford Park Avenue, Burnley, Sunderland and England, was a left-winger so tough and fearless – some would even go so far as to say dirty – that he used to frighten full-backs. That unusual role reversal was easy enough to imagine from the plain, unvarnished nature of his answers to my questions. Though in his eighties, he still exuded a slight air of menace; and despite having known Shack since they were teenagers together at Park Avenue and aware that it had been his fellow-Bradfordian who had urged Sunderland manager Billy Murray to sign him from Burnley, Elliott clearly felt under no obligation to gild the lily.

As someone who had played with and against Shackleton, Elliott is ideally placed to assess him as a player. But there was certainly no gushing praise. 'For the first few games, it was a little bit difficult because you just didn't know what he was going to do,' he said. 'I mean, he was a very good player; on his day, he was probably as good as anyone in football at that particular time. But he didn't have that consistency you would expect from a fellow with that ability.' So, I asked, how did he rate with the other great players English football has seen? 'Well, he's got to be up there with them,' was the terse reply. As good as George Best, perhaps? 'Best, I've got a lot of time for. On his day, Best was good, but so was this fellow as well. No doubt at all about that.'

Elliott also challenged the received wisdom that Shack was two-footed, a contentious stance in which he was joined by Ivor Broadis. 'I'm not saying he couldn't use his left,' said the man who played in all the positions down the left side of a team, 'but he had the skill to control stuff with his right foot.' Broadis concurred by saying: 'The strange part about it is that his skill always came from his right foot. I can't honestly say he was blessed with a great left foot.' In the light of this, Elliott drew attention to the fact that Shackleton played mostly at inside-left during his career. 'He used to say that, as a right-footer, the goals were larger when he was coming in from wide positions on the left,' he added. 'And I suppose he's got something there, when you think about it. There are several players who do that now – right-footed playing on the left.'

Elliott even went so far as to suggest that Shackleton was a bit 'tight' with his money – quite an accusation to be levelled by one Yorkshiremen at another, never mind friend against friend. 'He was a nice bloke,' he said, 'but he used to keep his hand in his pocket a little bit at times.' Mike Langley, the journalist who worked with Shack on the *Daily Express* and *The People*, corroborated that to some extent, saying Shack was 'careful' with his money, but added that professional footballers did not have that much to spend in those days, anyway.

Vince Wilson disagreed vehemently, however. 'I've heard such things, but I never found him to be like that,' said the former *Sunday Mirror* man. 'I've also heard that he didn't have the biggest appetite when the boots were flying, but I know he did retaliate after being kicked by Manchester City's hard-man centre-half, Dave Ewing. "I never did it again," he confessed to me. "I hurt myself more than him!" '

Charlie Crowe, too, played with and against Shackleton, and he recalls the contrasting experiences with more obvious fondness than Elliott. 'Sometimes,' said Crowe, 'it was harder to play with Shack than against him. Everything had to be different. When I took a throw-in to him, for example, he would pass it back to me with his backside – just because nobody else had done it. There was a school of thought that he never won anything, and stuff like that, but Shack took a delight and enjoyment out of the game that meant other players enjoyed it with him.'

Roy Bentley, who played with Shackleton at Newcastle before moving on to Chelsea, also recalled him getting up to his tricks with a throw-in, but not just for the hell of it. 'It was at Stamford Bridge,' he said, 'and there was a disputed throw-in that Shack thought was Newcastle's. Ken Armstrong, our [Chelsea's] wing-half, who always used to take the throw-ins, had gone over to take this one, but the referee ruled in Newcastle's favour. Ken came from Bradford and was a pal of Shack's, but as he was walking away, Len threw the ball against his back, got the rebound and went on the attack. People called him a clown, but I never did. He was the most excellent player.'

Bentley was a witness, though, to the more mischievous side of Shackleton's personality. The example he gave was of a penalty awarded to Bradford City when Newcastle were playing them at Valley Parade. 'One of the Milburns came up to take it,' he said. 'I can't remember which one it was because there were quite a few professional footballers in the family, but I think it might have been Jim or Jack. Anyway, we were playing in about six inches of mud and this Milburn came up to take the penalty. As he put the ball down on the spot, Shack took a big lump of mud off his own boots as though he was just cleaning them. Then, as Milburn came through to hit the ball – he had a very long run-up – Shack just flicked the mud in his face! "Stop!" shouted Milburn, because he couldn't see a thing. He blamed Len, of course; but when the referee went over to sort it out, Shack swore blind the mud had come off Milburn's own boot!

'There was also the time when we [Newcastle] were playing Fulham and their wing-half, Len Quested, who was very physical, was sticking close to Shack. He was tackling poor Len so strongly that he couldn't really do anything. So when we got to the dressing room at half-time, Shack asked for a bit of string from the trainer, who thought he needed it for his socks. But as we went out for the second half, and the teams were lined up, he went over to Len Quested, gave him the string and said: "Tie this to the back of my shirt and keep hold of it. That way, you can keep on my back for the whole of the bloody game!" '

On the whole, Shack's breezy personality and ready wit seem to have beguiled most of the people he played with and against. Bingham, Anderson, McSeveney, Broadis, Crowe et al, insist he was great company and a natural leader off the field. 'I used to watch people, listen to them, because when you're young you don't talk a lot,' Bingham recalled of his early days as a teenager in that star-studded Sunderland dressing room. 'Shack always dominated the conversation with his funny remarks and laughing. He kept good humour in the dressing room. For all his glory and his failings, I liked him. What I liked about him was that he was his own man. In fact, you can say that I loved him in a way, a strange sort of funny way. He didn't do everything he should have done, but he was a great character.'

Rather like the dashing head boy who is good at everything, Shackleton not only got on well with most of the players of his own age at Roker Park, but attracted a following among the younger ones. 'When we went to America [on a close-season tour], I used to knock around with Shack,' said Anderson. 'I thought I'd get in with the senior players, who would show me all the ropes. He was wonderful to be with: he was a real character. I don't quite know how, but he seemed to know all the places to go to in America, too. He'd probably never been there before, so he must have asked people about the best places.'

As far as McSeveney was concerned, it was a question of marvelling at how a footballer as extravagantly gifted as Shackleton could also be such a pleasant, likeable individual. 'His favourite trick was to nutmeg people,' said the former left-winger. 'He was brilliant at it. When it looked as if he was going to go past you, you'd open your legs to go after him and he'd put the ball through your legs – one, two, nutmeg! I used to watch him dribbling the ball along the touchline, too, and think: "I could never bloody do that!" But he was such a nice person with it, as well. It wasn't just that he was an artist, the Clown Prince or whatever; it was the fact that he was a genuine person and wanted to do well at football. He would help anybody, especially anybody in trouble. He was pure genius, was Len.'

Sir Tom Finney is another contemporary who believes there was no malice aforethought in the trickery with which Shackleton was capable of making opponents look very silly indeed. 'People thought he was deliberately taking the mickey,' said the former player many still regard as England's, or even Britain's, finest, 'but I think that was the furthest thing from his mind: he just felt that it was his job to go out and entertain. As for the complaints about him being unpredictable and selfish, he brought that on himself a lot because he used to do so many things on the field of play that you wouldn't see in the ordinary sort of player.'

Shack's problem, if problem is the right word, was that he had become instinctively unorthodox by the time he reached his peak as a footballer with Sunderland. Whether this was a congenital trait, or just an attitude that had developed along the way, is difficult to determine. There is certainly no evidence of any unorthodoxy until he began playing for Bradford Park Avenue during the war: when he was a schoolboy footballer there was no talk of tricks, only of great ability. The most likely explanation is that he was unorthodox by nature, behaved himself as a schoolboy because he wanted to be the first lad from Bradford to win an England cap and subsequently developed the confidence to exploit his amazing ball control to Music Hall standards.

Football of that showy kind may have wowed the crowds, but it did not always find favour with hardened professionals or other legends of the game. Raich Carter, the brilliant inside-forward who preceded Shackleton as the idol of Roker Park, was a case in point. Journalist Vince Wilson vividly recreated the time he and Shack went together to interview Carter, by then manager of Middlesbrough. 'Raich looked Len straight in the eye,' wrote Wilson, 'and said: "I wouldn't pick you in any team of mine! You messed about with the ball too much for my liking: you're more of an individual than a team player. No, I wouldn't have had you in my team, but I would have had you topping the bill at the Sunderland Empire – just you, a stage and a football. I'm sure you would have filled the house.'

Although he maintained that the atmosphere in Carter's Ayresome Park office remained warm and friendly throughout, Wilson, understandably, was a slightly uneasy witness to that frank assessment of one iconic footballer by another. As a journalist, he was delighted by the exchange; but as a lifelong Sunderland fan it was not something he wanted to hear. Not only that, but as a friend of Shackleton he was concerned about the effect Carter's characteristically brutal outburst might have on him. He need not have worried. 'Shack took the criticism without blinking an eyelid: he'd handled all those accusations before,' reported the man from the *Sunday Mirror*. 'He'd known ultimate worship of his skills, too, and realised that euphoria and criticism were travelling companions. He'd been a legend in his own lifetime!'

Later in his newspaper article, Wilson suggested that Carter might have formed a kinder opinion of Shackleton had he overheard the conversation the two journalists had had once on a trip to Yorkshire. 'I was bending his ear about his five paltry England appearances – such a scanty reward for the natural talents bestowed upon him,' Wilson recalled. ' "Was it five?" he questioned. "I knew it was somewhere between five and eight." Numbers, clearly, were not that important to him. "All footballers want to see the word 'international' after their names," he explained, "but one cap, that's all, entitles you to wear a crown.

'"Mind you, I don't think I was too popular with the establishment because I was not a football conformist." He started to reinforce his point by recalling that one star, Billy Wright, picked up 105 caps, and he didn't envy one of them. "Billy mastered the orthodox game. He tackled hard, headed well and passed accurately when the opportunity was there, but that was never enough for me. I wanted to spin and swerve the ball, a heavy one in those days, to the right and left of defenders. I wanted to play the ball into space and beckon it back to me with my finger; sometimes it worked! I could never have been a 'straight' player." '

It is precisely for that reason Jimmy Hill questions Shackleton's right to be regarded as a truly great player. Hill, who played for

Fulham and Brentford towards the end of Shack's career with Sunderland, tried to put it all into perspective by saying: 'Even with the old ball, he had the confidence to do tricks that left the rest of us slightly open-mouthed. But that's sort of diminished now when you see the quality of some of the players who come in from abroad. Henry, for instance, is amazing because of the pace at which he achieves it. But, of course, the actual capacity to play tricks with a football has become more feasible because of the nature of the ball.

'Shackleton had the capacity then to do things that other players couldn't. Whereas others were happy if they got that old ball within two yards of them when they brought it down, he would be playing with it. But there were other players, like Tom Finney, who were playing quietly in the same era and had that extra bit of pace and trickery to go past opponents: I saw Finney leave three or four players, one after the other, stone-cold dead playing for Preston at Brentford. And Tom would not go back and beat you again, for the sake of it. I think that was the subtle difference between him and Shackleton.

'Finney was devastating: he was the one to get near the goal so that he could lay one back for somebody to slot in the net. I don't want to diminish Shackleton's ability in any kind of way, because football is supposed to be part of the entertainment business and he was the best at that. You'd go a long way to see him do something with the ball that would get your admiration and astonishment; but occasionally, maybe, falling in love with his own artistry might mean him missing a guy who was standing there, waiting to tap it in from five yards. That is the only difference one could make between him and somebody like Tom Finney.'

Finney was such a natural athlete and complete footballer that few would doubt his ability to adapt to the heavier physical and mental demands of today's football. But what about Shackleton?

Would the Clown Prince, the defiantly unorthodox midfielder, have been successful in the modern game, where clowning and nonconformism are not encouraged? Never mind successful; would his clever manipulation of the ball have been able to survive the rigours of today's intense, high-speed contests? Johnny McSeveney and Stan Anderson have no doubts on that score.

'Len Shackleton would always be a star,' insists McSeveney. 'His concept of football and his football brain were something special. There is no doubt that, in those days, he was as good as anybody who was around. And I think that, if he had played today, at this standard of football, he and Matthews and Finney – players like that – would have adapted to the speed and the tactics. People say football was slow back then, but it wasn't. I'm not saying it was as quick as it is now, and they probably had more time then. But they made a lot of time because they were good players.'

Stan Anderson insists: 'Len would have been an absolutely outstanding player in present day football. We talk now about David Beckham bending the ball, but Shack could bend that old, heavy ball then just as well as David can today's much lighter one.' Indeed, McSeveney actually remembers him doing it for Sunderland at White Hart Lane. 'He took a free kick once at Tottenham and bent the old ball, which was difficult to master, around the wall and into the corner of the net,' he recalled. What sorcery Shackleton might have weaved with today's lighter ball is almost unimaginable. He certainly regretted not having had the chance to show what he could do with it and reckoned, self-confident as ever, that he would have been 'an absolute sensation'.

Malcolm Macdonald agrees entirely. 'Really,' says the former Luton Town, Newcastle United, Arsenal and England centre-forward, 'the time for Len Shackleton to have been born was 20 or 30 years ago. That would have allowed him to play the game today, and I think he would have been an absolutely stunning revelation in it.'

Stan Anderson reckons there is a reason other than a keen intelligence and outstanding skill to believe Shack would have flourished alongside the David Beckhams and the Michael Owens of the modern game. 'Len would have been an even greater player in those days if there had been TV, because there's no way he would have allowed himself to be shown up on television! Playing away from home, if he'd seen the cameras, he'd have said: "Right, I'll put on a show today!" It's a shame, really, because he was born perhaps 15 or 20 years too early. He'd have been an absolute riot in the game today. The tragedy is that that we can't see somebody like him playing in present-day football because the art of dribbling has gone out of the game. It's all passing and moving now. You wouldn't put Len on a par with George Best and Pele because those two were great players, but he would be somewhere near.'

Johnny Downie agrees. 'Len was a wonderful, wonderful player,' said his old Bradford Park Avenue team-mate. 'I cannot compare him with any other player of his time, but he and George Best, in my world, are the two players who stand out. They would beat men, they were creators and that takes a bit of doing. I bet over the last few years before he died, he'd have thought: "I would have been a billionaire, not a millionaire, if I'd been playing now!" He'd have been much more of a personality than Beckham, and a much better player in a position where he could score goals. It wouldn't have been just a question of how much he could earn, either. Which country do you think he would have been playing in? He could have held his own anywhere.'

Perhaps the final word on what made Len Shackleton special should be left to another of English football's legendary players. 'As a man,' said Tom Finney, 'Len was a very pleasant type of lad. He was down-to-earth and a very sociable and likeable sort of person who liked a joke. As a player, he was outstanding in the sense that he was what I'd call a really natural footballer. He played the game as it should be played: he enjoyed every minute of it.'

CHAPTER EIGHT
A TRUE ALL-ROUNDER

A NY sport involving a moving ball was made to be mastered by Len Shackleton. So it should come as no surprise to learn that he was almost as good at cricket as he was at football. Some would say even better, in fact. No need, either, to wonder where his ability at this game came from. When his grandfather, Francis Shackleton, died at the comparatively early age of 53, the obituary in the local paper was lavish in its praise for this stalwart of village side Queensbury Cricket Club. 'It is questionable,' it said, 'whether Queensbury ever produced a better batsman; certainly never a more enthusiastic cricketer, his active fielding being no less brilliant than his batting.'

Blessed with lightning reflexes, wonderful hand-eye co-ordination, big hands, good balance and natural athleticism himself, Leonard Francis Shackleton might well have gone to the very top as a professional cricketer had he not been so outstanding as a footballer. As it was, he occupied himself – and supplemented his relatively modest earnings from football – during the much longer close seasons of the 1940s and 1950s by playing professional cricket in high-class leagues in Yorkshire and the North-East of England.

A fast-medium bowler who could also bat a bit, Shackleton began playing the game in organised fashion at grammar school, where his early promise was soon evident. 'The batting honours were carried off by Varley, Baron and Aldred, with Rhodes, Barraclough, Denison, Shackleton and Gatenby as promising. The best bowlers were Shackleton, Varley, Gledhill, Earnshaw and Greenwood,' said the report on Carlton High's junior cricket XI's season in the July 1935 issue of the school magazine, *The Carltonian*.

That same month, Shack's prowess with a cricket ball even got him noticed by the national press. Roger, his middle son, has inherited a framed certificate from the now defunct daily newspaper, the *News Chronicle*, marking one of his father's achievements. Entitled *News Chronicle Cricket Scheme for School Boys*, it was presented to Shackleton by Herbert Sutcliffe, the famous Yorkshire and England opening batsman, for 'the best bowling performance during the week ended July 6, 1935'. Sutcliffe also signed the certificate for good measure.

Young Shack, and one or two of the other juniors, must have played the odd game for the school second XI, too, because the school magazine report on that team mentioned the improved fielding (the significance of this will become clearer later) and added: 'Aldred has been the most successful batsman, and Shackleton and Bennett the most dangerous bowlers, each keeping an excellent length.' In that same issue of the magazine, the report on the junior football team recorded that Shack, then only just 13, had represented the Bradford Boys' side on several occasions. So, from an early age, he was developing as quite the all-rounder in more ways than one.

By turning out for the Dartford Paper Mills' works team, Shackleton kept on playing cricket during that 'lost' year after being rejected by Arsenal. Then, when he moved back to Bradford at the beginning of the Second World War and rejoined Bradford Park Avenue, he played for Lidgett Green in the 'no-holds-barred'

Bradford League during the summer. As with his football career, the hostilities worked in his favour to some extent. They did so in the sense that the suspension of county cricket for six years meant that the country's leading cricketers, when not serving in the armed forces or contributing to the war effort in some other way, sought employment and an outlet for their talents in league cricket instead.

As a result, the teenaged Shackleton was understandably 'thrilled' to find himself playing at Lidgett Green with and against cricketers of the stature of Yorkshire and England captain Len Hutton, Kent and England wicket-keeper Leslie Ames, Lancashire captain and England batsman Cyril Washbrook, Derbyshire and England all-rounder George Pope and the Derbyshire and England bowlers, Cliff Gladwin and Bill Copson. Just as wartime football must have accelerated Shack's development by bringing him up against star 'guests' from the country's bigger clubs, rubbing shoulders with cricketers of that quality cannot have done anything but improve his ability at his second sport as well. As a matter of fact, Shackleton admits that it was fast bowler Gladwin who first showed him how to swing the ball, something he had not had a clue how to do beforehand.

At all events, he was fully equipped to play professional cricket by the time he was transferred in 1946 from Park Avenue to Newcastle. There, he joined Benwell, in the Northumberland League, and enjoyed a lot of success. One of his most prized sporting souvenirs was the ball presented to him for scoring 117 not out and taking 8 wickets for 35 runs in a local derby against Benwell Hill on 2 August 1947. Fortunately, that mounted ball was one of three to escape the attentions of son Roger when he was ten years old and playing cricket in the back garden with friends from next door. In his innocence, Roger had taken one of the mementoes, a ball commemorating Shack's debut for Wearmouth against Chester-le-Street in the

Durham Senior League, out of his dad's trophy case to play with. But next door's dog had chewed it up while acting as a fielder, and Shack only just stopped Roger in time when the boy returned to the trophy case for a replacement.

Wearmouth was the cricket club Shackleton joined after he had moved from Newcastle to Sunderland in 1948. 'And what a good club it was,' he said. 'Most of the other clubs in the Durham Senior League came to sign me but I wouldn't move from Wearmouth because, once you get a good club, you stay there.' In fact, he was their resident professional for seven years and, as those other mounted balls in that trophy case proved, he certainly made his mark on the game in the North-East.

On 4 June 1952, his bowling figures of 4-32 in a local cup-tie against Whitburn included a hat-trick of wickets. Then, on 4 August that same summer, he took 9-12 against Philadelphia. Little wonder, then, that he was chosen to represent both Northumberland and Durham in Minor Counties cricket. Alec Coxon, the former Yorkshire and England cricketer, is reported by Johnny McSeveney, Shackleton's left-wing partner at Sunderland, to have said that Shack, with the new ball, was as good as any other bowler in the country for the first five overs.

That was quite a tribute, considering world-class opening bowlers such as Freddie Trueman, Brian Statham, Alec Bedser and Frank Tyson were either in their pomp then, or just approaching it. Unfortunately, Coxon, in his eighties at the time of writing, is not the most approachable of men and was unwilling to co-operate when I tried to get him to confirm the story and expand on it. Greatly respected as a coach in North-East cricket circles, Coxon was just one of several former Test cricketers who were working as professionals in the Durham Senior League at the same time as Shackleton was doing the equivalent job at Wearmouth. His counterparts included the West Indian, Dick Fuller, and the Indian, C.S. Nayudu, both of whom had played for their countries. So he was holding his own in quite exalted company.

Those who played in the same team as Shack at Wearmouth feel that Coxon's flattering assessment of him was not at all outrageous. Nobody had a closer look at his bowling than Tom Moffat, MBE, a Sunderland supporter who kept wicket to him throughout his seven seasons at the club. Moffat, later one of the driving forces behind Durham's successful quest to acquire first-class status and a director of that club from day one, said: 'I don't doubt that's true,' when I told him what Coxon was reported to have said about Shackleton. 'I remember keeping wicket for the Durham Senior League against a touring Bradford League side and we beat them quite well,' he added. 'And our first three bowlers were Alec Coxon, Ronnie Aspinall and Len Shackleton – all of them Yorkshiremen.

'Len was a superb player, you know. He played for both Northumberland and Durham, and I think he could have played first-class cricket if he'd wanted to. I don't think it would be true to say he was as good a cricketer as he was a footballer, because he was a genius as a footballer; but if he'd applied himself, who knows? He had offers of first-class cricket, but Len didn't want to do it. He was a bit quirky in some respects: that comes through in his autobiography where he says it wasn't the end of the world if he didn't play football for England, that sort of thing. But he was a very fine cricketer and I always liked keeping wicket to him. He was ideal for a wicket-keeper because he used to bowl out-swingers quite fast. As a bowler, he was on the fast side of medium.'

And as a batsman? 'I don't suppose he ever scored a century, but he scored lots of fifties. It's funny, but there weren't many people who scored centuries in League cricket in the 1950s. There were all kinds of reasons for that – the level of umpiring, the standard of wickets and so on – but Len did score a lot of half-centuries. He wasn't exactly a hitter but, when he got in, he liked to entertain. Even so, he was principally a bowler who batted, rather than a batsman who bowled. He batted quite high, though – usually at four or five – and once or twice he opened. I remember he once scored 15, got out and said: "They don't put me there any more! I'm bored stiff opening the batting!" Psychologically, it just wasn't his forte, you see.'

It is an interesting point that Moffat makes. Although Shackleton obviously enjoyed playing cricket, a game for which he had a natural aptitude, some aspects of it did not really suit his mercurial nature. As we have seen, the patience and intense concentration required to open an innings was one of them. And he admitted that he found the drawn-out nature of two-day games in the Minor Counties Championship a mental and physical strain. No doubt that was as responsible as anything else for putting him off the idea of wanting to try his luck in the first-class game.

Shackleton explained his reluctance to play county cricket by stressing that he was totally committed to football. Cricket, he said, was just a 'pleasant recreation', a way of keeping his body fit and his mind off football during the summer. In fact, he went so far as to argue that it was impossible to combine first-class careers in the two sports and do justice to both. They could not be combined, he contended: 'without neglecting, even slightly, one or the other.'

These, of course, were the days when the longer duration and relatively uncluttered nature of football's close season meant it was feasible to pursue a first-class career in both sports. Several famous players did it, among them Denis Compton (Arsenal and Middlesex), Willie Watson (Sunderland and Yorkshire) and Arthur Milton (Arsenal and Gloucestershire). While accepting that those three had done very well at both games, Shack wondered how much more successful they might have been had they concentrated on just the one and treated the other as light relief.

He supported his argument by claiming that Compton could have been one of the greatest left-wingers in the world if he had devoted himself mainly to football; that Watson, one of the few double internationals, could have been 'a world-beater' at either game, but fell short of that exalted standard because he split his time between the two; and that Milton, another double international, was transferred from Arsenal to Third Division Bristol City before he was 27 because he did not devote himself sufficiently to his football career.

One of that trio, the elegant wing-half and left-handed bat, Willie Watson, tended to agree. A few months before his death in April 2004, and not in the best of health, Watson was kind enough to speak to me from Johannesburg, where he and his wife settled after he went out to South Africa in 1968 to become sports manager at the famous Wanderers club. He made it quite clear that, even back in the comparatively sedate 1950s, it was not easy to combine careers in top-class football and cricket. 'I remember that, at the end of the cricket season,' he said, 'I was looking forward to playing soccer; and, you know, maybe something went out of the cricket, but then came back the other way. You'd played long enough at soccer, so you were looking forward to the cricket season coming.

'To play and survive at either game continuously takes some doing – to keep your mind right, you know. The biggest problem was the mental aspect of it. I think I went quite a few years without any alcohol throughout the season, and that could be difficult. I went a few years and never had a family holiday because of the seasons overlapping.' All along, though, you cannot help but feel that Shackleton did not attempt the combination himself simply because he did not have the right temperament for county or Test cricket.

There is another factor to be taken into account here, however. 'I have been told by more than one person "in the know",' said Roger Shackleton, 'that my father would have made an even better cricketer than a footballer; but LFS told me that he felt sorry for double internationals such as Willie Watson and Arthur Milton because of the extra touring commitments needed in their careers and the resultant time away from home. One is or one isn't a family man, and LFS regarded it as unfair to have a family, then "neglect" it.'

Whatever the reasons for Shackleton's reluctance to try to become one of the few double internationals himself, he clearly relished one-day cricket. All he really seemed to want from the game was the opportunity to bowl a few overs, thrash a few runs, show off and have a bit of fun in the field. In cricket, as in football, Shack found it impossible to repress the unconventional urges that defined him as a performer. At the wicket, for instance, he was quite likely to break all the rules of batsmanship, given the chance.

Johnny McSeveney remembers watching him bat in a benefit match and seeing him, a right-hander, play forward with his right leg instead of his left. Brian Clough, too, has an example of how Shackleton carried his taste for the unorthodox into cricket. 'I went to watch him once, and he played a stroke then that I've never seen since,' recalled the former Derby County and Nottingham Forest manager. 'When the bowler let fly with a short one at him, he didn't duck under it. He ducked sideways and got his bat so that he flicked it over his shoulder, over the slips and over the wicket-keeper for four!' Bob Stokoe, too, was witness to Shack's unorthodox brilliance on the cricket pitch. 'I've seen him lift his left leg up and knock a four through his legs,' marvelled the former Newcastle United player and Sunderland manager. 'He was an excellent cricketer.'

But it was in the field that the true Shack came out most often. 'We knew he was there all the time,' said Frank Forster, an opening bowler who played with distinction as a professional for 20 years in the Northumberland League (with Benwell) and Durham Senior League (with Wearmouth, immediately post-Shackleton, and Philadelphia). 'He was a live wire, you know. He had a way of curling his toes: he was very, very wily. Sharp's the word, I think.'

For very particular reasons, Forster remembers the year, 1953, he played against Shackleton for Seaham Harbour, Wearmouth's local rivals. 'We won the Durham Senior League that year,' he said, 'and we'd been putting a half a crown away each week for a bus trip at the end of the season. By coincidence, the chap in charge of the pool organised seats in the stand at Roker Park for Sunderland's game against Arsenal. I think Sunderland won 7-1 and Len Shackleton ran amok.'

Shack could run people out on the cricket field just as easily. 'Len was the most brilliant fielder you've ever seen,' declared Tom Moffat. 'I remember him being at cover point in a game at Bradford when the batsman played a shot that looked as though it was going to go past Len. The fellow took an involuntary step, then realised his mistake. The ball sort of leapt into Len's hands and, almost in one movement, he ran the bloke out. It was like seeing a rabbit trapped in the headlights, because the batsman never moved. Len would do things like that: he was just phenomenal.'

Shackleton also excelled close to the wicket, as Doug Weatherall, the former *Daily Mail* football writer, remembers with awe still in his voice. 'I was playing in the same team as Shack in a groundsman's benefit match at Ryhope,' he recalled. 'It was, for the want of a better word, a personality event. Anyway, I was fielding at first slip and Shack was at backward point, sort of gullyish, when the lad batting unleashed a wonderful square cut. One or two of us joined in the applause for a very good shot, as did Shack, who was looking towards the boundary while applauding. Then, having finished clapping, he produced the ball from his pocket. In the same movement as he'd taken a wonderful catch, he'd slipped the ball in his pocket without anyone noticing!'

Maybe Shackleton restricted his tomfoolery just to non-competitive matches, because he made it quite clear in his autobiography that he did not believe in clowning at cricket. But never able to keep a straight face for long, he promptly admitted with obvious relish that batsmen were disconcerted, and the crowd delighted, when, fielding at cover point, he looked at one wicket and threw the ball at the other. As Tom Moffat said: 'Oh, he did all sorts of funny things, Len. He was so quick-witted, you know.'

His 'funny things' also had the same pulling power in cricket as they did in football. Moffat, an opening batsman who got his best bat from Shack and was given lifts everywhere by him in his 'little, black, clapped-out Ford', says the footballer's presence would fill entire cricket grounds. He recalls that Wearmouth, for instance, took record receipts of £200 when 3,000 people crowded into their ground to see them take on local rivals Sunderland. 'I still remember going to Carley Hill [the Wearmouth ground] quite early that day,' said Moffat, 'to find that the queue for the one paying gate was right along Thompson Road. In all the years I played cricket, I never again saw such a large crowd at a league cricket match.'

Mike Langley, the distinguished former sports journalist, caught a first-hand glimpse of Shack's excellence as a cricketer. Langley, deputy sports editor of *The People* when Shackleton was one of their football columnists, also worked with him on the *Daily Express*; and it was in those earlier days that they went together for some practice at the famous cricket school run by Alf Gover, the former Surrey bowler, in Wandsworth. 'We used to go down there because we were quite keen cricketers on the sports desk at the Express, and Len, of course, had played the game professionally,' explained Langley, now in his seventies and retired.

'So Tony Lock, the Surrey and England spinner of Laker and Lock fame, was batting and Shack was bowling to him. Then Len let go with a fairly quick one with which he had high hopes of "doing" Tony. In fact, Shack had turned away thinking: "That's got him!" when Lock drove it back with great power and shouted a warning to Len. But this shows how good these fellows are – Shack, without even looking, put out his hand and caught the ball! I thought to myself at the time: "Here's two great talents!" '

But it was not just at football and cricket that Shackleton excelled: he had this extraordinary ability to master any sport that involved a moving ball. His ball sense, his feel for a ball, was quite phenomenal. 'He had a good eye for everything,' said Bob Stokoe. 'Good golfer, played squash, badminton – all these sort of games he could handle with no bother.' Johnny McSeveney, for his part, recalled seeing Shack play table-tennis brilliantly with the *edge* of the bat, then catch the ball in his mouth and blow it back.

Roy Bentley, on the other hand, remembers him doing a trick on the snooker table. 'He had terribly long fingers,' said Shackleton's former Newcastle and England team-mate. 'When I was a kid, they used to call them piano fingers. As a result, he could do terrific things with a cricket ball or a snooker ball. He used to put the black ball on the spot on the snooker table, get down the far end and skim the white ball up towards the black. He didn't manage it every time because he could be just a few inches out; but, more often than not, he'd spin the ball around the black and back to him without touching anything'

Shack had learned this party piece from Tommy Mitchell, the Derbyshire and England leg-spinner, who was another of the top-class cricketers who played for Lidgett Green during the war. He was staggered by the amount of skill involved when he first saw Mitchell perform it, and he was modest enough to admit that he had never seen anyone – himself included, presumably – do anything that was anywhere near comparable. Nevertheless, with his usual appetite for practice and perfection, he had obviously mastered it sufficiently over the years to impress the likes of Roy Bentley.

Shackleton himself revealed in *Return of the Clown Prince* how quickly he took to the games of tennis and baseball. During the war, he and Jimmy Stephen, his Bradford Park Avenue team-mate, were on holiday with their wives in Morecambe, the Lancashire seaside resort, when Stephen announced he was going to enter the open tennis tournament in the park. A keen tennis player, Stephen invited Shack to join him using Mrs Stephen's racket. The trouble was that Shackleton had never played the game before and, in the absence of any television coverage of it at that time, did not even know how to score. Needless to say, the complete novice went on to win the tournament by virtue of his God-given ability to control and manipulate a moving ball better than most people. Shack hastened to add that he was not boasting, just pointing out that he had been lucky enough to be born with a heightened ball sense.

His brush with baseball was equally startling and instructive. It took place in 1957, when he and his wife, Marjorie, went on holiday to the USA with their friends and business partners, George and Dorothy Childs. Staying with relatives of the Childs at Corning, New York State, they were introduced to the owner of the local Minor League baseball team and invited by him to attend one of their games. Not for the first or last time, Shack's tongue must have run away with him because, clearly irked by his contention that top-notch cricketers such as Brian Close and Willie Watson could easily have played Major League baseball and that he himself was quite capable of playing reasonably well at Minor League level, their host marched him out on to the field after the game was over.

They took with them several of the players, a pitcher and catcher included, and Shackleton was invited to see whether he, a professional cricketer, could do with a baseball bat what he had been claiming he could. To his horror and embarrassment, he did not even see the first two pitches as they whistled past him. Desperately trying to work out what was wrong, he realised he was holding the bat incorrectly. It dawned on him that, instead of leaning it on the ground, cricket-style, he should have been standing upright watching the ball, with the bat cocked at the ten past two position. Once the penny dropped, Shack was away. In no time at all, he was not only striking the ball cleanly, but actually placing it wherever he wanted in the stadium. In fact, he showed himself to have such a natural aptitude for baseball, it was suggested that, even at 35, as he was then, he could make a very good living at the game.

However, although his football career was coming to an end and baseball's much greater financial rewards must have been tempting, he declined to pursue the matter. He did not fancy 'the foreign way of life', he said, and preferred living in the North-East of England. Less convincingly, this tireless campaigner for the abolition of English football's maximum wage, and improved payments all round, also insisted that he had never been motivated solely by money. This, after all, was the footballer who, at 29 or 30, had told Stan Anderson that if he could only make £25,000 clear profit from his newsagent's shop in Sunderland, he would give up the game like a shot!

No doubt the pay for playing even Minor League baseball would have been considerably greater than the £7 a match Shack received from Wearmouth Colliery as their resident cricket professional. But considering there might be as many as three games a week, his earnings from the summer game were a more than useful addition to the £14 or so a week he was getting from Sunderland FC as well, and must have added to his contentment with life on Wearside. In fact, if you do the multiplication, you will see that he was earning more as a professional cricketer than he was getting as a professional footballer; and that says everything about how poorly footballers were paid before 1961. Monetary issues apart, the truth of the matter is that Shackleton could not have begun to contemplate a new career in baseball because the chronic ankle injury that was about to finish him as a professional footballer and cricketer in 1957 would have precluded anything athletic elsewhere.

Something else Shack discovered, in his fascination with the difference between the moving and the stationary, was that his razor-sharp reflexes also served him well when it came to using guns. Out hunting with his friend, George Childs, he had little difficulty in hitting a moving rabbit, while Childs, a crack shot when aiming at a stationary target, could not hit one, hard as he tried.

In fact, golf seems to have been the only sport that presented Shackleton with any difficulties at all. 'Following a round,' said Roger Shackleton, 'he frequently used to claim that he had just played like his mother. He was rarely fully satisfied with his golfing performance, but he did enjoy playing regularly. As a columnist, he used to play weekly with former football colleagues. I caddied for him many times and recall that, when I was at secondary school in the late 1960s, there was a regular four-ball between LFS, Joe Harvey, Jackie Milburn and a pal of dad's called Tommy Mervin.'

Shack blamed his struggle to master golf mainly on the fact that it involved a stationary, and not a moving, ball. He did not bother to learn the correct techniques for hitting it, either, but constant practice and that innate ball sense of his enabled him, in his words, to 'fiddle' his way around a golf course so well that he succeeded in getting his handicap down to as low as five at one point. And, of course, he remained as unconventional as ever in his approach to the game.

Johnny McSeveney used to play golf with Shack regularly and

remembers him putting with just one hand. 'He'd putt with his right hand,' he says. 'He wouldn't put his left hand on the club at all. When I asked why he didn't use both hands, he replied. "Well, people keep saying that your hands get in the way of each other, so I just use one." Significantly, though, his golf party piece was to throw the ball up in the air with his left hand, then hit it two-handed on the half-volley with a driver. Astonishingly, that breathtaking demonstration of hand-eye co-ordination and total mastery of the moving ball enabled him to outdistance accomplished golfers playing off the tee.

Shack had a pretty good short game, too, as Malcolm Macdonald would testify. 'Supermac', as one of Newcastle United's most famous centre-forwards is still known, was in his prime when he came out of St James' Park one day to find Shackleton, by then a football reporter, waiting for him. 'He asked me if I'd got a minute,' said Macdonald, 'and we stood talking for about ten or fifteen. All that time, he was bouncing a golf ball up and down on what I think was a seven iron, which is fairly narrow-shafted, in his right hand. Not only that, but he never took his eyes off me for a second. That's phenomenal ball skill! I was so mesmerised by it, I hardly heard what he was saying.'

Some of the tales told about Len Shackleton's ball control are so outrageous as to be scarcely believable, were it not for the fact that he is the subject of them. In that sense, he was clearly an athlete on some much higher plane than ordinary mortals. As Johnny McSeveney put it: 'With Len Shackleton, when you tell people the stories, they look at you as if you're telling them a fairy tale. They don't believe the things you are saying. The look on their faces! They just don't believe it. But, with a ball, he was a genius.'

Shack was even good at cards. Billy Bingham, then just an impressionable young member of Sunderland's 'Bank of England' team, recalls how Shackleton was always sitting behind the biggest pile of money when the players' card school got under way on the train going to away games. Since Sunderland, along with Newcastle and Middlesbrough, was situated so far away from the country's other First Division clubs, most journeys were long and playing cards was an obvious and traditional way of whiling away the time.

Although cribbage and dominoes had brief periods of popularity, brag and poker were the players' favourite games and the stakes, says Bingham, could get frighteningly high for those days. 'Some players thought nothing of writing IOUs for £50 or more,' he revealed in his own autobiography, 'and I myself lost a whole week's wages more than once before I saw the light and dropped out.' Almost invariably, reported Bingham, Shackleton was the winner. 'Len even had the odd game in Willie Watson's more select bridge school, but he was soon back behind that familiar pile of money on the poker table.'

According to Vince Wilson, Shackleton had some interesting theories about the gambling that took place between the members of football teams at the time the maximum wage was in force. 'He used to say that gambling could be good or bad,' recalled Wilson. 'Some players, naturally enough, were affected if they lost a week's wages going down to a game, which was quite common. They'd go flat and that would affect their performance quite seriously. But others would say to themselves: "I've got to get that bloody cash back!" and fight like hell to do so. So he felt it would have been wrong to ban card-playing altogether. In some cases, it didn't work well for the team, but in others it did.'

But even Shack, Sunderland's king of the card players, was a little daunted when he went on a ten-day trip to Las Vegas in the late 1960s as a guest of the North-Eastern Sporting Club. In the world capital of gambling, he soon realised that he was out of his depth –

and not just financially. Having observed the clever, tough high-rollers at work, staking thousands of dollars on the turn of a card or roll of a dice, he was forced to admit that: 'As far as encountering the "pros" is concerned, the most entertaining thing to do is watch!" In fact, he must have felt then much the same sort of inferiority and awe that most people experienced facing him on the field of play, the tennis court or across the card table.

CHAPTER NINE
HOLD THE BACK PAGE

When injury forced him to retire from football in 1957 at the age of 35, Len Shackleton had not the slightest desire to become a coach or manager. He had made it quite clear in *Clown Prince of Soccer* that the very idea appalled him. In fact, he said he could think of no more precarious occupation or quicker way of ruining his health. Therefore, with few more attractive options available to him, Shack did what so many other players have done down the years and went into football journalism. He stayed in it, too. Despite disliking the job, or so he said, he spent 27 years in all on, first, the *Daily Express* and then, for a much longer time, *The (Sunday) People*. He said his wife summed the job up best when she described it as being like 'schoolboys telling tales'. But he had to agree that it paid good expenses and it paid good wages. Not only that but, as he added with his usual wry humour: 'I was associating with people that I knew and I liked and it was better than working!'

The great advantage of the job, as Shackleton readily acknowledged, was that it kept him in touch with football and footballers. That, in turn, was advantageous to the newspaper employing him, because those in the game would be more likely to confide in him, one of their own, than in a professional journalist.

Therefore, by employing famous ex-footballers like Shack, there was a greater likelihood of a paper getting 'exclusive' stories on the ongoing soap opera that is professional football. That was the theory, anyway, although it did not always work out according to plan in his case, as we shall see. In addition, the former star player was – and still is – useful to a paper because of the authoritative voice he can bring to issues of the day through a regular column of some sort. And Shack, of course, was never short of an opinion or three.

But, here again, he was different; exceptional even. What set him apart from most of the other ex-footballers working as journalists then or now was his ability both to write his own stuff (whisper it quietly, but the majority need a 'ghost-writer' to turn their thoughts into the written word) and make it amusing. Getting a laugh from the reader, I can assure you as a professional journalist myself, is one of the most difficult things in the business to achieve. It has to count as a real and precious gift, and Shack had it. He proved that most often in his match reports, especially their 'intros' (i.e. introductory paragraphs), some of which became legendary among the hard-bitten, seen-and-heard-it-all-before denizens of the press box in the 1960s, 1970s and 1980s.

It is difficult enough just learning how to write a report on a football match. No matter how much you know, or think you know, about professional football, it takes a lot of hard work and practice to be able to condense 90 minutes, or more, of football action into anything between 500 and 1,000 words. Not only that, but you have to pick out an angle, make it interesting to read – no mere recitation of the facts will do – and complete all this at least twice against a tight deadline.

In most cases, a football writer will first have to file what is called a 'runner': that is to say, a running report on a game while it is taking place. It means he has to try to keep one eye on the pitch and the other on what he is writing, either in a notebook or, these days, on a laptop. It is not easy, and occasionally you need the assistance of colleagues to fill you in on any action you have missed. This initial report also has to be sent – by telephone or cyberspace – to your newspaper by the final whistle, or soon afterwards.

That done, the reporter then has to go behind the scenes to seek the opinions of the two managers and any relevant players on the result, its consequences and anything controversial that might have happened. Having gathered all this in, he or she sits down to write a considered piece on the game that has to be completed and filed within about an hour and half of the final whistle – less than that in the case of night matches. This is just a generalised picture of the football reporter's task on match days. It varies in some respects from paper to paper, journalist to journalist, and I'd be surprised if Shack ever had to go and get the 'quotes'. Even so, it is not an easy job to do in any form; and he managed to do it well enough to make people laugh.

One of Shack's most memorable 'intros' was recalled fondly for me by Norman Wynne, a retired football writer who worked for the *Daily Express* and *The People* at much the same time as Shackleton. 'One of the things about Shack that always sticks in my mind,' said Wynne, 'is that, although he wasn't strictly a journalist as such, he produced one of the best football-match "intros" I've ever read. It was when Sunderland played Northampton on one occasion. It went: "Northampton, the place where boots and shoes are made, brought their own brand of clog to Roker Park." He was very dry-witted was Shack!'

The wit was not confined to his 'intros', either. Several of the veteran journalists interviewed for this book recalled with great glee the phrase with which he dismissed the ball control of one player of whom had a very poor opinion. He was George Herd, the Scottish international inside-forward Sunderland bought from Clyde for £40,000 in 1961, an enormous fee back then. 'The ball,' wrote Shackleton contemptuously of Herd, 'went to his wrong feet.' It is claimed, too, that he actually invented the now well-worn put-down: 'There are two things wrong with this team – the defence and the attack!' My own favourite, though, is the phrase Shack once used to describe an attacking run by a star forward: 'He went past two players like a magician, then shot like Tommy Cooper.'

Ken Jones prefers another of Shack's little gems. Ken, who was chief sports writer on the *Sunday Mirror* before joining *The Independent* in the same capacity, says the old staff members of *The People* were still talking about what Shackleton used to write when he, Jones, joined them at their Christmas reunion in 2003. His favourite example involved the hapless George Herd, who had a reputation, rather like England's Ray Wilkins, for playing the ball square. 'At about 4.20 yesterday afternoon,' wrote Shack laconically, 'George Herd played his first forward pass of the season.'

What must be refreshingly obvious from the above is that Shackleton was not one of those tiresome former players-turned pundits who are reluctant to criticise current practitioners of the profession for fear of breaking some unwritten code of silence. Although a few former playing colleagues praised him for not having been unduly critical of other professionals in his journalism, there does seem to have been a welcome absence from his work of the mealy-mouthed: 'He'll be disappointed with that.' The Clown Prince named names and called it as he saw it. Even when he was playing, Shack's humour had had a sharp edge to it; and he was no different as a journalist.

'He didn't suffer fools gladly and he was forthright in his opinions,' said Ivor Broadis, Shackleton's former Sunderland team-mate, who also became a football writer when he finished playing and used to run into him on the reporting circuit. 'If a fellow couldn't play, he couldn't play, so far as Len was concerned. I think what annoyed him was that people didn't try to improve.'

Malcolm Macdonald, a player with Luton Town, Newcastle United and Arsenal at the time Shackleton was writing about the game, was also conscious of his unwillingness to temper his views, or offer special treatment, simply because he was a former footballer himself. 'With writing for *The People*, he was always around at Newcastle during my five years there,' said Macdonald, 'and Jackie Milburn had a similar role with the *News of the World*. But we would see an awful lot more of Jackie, who made himself "big mates" with the players. That was his way of doing the job, and it was always very protective.

'Len, on the other hand, took quite a different view. I suppose his was a more critical eye: he couldn't speak kindly of somebody he believed had little or no talent. In fact, I see a great similarity between Shack and Alan Ball inasmuch as both of them had no time for people without ability. I always got on extremely well with the two of them; but whenever you talked to Shack, you always knew there were another dozen angles in his mind that he was never going to bring into the conversation. Jackie Milburn was a straightforward type of man who would say: "This is what I'm going to do, and I'd like you to talk about such and such a thing." So you knew exactly where you stood with Jackie. But with Len, you could give him a piece of info and it would be twisted and turned and manoeuvred into something totally different to what he'd originally said to you.'

As when he was a footballer, Shackleton needed careful handling. 'He was brilliant, absolutely first class,' says John Maddock, northern sports editor of *The People* for many of the 21 years Shackleton worked on the paper. 'His contribution to *The People* was enormous. Some of his 'intros' were superb. In fact, he should have been a feature writer. You used to look at Mike Langley, who would rip up piece after piece of paper until he got the right "intro". But Shack would just sit there, get out his pipe, light it and do it. It was in his head, and that was it. I never saw him alter an "intro".

'His journalism, though, was like his football – brilliant but lazy. Shack, if you told him to go and do something, would go and do it: he would never, ever look for it himself. He was original and his writings were exceptional, but he was never a news gatherer and he only did what he had to do. He had a tremendous brain, but was reluctant to use it. Sometimes, you'd say to him: "Shack, you're about 150 words short here. Have you got something else?" "No!" he'd say, and that was the end of the matter so far as he was concerned. He was a lovely chap, but he could get very awkward.

'Basically, he resented authority. He was like that all his life, wasn't he, with his directors and his managers? So you had to be careful how you approached him. You didn't go up to Shack and say: "Look, do this, do that, do the other." Instead, it was a case of: "Shack, only you can do this. Go and see Jimmy Scoular or go and see Joe Harvey. We're looking for this or that", and then he'd go and do it. But if you gave him a direct order – "You've got to go and see Joe Harvey!" – he'd say, "Bollocks!"

'In the same office, we had Harry Johnston, the former Blackpool and England centre-half, and Tom Holley, the ex-Leeds United captain. Harry was a gentleman who wouldn't use his contacts, whereas Tom, a qualified journalist, used his to the utmost. The other two – Harry and Shack – never would. They were always apprehensive about it.

'That said, Shack did use Cloughie [Brian Clough] a lot. One day, though, I think they fell out over something minor, and Shack was the type to say: "Well, if he doesn't want to speak to me, I'm not bothered!" So when I pointed out that contacting Clough was for the paper's benefit, not his, and would he mind going to see him, he replied: "Oh, I'm not going all the way from bloody Sunderland to Derby to talk to that bastard!" That was his type of attitude.'

The odd spat apart, Shackleton and Clough were close friends. That is hardly surprising since Shack played a major role in getting Clough his first two managerial jobs in football, at Hartlepool United (then Hartlepools) and Derby County. In other words, the Clown Prince got 'Old Big 'ead' started on the road that led to fame, success and fortune at Derby and Nottingham Forest. Derby's two League Championships, in 1971-72 and 1974-75 (albeit with Dave Mackay in charge in the second instance), and Forest's one in 1977-78 – not to mention the two successive years, 1979 and 1980, in which Clough's team took the European Cup back to the City Ground – can be traced directly to the time in 1965 that Len Shackleton recommended Brian Clough to Ernest Ord, the eccentric chairman of Hartlepool United, as a candidate for their managerial vacancy, then did the same with Sam Longson at Derby two years later.

Although both footballers famously played for Sunderland, Clough arrived at Roker Park four years after Shackleton had retired. So the relationship between them began as football reporter and player. 'When I went to play at Sunderland, Len had finished as a player and was in your particular field,' Clough told me, before adding in typically caustic fashion, 'although he wasn't that much good as a journalist. Not many people are unless you're trained to be, and even the ones that are trained don't turn out too good!'

'The first real meeting I had with him was when he was a journalist and he would come to Middlesbrough while I was still playing for them. Obviously, there were only three clubs – Middlesbrough, Sunderland and Newcastle – in the North-East, and he used to cover them for *The People*. I think he worked for the

Express before that as well. In fact, I remember that when he told me he'd gone from the dailies to the Sundays, I asked him what the next step would be. "I want to work for a monthly!" he said. Now that was typical of Len. He was unbelievable. If there had been a six-monthly one, he'd have worked for them!'

Clough's poor opinion of Shackleton's work ethic is borne out by a story still told with relish by veteran football writers in the North-East. It concerns the time Shack and Jackie Milburn, another ex-footballer who turned to journalism after he retired, were sitting together in a press box before a match in the 1970s discussing the industrial strife currently gripping the country. 'I see the government are thinking of introducing a three-day week,' Milburn is said to have remarked. 'Bloody hell,' Shack replied, tongue firmly in cheek, 'I'm not having that! I'm not working that much!'

But back to the Clough-Shackleton relationship. 'So I teamed up with him as player/journalist, so to speak, with him based in Sunderland and me in Middlesbrough,' added Clough. 'When I was transferred to Sunderland it was easier for him, obviously, as he didn't have to go the 20-odd miles down the road to Middlesbrough. There was quite a big age gap between us. I was in my early twenties and he was in his mid-thirties. In fact, I vividly remember playing in his testimonial. So that was how we got to know each other.'

It was a mutually beneficial relationship. Clough lapped up Shack's iconoclastic opinions and Shack, the reporter, thrived on the football gossip the talkative, self-confident striker could supply. The bond extended to practical matters, too. Clough says that Shackleton even fixed him up with his first car, a little Morris, when he was 25. 'Len came to me and said: "It's about time you had a car and learned to drive." He took me to the garage, introduced me and, of course, everybody knew him.'

Shack, the old pro, also advised the young Brian Clough on

financial matters. 'I was battling away with about four centre-forwards at Middlesbrough,' said Clough, 'and I was fourth on the list, believe it or not. I was on 11 quid a week during the season and £7 during the summer, something like that; but Dougie Cooper, a centre-forward they thought could play – big lad, strong shoulders, typical build of a centre-forward – and somebody else, they were on 11 quid all the year round. I was a ninepenny rabbit by comparison, and people used to say I got knocked off the ball too easily. The only thing was, Dougie Cooper couldn't score goals and I could. So Len told me to ask for a rise; and when I asked him on what grounds, he said: "Tell them you're just as good a player in the summer as he is." I would never have thought of that; but Len did.'

It was a friendship that was to prove particularly valuable for Clough after he tore the cruciate ligaments in his right knee in a collision with Bury goalkeeper Chris Harker while playing for Sunderland on Boxing Day 1962. As we know from the example of Paul Gascoigne and others, that kind of serious injury can be repaired these days; but, back then, it was a savage, career-shattering blow.

Only 27 at the time and approaching his peak as a player, Clough was at his wits' end. 'So, I'm out of work, no trade at my fingertips and worrying,' he recalled. 'I loved cricket, but I could do nothing else apart from football. Anyway, I went to see Raich Carter, the manager of Middlesbrough, because I'd been there since I was 17 or 18. He said he'd think about giving me a job; but when I went back in two or three weeks' time, he said there was no room for me there.

'So I went back and tried to hang on at Sunderland because George Hardwick had become manager of the club. George was an ex-Middlesbrough player and I knew him better than most people in football. In fact, I used to idolise him. But while I was trying to get fit – I spent about 18 months doing that – George grabbed me and said: "Hey, if you think you're going to walk around drawing your wages for the next 12 months, you've got another think coming! Get on a coaching course and go and help with our third team.'

Sunderland did grant Clough a testimonial, however, and it was at about that time Shackleton told the crocked striker he thought he could get him the Hartlepool job and asked if he was interested. 'Well, it's a bit thin on the ground round here with Middlesbrough and Sunderland,' replied Clough. 'So the answer's "Yes".' As a result, within a week of having had his testimonial, the young firebrand was installed as manager at the Victoria Ground in succession to Geoff Twentyman, the former Liverpool wing-half.

'Len was as influential off the field, being a big star in a small place like the North-East, as he was on it,' reflected Clough. 'So he could talk to chairmen like Ernie Ord, and he got me the job. But Hartlepool weren't just bottom of the Fourth Division, as it was in those days: they were cemented there! They had to apply for re-election six times out of seven, so that's how bad it was. I worked hard at it, kept them afloat, so to speak, and survived a human villain called Ernie Ord. Oh, he was a horrible man! We can't libel him because he's been dead 20-odd years: I just wish it had been a 120-odd years!

'Len knew the problems, obviously, but at least he got me through the door. And, as you well know, to get through the door is hard enough sometimes. I then continued to be the same ignorant, conceited – you name it – things that I was as a player, and got away with it! Actually, though, I'd talked football management for five years before I got injured because I'd teamed up with a bloke called Peter Taylor from Coventry.'

Pat Murphy, the experienced and knowledgeable BBC5 Live sports reporter, suggests in his study of Clough, *His Way – The Brian Clough Story*, that Shackleton was the first to spot the potential of the Clough/Taylor managerial partnership that was to make history in

English football before ending in bitterness and recrimination. Clough, however, insists that the idea was his and his alone. 'Peter Taylor had gone before I'd even transferred from Middlesbrough to Sunderland,' he explained. 'I spoke to him a couple of times over the telephone. We were reasonably close, but a bloke like him wasn't the type to keep close. Anyway, he kept complaining that he couldn't get into League football, couldn't even get an interview. "I can't get a job. I can't get this, can't get that," he'd say. And it was difficult to break into because there were so many people floating around wanting jobs. The idiots used to go for big names: they still do nowadays.'

When Shackleton opened the door at Hartlepool for Clough, the managerial rookie persuaded Taylor, then manager of non-League Burton Albion, to join forces with him at Victoria Park. Taylor hailed from Nottingham; so when, a couple of years later, Shack told Clough he thought he could get him the manager's job at Derby, the other half of the partnership could hardly wait to get back to his native East Midlands. As for Clough, Middlesbrough born and bred, he wasn't even sure where Derby was. 'Derby? Where's that, like?' was his response to Shack's news that he thought he would be able to work the oracle for him a second time.

Even now, Clough is not sure how Shackleton came to know Sam Longson, the Derby chairman, so well. He believes a friendship must have blossomed through journalistic contact between the two of them. But there was a potential hitch when Clough refused to go all the way down to Derby for the job interview. Typically cussed and confident, he insisted on meeting his prospective new employers at some kind of halfway point between Hartlepool and Derby. In the end, he got much the better of the deal, since Shackleton somehow succeeded in sweet-talking Longson into making the long journey up to Scotch Corner on the A1, which is a great deal nearer Hartlepool than it is to Derby.

'They settled on a hotel called the Scotch Corner Hotel, which was a racing hotel," said Clough. 'And I said to Len Shackleton: "Why the racing hotel?" "Well," he said, "a lot of people go there." And, you know, to this day I don't know one end of a horse from the other! So I said: "OK, we'll go there." Sam Longson, to his credit, came up, with the vice-chairman. We had an hour, an hour and a half, then two hours together, and it got to the stage where I said: "Look, I've got to go and you've got to get back down there. What's the procedure?" To which Longson replied: "Oh, you've got the job now! I'd like you to come down to Derby to a board meeting to confirm it. Just a rubber stamp." So I must have said something right in those two hours!

'But I only got the job through Len's introduction to Derby. I went there, stayed there and then it all took off from there, managerial-wise. So that's what I owe Len Shackleton. If I had threepence in my pocket, I'd owe him tuppence of it, because one penny was my contribution. Len, initially – and this is so important – was the breakthrough. He got me through the door, and I did the rest.'

In his book, *Clough: A Biography*, Tony Francis claimed that Shackleton was decidedly miffed at not getting anything at all – not even a free lunch at the Scotch Corner Hotel – in return for the major part he had played in bringing the young Hartlepool manager and Derby together. He quoted Shack as saying that Clough sent a tin of biscuits and a box of chocolates for Mrs Shackleton every Christmas after Derby won promotion to the old First Division in 1968-69, but that those gifts stopped when Clough and Taylor moved on to Nottingham Forest in 1975. 'I'd given a millionaire something money couldn't buy and didn't get so much as a "thank you",' Shack is reported to have complained.

However, it is a questionable quote if only because Clough was nowhere near being a millionaire at the time he moved from

Hartlepool to Derby. Not only that, but Clough insists vehemently that they never fell out over the deal and that Shack did not expect any recompense other than an exclusive story for *The People*. 'I don't know how I could have thanked him,' said Clough, bristling. 'What was suggested? Do you mean I should have sent him some money? That was the last thing Len wanted – money! How do you thank somebody apart from friendship? And that's the best "thank you" there can be.'

Subsequent events appear to support Clough's version of the story. There is nothing at all in *Return of the Clown Prince*, published in 2000, to suggest that Shackleton bore any kind of grudge against Clough for not getting anything monetary out of the Derby deal. As a matter of fact, Shack went out of his way in the book to sing his old friend's praises in a loud voice. He celebrated his uniqueness as a player, manager and human being and lamented the fact that the FA had never had the courage to appoint him manager of England. Significantly, he also quoted Clough as having left him with these words in a then recent conversation: '…and don't forget, my door is always open to you.' That exchange smacks of anything but ill will.

It was not a friendship entirely without friction, that is for sure; but how many friendships are? Clough says he did have words with Shack from time to time, but only because he was going round with a couple of other journalists, one of whom was the *Daily Mirror*'s man in the North-East, Charlie Summerbell. 'Charlie Summerbell was the hardened journalist, and Len wasn't,' Clough recalls. 'Len used to tag people on to his shoulders, so to speak: he did the same thing when he was a player. Shack was an amateur in journalism, and he used to go around with Charlie. So, whenever Len wanted to talk to me about anything, there was always a couple of them. I never really fell out with him, but I did say to him occasionally: "Hey, if you want to talk to me, talk to me; but not bringing half the bloody press round with you! He'd got *carte blanche* with me, Len had: he could do anything he liked. But when I invited him into my house, I didn't want to invite half of bloody Fleet Street with him! I didn't fall out with him as such, though.'

Clough and Shackleton kept in touch even after Shack had retired as a journalist. 'I used to get occasional photographs of Len fishing in a serene, calm Mediterranean or somewhere sea,' said Clough. 'That was Len's idea of retirement: shut away completely with his fishing line. I met up with him once on holiday and asked him what he did all day long. "Oh, well," he replied, "I go fishing for two or three hours a day." He was content with that. Deep down, he was a lazy bugger, you know. He certainly didn't push himself in any walk of life, as far as I know. He had this outstanding ability as a footballer, but it came easy to him. I don't know how best to describe him as a bloke, though. Nothing fazed him and he had this off-the-field approach of: "All right, then; so what?" '

Brian Clough was not the only ex-footballer Shackleton found a job for in his role as a football reporter. Johnny McSeveney, his old left-wing partner at Sunderland, was another beneficiary of his kindness and contacts. 'We always kept in touch,' said McSeveney, 'and I remember ringing him after I came back from working in the Emirates. When he asked me what I was doing, and I told him I had nothing lined up, he advised me to ring Ian Porterfield, who was going to Rotherham as manager. But I didn't know Ian very well, so Shack told me to leave it with him. Next thing, Ian 'phoned me and I joined Rotherham.

'He was always helping people to get jobs. Prior to the Rotherham business, he'd got me the manager's job at Darlington. He'd got me the interview with the chairman and I'd met him, a local man called Tate, in Newcastle. He more or less offered me the job – told me the terms, everything – and I turned it down. Ralph Brand got the job in the end, but I could have had it if I'd wanted it. Len would help anybody: anybody in trouble he would help. And as a reporter, he was very sensible; he didn't always give his own opinion, he just wrote what went on.'

Contrary to what John Maddock, his sports editor on *The People*, claimed, there is evidence that Shackleton did try to use his many contacts in the game to get stories for the paper. Stan Anderson, for example, confesses to having been one of Shack's sources of information. 'You either trusted people [journalists] or you didn't,' said Anderson, who played for Newcastle and managed Middlesbrough after leaving Sunderland. 'So when he used to ring me up and ask if I'd got any information for him, I'd say: "Well, you can't mention my name, but why don't you take on this thing?" "Right," he'd say, "fair enough!" Of course, it didn't stop him ringing Newcastle or Middlesbrough and saying: "Well, I've heard this about whatever…", and they'd say: "Where the hell did you get that information from?" In fact, I spoke more to Len after he'd finished playing, when he was a reporter, than when he was actually playing.'

It does seem to have been very difficult for anyone, Trevor Ford excepted, to fall out with Shackleton. Although he did not suffer fools gladly and his droll sense of humour could be a touch cruel at times, he was enormously popular with most of the people with whom he came into contact. Vince Wilson, for example, could not speak too highly of Shack after spending many journalistic years on the road with him. Vince, whose appointment as football columnist for the *Sunday Mirror* in the North-East prompted other Sunday newspapers, including *The People*, to follow suit, was clearly fond of the man. It helped, I suppose, that Wilson was a committed Sunderland fan who had idolised Shackleton from the terraces; but all too often you can discover that your idols have feet of clay when you meet them close up. Happily, this did not happen when Wilson found himself working alongside his hero.

'I found him fascinating company on our travels while we were covering the same sporting events in the North-East,' said the now-retired *Sunday Mirror* man. 'He was warm, expansive and quick-witted, and he had a marvellous recall for funny stories from his playing days. They were largely about his Sunderland/Newcastle team-mates and my early heroes. To have one-on-one discussions with him in those days was priceless. We went to a lot of games together while we were in the North-East, so I had a great chance of just talking to him. Oh, to travel with Shack! It was a joy to do that with somebody you had idolised in your youth, you know.'

Wilson has his own treasured store of Shackleton 'funnies' to draw on from his long friendship with the Clown Prince. He recalls the man from *The People* writing: 'Sunderland began with a bang – like a puncture!' when they started the season after relegation to the Second Division in 1958 with a defeat. Another one from around that time was: 'Don't worry, Sunderland are going places... to Rotherham, Barnsley...' Shack used to keep the press box in stitches, too. 'One day at Roker Park,' says Wilson, 'a fan to the left of the box was complaining about cigarette ash being dropped on his head from the tier of the stand above. The Sunderland directors used to sit directly above us, and Shack said: "There you are: we're being spoiled again! At least we're getting cigar ash dropped on us. That poor bugger's only getting Woodbine ash!"'

Although Wilson stresses that Shackleton's conversation was always highly entertaining, he does concede that he could be quite critical and cold in some ways about people he didn't rate. 'He was good fun to have in the press box,' says the ex-*Sunday Mirror* man, 'and, as a former professional footballer, he was quite enlightening about the game, too. But he had very strong views about players who could play and those who couldn't: very much so.'

One of the problems entailed in employing ex-pros as football writers is that, not having received any training as journalists, most are not too familiar with the laws of libel. In Shackleton's case, Wilson cites as an example the tale Shack told him about a letter he had received from a Sunderland fan for his weekly letters column. 'Shack, of course, detested Alan Brown, who had arrived as manager of Sunderland as he departed. Anyway, a fan had written to him saying that, as Brown was so unpopular and unsuccessful – which he was – he was thinking of organising a whip-round to pay him off. Asked what he thought of the suggestion, Shack had replied: "Yeah, I am sure the fans would respond eagerly; but what would you do with the leftovers? Buy Alan Ball, Bobby Moore and somebody else?" You know, I don't think that would ever have got in!'

Shackleton never pretended to be a committed journalist, of course. As far as he was concerned, it was just a means to an end. It paid well, kept him in touch with football and didn't make too many demands on his time. Other than that, he had no interest in the profession whatsoever. 'I was in his presence on one occasion when he had to go down to some function in London with the *Sunday People*,' recalled Wilson. 'So the sports editor suggested that he might like to stay behind on the Saturday night to see how the paper was put to bed and what the work was like on the "stone" [the "stone", for the benefit of those unfamiliar with old-school, pre-computerised journalism was where the pages were assembled in hot metal by skilled compositors]. "Christ!" replied Shack. "I live at bloody Roker, where there's ten million bloody stones on the beach. I'd rather be there!"'

That harsher side of Shackleton's nature does not appear to have made him many enemies, as John Maddock would testify. 'We had a "Shack's Club",' said his former sports editor on *The People*.

'Readers used to send him letters, and we'd put on a dinner for the winner every year in Newcastle. I'll never forget one year because I rang Gordon Richards, the racehorse trainer, and told him we were looking for one or two big names to attend Len's dinner. Having agreed to be there, Gordon did his training, got to the dinner at seven, stayed 'till well past midnight, didn't drink and then drove all the way back to Penrith, in Cumbria, because he had to work with his horses in the morning. And when I thanked him for coming, he said: "I'm only doing it for Shack. I think the world of him."

Any number of personalities used to turn up – all the big names from the North-East. You just rang them up and said: "It's Shack's do" and the reply was always: ' "I'll be there!" ' '

That bad ankle and a change of career did not stop Shackleton playing football wherever he could. Even when he had been a journalist for some years, he did not need much encouragement to pull on a pair of boots. 'The last game I saw him play in full-scale professional company,' recalled Vince Wilson, 'was in Germany after Newcastle United won promotion to the First Division under the captaincy of Stan Anderson in 1965. They played five games in two weeks after that memorable season had ended, and Shack unexpectedly appeared in a practice game which was played between their fixtures.

'Like me, he was a travelling reporter covering the Newcastle tour. He was also in his early forties, a little heavier and a little slower than in his heyday; but his trickery and control – in borrowed boots – left a special memory or two with young United lads who had never seen him play. His kind of genius, original talent, refused to desert him even then. Much later than that – at 78 – he would still kick a ball 30 yards accurately provided there was nobody around.'

Doug Weatherall and John Maddock also have vivid memories of Shackleton on the football field when he was a journalist. 'Long after he had finished playing,' recalled Weatherall, 'he appeared in a testimonial match – for Stan Anderson, I think it was. And, just towards the end of the game, he went in goal for a rest. But when he got the ball and someone was threatening to challenge him, almost Trevor Ford-like, he had the confidence and the eye to throw the ball at the left-hand post and take the return off it. I've never seen that sort of skill at any level of football, or anywhere else for that matter. It was just astonishing. He could have thrown the ball into the net, but he didn't because he was so confident of where he was putting it.'

If Weatherall's story underlines yet again Shackleton's extraordinary ability to make a ball do exactly what he wanted, Maddock reminds us how unwise it was to mess with him. 'My first recollection of Shack,' said the former sports editor, 'was playing for *The People* with him in a Wednesday League match, and Jack Bentley, our Rugby League writer, kept criticising him. "Give me the ball!" Jack was shouting at him: "Do this, do that!" So Shack deliberately put the ball a yard in front of him every time, and made him run. At the end of it, Jack Bentley threw up!'

Shackleton had much the same effect on football's establishment when, as we have seen, he supported George Eastham over the inside-forward's successful campaign to obtain a transfer from Newcastle United to Arsenal and challenge the archaic retain and transfer system. It was Shack, as a sympathetic journalist, who introduced Eastham to Ernie Clay, the wealthy businessman whose financial backing, crucially, enabled Eastham to take the fight to Newcastle and eventually win a court ruling that is a landmark in the history of the game.

'They were very close, and he [Shack] created a lot of Ernie's thinking,' reports Malcolm Macdonald, who knew Shackleton as a newspaperman in the North-East and was Fulham's manager under Clay's chairmanship for four years. 'When Ernie was involved with

George Eastham, Len Shackleton was there pushing them: he was creating a thought process. Len, after he finished playing, found he could be more effective by manoeuvring behind the scenes; and manoeuvre he did – all his life. As a player, he was in the forefront; so the spotlight was always on him. But he found, later in life, that as an ex-pro he could have more effect on the game. He knew he was better totally in the background, where he could have a marked effect on the game without people being aware it was he who was creating a huge amount of thinking.'

The George Eastham case was not the end of the relationship between Shackleton and Clay. They met again about six years later, when Newcastle were in Portugal defending the Fairs Cup they had won in 1968-69. Clay had a hotel at Sintra, some 30 or 40 miles from Lisbon, and Shack was one of those who stayed there when he went out to cover the match for *The People*. Clay was on the board at Fulham by then, and the two of them had long talks about football. From their discussions, Shackleton sensed that Clay was on the same wavelength as himself, but his innate mistrust of football directors made him cautious. He got the impression that Clay's knowledge of the game was quite thin and that the businessman, like so many others, was in the game simply for the kudos it brought.

Nevertheless, Clay continued to court Shackleton. Having paid several visits to the famous ex-player's Sunderland home, he eventually invited him to become a member of the Fulham board. Shack declined, saying that he had no ambitions or aspirations of that sort; but Clay persisted. He even went so far as to offer to lay on a helicopter to take Shackleton from a field opposite his home to London for Fulham's weekly board meeting. From Shack's account of the episode, it is clear that he was acutely embarrassed by all of this. Not only that, he felt that Clay was keen to recruit him just because he wanted to pick his brains. But such was the

Fulham director's determination to get his man, Shackleton finally gave in and agreed, against his better judgment, to go along with Clay's proposals.

He did fly down to London for his first board meeting, but by scheduled flight and not helicopter. At Craven Cottage, he recalled meeting some 'very interesting' people, among them Ted Drake, the former Arsenal centre-forward and Chelsea manager, and Bertie Mee, manager of Arsenal when they did the League Championship-FA Cup double in 1970-71, but did not return to Sunderland 'thrilled' by the experience. What is more, a creature of habit, he did not relish having to break his normal journalistic routine to make the weekly trip to London.

So Shack was clearly relieved when the editor of *The People*, Sam Campbell, ruled that, because of the danger of bias creeping into his reporting, he could not combine his work for the paper with being a director of a professional football club. While a little miffed that anyone should think him incapable of remaining totally objective about Fulham, Shackleton was grateful for the chance to withdraw from the arrangement without causing personal offence to Ernie Clay. What a pity, though, that he did not last more than one board meeting at Craven Cottage. Now we shall never know whether Len Shackleton would have backed up his famous blank page jibe by showing just what a director with plenty of knowledge about football could do. The odds are that he would not have been 'average': that was not his style in anything he tackled.

CHAPTER TEN
FAMILY MAN

Len Shackleton, one imagines, would have been thoroughly shocked by the sex, drugs and rock 'n' roll lifestyle displayed in the television soap opera *Footballers' Wives*. Not because he was some kind of prude or keep-fit fanatic – smoking and gambling were two of his vices and his closest friends at Sunderland were three of the most roguish members of the squad – but because the programme would probably have offended his strong sense of family. Read *Return of the Clown Prince* and you cannot help but be struck by the frequent references to his wife, Marjorie, and his three sons Graham, Roger and David. They, you get the impression, were what really mattered to him in life. Indeed, Roger made it crystal clear in a previous chapter how important family life was to his father.

Shack lived in a totally different era, of course; an era at the other end of the social and behavioural spectrum from *Footballers' Wives* and that disgusting new players' party game, 'Roasting'. But it was not so different that no footballer ever misbehaved. My father was a close friend of Tom 'Pongo' Waring and the stories he told me about the former Aston Villa and England centre-forward's wild, off-the-field behaviour made George Best look like a choirboy. Nobody knows what goes on behind closed doors; but there was never the slightest public whiff of scandal about Shackleton, and it is extremely difficult to imagine him ever wanting to step out of line as a husband and father. An innovator and iconoclast as a player, Shack seems to have been very much the conformist as a private person.

It is a matter of record that he took his family with him whenever he could. When he went on that controversial coaching trip to Kenya in 1955, for instance, he was accompanied by his wife and his eldest son, Graham, who was then about nine years old. In fact, he made a point of asking the Kenyan FA to allow him and his family to travel by ship, instead of by air, because he was away from home so much with Sunderland during the football season and wanted to make up for lost time with Marjorie and Graham. We have seen in an earlier chapter, too, what a torment of worry and guilt Shack went through when Graham was taken seriously ill as a young child and he, questionably, felt he had to go off to London to play for Newcastle United. He could hardly wait to get back to Tyneside.

There is no doubt that Shackleton was enormously proud of his three sons, all of whom forged careers in the respectable professions. The eldest, John Graham, but known as Graham, was born in Bradford in 1946, the year Shack was transferred from Park Avenue to Newcastle, and became a lawyer. Married with two children, Graham lives in Shropshire and, at the time of writing, was working for the Crown Prosecution Service. Not a particularly sporty type, he is said to have turned down the chance to go to Cambridge University on a sports scholarship allegedly made available through connections of Shack's old Sunderland team-mate, Don Revie. Graham needed to develop his proficiency at cross-country running to take up the scholarship, but preferred to become an articled clerk instead.

Roger Anthony, the second boy, was born in 1955, when his father was playing for Sunderland and nearing the end of his career there. Roger, a chartered valuation surveyor, confesses to having little or no interest in sport. He says he was forced to play rugby football at school, and his only sporting activity now is regular swimming, 'simply to remain fit'. He is married with two daughters, neither of whom has any significant sporting interest, either. 'My real interest and passion is motor cars, not football,' says Roger. 'I wish, when my father was showing me in the back garden how to trap balls and do this, that and the other, I'd taken more notice, because he reckoned I'd got the natural ability. My father would always maintain that it's a good way of earning your living – being paid to keep yourself fit – but I just had no interest in it.'

David Andrew, the youngest, is four years younger than Roger and a GP in Perth, Australia. He is also the only one of Shackleton's three sons who has inherited his father's and grandfather's aptitude for, and love of, sport. 'You could fill a whole book about his sporting activities,' said Roger. 'It's soccer mainly, the others being golf, swimming, bungee jumping, paragliding et al; he's the veritable "Mr Energy" or, as my father used to put it, a bit of a "one off".'

A keen and talented schoolboy footballer, David played abroad while doing his A-Levels. One year it was with Washington Diplomats in the USA, then a Finnish team. He played for the university while at Manchester University Medical School and trained with Fulham and Queens Park Rangers while at the British School of Osteopathy. At the time of writing, he was still playing the game in local and regional amateur league tournaments in Australia. 'Most of my school pals who were keen on soccer seemed to have "retired" with injury problems by their early twenties,' said Roger Shackleton. 'Brother David has always led something of a charmed existence and is still fit enough to play now that he has reached forty-four years of age.'

Like the offspring of all celebrities, the Shackleton boys had to come to terms with the fame of their father. At least one of them –

David – seems to have had few problems; but the adjustment was more difficult for somebody like Roger, who was the son of an iconic footballer in a football-mad area like the North-East and did not have the slightest interest in the game himself. 'People started calling me "Young Shack",' he recalled, 'and I just used to say: "Yeah, fine!" Without being patronising, I shied away from it.

'It's a mixed position and probably beneficial and troublesome in equal part. Being known by reference to one's parent's position seems to "displace" one's own identity. This can make the normal difficulties encountered whilst growing up seem more difficult to deal with than they may perhaps otherwise be to "normal" people. Whereas North Americans seem to all want to become famous, I would personally find this highly undesirable. It seems to me there is nothing wrong with anonymity. Indeed, it makes it easier to get on with things in an undistracted way, so that one is more likely to be in control of a situation, rather than it you.'

The depth of Shackleton's pride in his sons was measurable from the reply he gave in that Radio Five Live programme about him in 1996 when Jimmy Armfield asked whether he felt envious of the hefty sums of money – £12-15,000 a week – footballers earned even then. 'Not really,' replied Shack. 'There's no sour grapes with me. My eldest boy is a solicitor, my middle boy is a chartered surveyor, my youngest is a doctor and an osteopath. So that's what football has given to me, to give to them.'

Shackleton certainly explored every avenue to ensure that his family had a good standard of living and his sons all the educational opportunities they needed. In addition to the money he was bringing in from his winter and summer careers as a professional footballer and cricketer, followed by his income as a journalist, he went into business in a variety of ways outside of his work. At various times between the end of the Second World War and the 1970s, he owned, or part-owned, an ice-cream parlour in Sacriston, County Durham, a sweet shop and hairdresser's, an off licence and general dealer's and a haberdasher's and wool shop – all three of those shops were in Sunderland – plus a gift shop, café and holiday flats in Grange-over-Sands, Cumbria.

The name above one of the shops in Sunderland still amuses Billy Bingham: 'There was a guy called Len Duns, who preceded me as a right-winger at Sunderland. In fact, he'd played in the FA Cup final for the club, pre-war. There was an age difference of about 14 years between us; so, as he was going out of the team, I was coming in. Anyway, Len Duns was a really nice guy, and Shack got him to open a shop with him. They called it "Shack's Snacks & Duns' Buns". Well, I cracked up when I saw it! It was down by the Roker seafront somewhere. All the people used to go to the shore at Sunderland then for their holidays: they didn't go to Majorca, they went to Roker! And there was this little place on the seafront.

'Shack was making money besides his football. He was also doing a few articles in the papers, and things like that. We were only getting £12 a week then [as footballers], for Christ's sake! Even though the working man was getting just £3, you've got to say that £12 isn't a fortune. Mind you, houses then were costing £600-£1,000, good houses. So you've got to put everything into perspective. But he opened that shop because he was enterprising and he thought he wasn't getting enough money out of the game.'

There was more to it than money, though, where Shackleton's family were concerned. Just as he tried to take his wife and first child abroad with him whenever he could while he was a player, and 'phoned home regularly when he was away with Newcastle or Sunderland, he went out of his way to ensure that he stayed as close to home as possible when he became a journalist. 'Following his retirement from the game, where he had to be away from home every other week or when on tour, he insisted on working as a journalist from an office at home,' said Roger Shackleton. 'I believe Henry Rose of the *Daily Express* had approached him about becoming a sports writer, rather than the other way round, so he was fortunate enough to get away with this requirement. It was then carried over when he was "head-hunted" by *The People*.

'No one in this life is perfect: we all have our faults of whatever type and combination. Nor would LFS (as he is wont to refer to his father to differentiate between him and his grandfather, Leonard Price Shackleton, or LPS) ever have purported to be the perfect parent. However, he was an intelligent, thoughtful, highly reasonable, humorous and energetic character. Although generally sociable, he was not a socialite; both he and my mother had a relatively small circle of close friends. My brothers and I knew them as aunties and uncles even though none were blood relations.

'As children, we always used to look forward to family holidays and we were taken away abroad – some years, a couple of times – significantly earlier than the modern era of package tours. LFS was also keen that we should all benefit from a good education. It is difficult to be wholly objective about such matters but, in overall terms, I think it true, fair and reasonable to state that one could not have wished for a better father were it possible to pick one in advance. If I am able to achieve a similar outcome with my own girls, I would consider this to be a great personal success indeed. Is there anything *more* important to *any* parent?'

In the latter years of his life, Shackleton finally tore himself away from his beloved North-East and went to live at Grange-over-Sands, in Cumbria. The main reason for the move, in the late 1980s, was that Marjorie Shackleton wanted to be nearer her sister, who lived over there on the west coast. In fact, the sister and her husband were in partnership with the Shackletons in the shop, café and holiday flats already mentioned. They ran the business and the Shackletons were the 'silent' partners. But when Shack retired from journalism in 1985, the business was sold. The proceeds funded the purchase of an apartment at Los Cristianos, in Tenerife, where the Shackletons had been renting previously for holidays and close to which Robert Maxwell, the controversial newspaper tycoon, went overboard from his yacht, sensationally and fatally. As he grew older, Shack suffered from mild emphysema; so, to avoid Britain's winter weather, he and his wife would spend six months in the warm and dry end of Tenerife before returning for spring and summer in the UK.

Shack was actually in Los Cristianos when he heard, in March 1999, that he had been included among the 100 best players 'ever to have graced professional football in this country', as the Football League put it in their letter of nomination. As such, he was invited to attend a celebratory 'Evening of Legends' at the London Hilton on 13 May 1999, and be honoured for his contribution to the game. The climax of the evening, he was informed, would be the award of a specially commissioned gold medal to each 'legend'.

This, of course, was the *only* medal Shackleton would have to show for all those years of entertaining crowds and striving to perfect his control of a football. Yet his family had enormous difficulty persuading him to return to England to attend the function. Naturally modest and 77 years of age by then, he did not relish the prospect of all the fuss and bother, let alone all that travel. No doubt he also thought it a bit late in the day to have his talent recognised officially as having been a bit special. Roger Shackleton remembers his father's reaction when he heard Newcastle United were thinking of putting up a statue of Jackie Milburn. 'They should have bloody well thought about that when he was alive!' snorted LFS. 'What good is it going to do him now?'

In the end, though, he relented and seemed glad he had made the effort to attend. In *Return of the Clown Prince* he expressed his pleasure at the opportunity the 'Evening of Legends' gave him to renew acquaintance with old friends such as (all of them listed in alphabetical order, note) Jimmy Armfield, John Charles, Tom Finney, Trevor Ford, Nat Lofthouse, Malcolm Macdonald, Wilf Mannion, Stan Matthews and Terry Paine. It was good to see Trevor Ford included in that list: it suggested that, at the very least, the two old Sunderland adversaries had decided to let bygones be bygones before they shuffled off this mortal coil.

It was also in Tenerife that Shack did most of the work for his final contribution to the gaiety of nations. Roger Shackleton had talked his father into producing *Return of the Clown Prince* in 2000 and helped him with the sequel to the famous *Clown Prince of Soccer*, published 45 years earlier. 'I persuaded LFS into the idea because his generally failing health, from normal ageing, meant that he was too old and tired to play golf, or even bowls, any more,' he explained. 'Compiling the book was a good excuse for re-establishing contact with many of his old pals and the time was propitious for looking back with the benefit of hindsight over all the changes in the game. I first started the research as long ago as 1994, but the project did not start in earnest until the autumn of 1999 and the book was published two or three weeks before LFS' death in November 2000.'

Bravely, and perhaps typically of a habitually individualistic family, the Shackletons decided not to take the project to a commercial publisher and opted for the do-it-yourself route instead. That meant they not only had to produce all the material, but pull it together, read proofs and edit copy, arrange for pictures to be included, get someone to design the dust-cover, have the whole thing bound and printed, then sell and distribute the finished article. It was a major undertaking masterminded by Roger and his wife,

Catherine, and helped along enormously by the willing assistance of a number of friends and acquaintances.

'His England caps were in brown paper bags covered in dust,' said Roger, looking back on the process of gathering material for the book, 'and if it hadn't been for my grandma cutting out newspaper articles when he first played in 1934, he would never have accumulated a scrapbook himself. There's very little from his journalistic career, but otherwise it's as comprehensive a collection of stuff as one would ever hope to have.

'Then there was this chap, John Feast, who was a collector of memorabilia and autographs and who introduced himself to my dad. His mission was to collect all of the post-war England players' autographs, and he only had about four or five left, one of them being my father. So when Dad learned this guy lived at Heysham, near Morecambe, just over the bay from Grange-over-Sands, he invited him round. And when John saw all my dad's stuff, he said: "We can't have that. I'll put them into shape for you." If he hadn't done that, my research job hunting through boxes and boxes and boxes of cuttings, and all sorts of things, would have taken for ever.

'My memory's not what it should be and I'm only 48, and my father's memory never was. It wasn't senile dementia or anything: he was just generally vague. Fortunately, he was readily accessible, and when people would write to him or 'phone him, he would see them if they wanted to come over. And he'd been good enough to see this chap called Brian Leng (of *The Wearside Roar*) quite a few times. So Brian would tell me what my father was referring to when I couldn't make out what he was saying.

'At each critical stage, there was someone who, if you'd scoured around for ages, you couldn't have picked a more apt person to deal with it. I'm not one of those ethereal, in-touch-with-the-spirit-world weirdos, but it was almost like an instance of where the truth is stranger than fiction. When we can now look back with the benefit of hindsight, the timing of everything, from start to finish, couldn't have worked out in a way that would have dovetailed any better unless we had been positively clairvoyant.'

Also prominent among the friends of the publishing venture was Bob Murray, the chairman of Sunderland FC and a great Len Shackleton fan. His decision to buy a large number of the books for sale at the club's new ground, the Stadium of Light, gave the project impetus. 'Everybody had rallied round,' said Roger Shackleton. 'Bob Murray had given some encouragement to it by buying 1,000 copies. It was a great underwriting of the project in that sense. It was like a cash grant. If he hadn't lent us support, maybe my father would have thought: "Erm, I don't know whether we really want to bother."

The book itself is an anthology. The final third of it, approximately, is a straight reprint of *Clown Prince of Soccer*, while the other two thirds consists of a collection of random pieces in which Shackleton is interviewed about his career, reminisces about it himself or expresses an opinion about developments in the game since he gave up playing. It could have done with the tighter editorial control a commercial publisher would have brought to the project; yet it is still good to look at, full of fascinating information and insights about Shack and, as such, reflects enormous credit on the publishing beginners who put it together. At the very least, we should be grateful to them for making the venerable *Clown Prince of Soccer* available again to the younger reader and anybody who missed it the first time round.

The sequel looks to have made a bad mistake, though, in trying to repeat the joke that came off so well in *Clown Prince of Soccer*. Michael Parkinson had been approached by Roger Shackleton to provide a foreword for the book and had agreed to do so; but, because of the pressure of work, the celebrated television interviewer, sports journalist and Len Shackleton fan had been unable to deliver the goods before the deadline for publication. He suggested that, instead, they use extracts from the uniformly flattering articles he had written about Shack over the years, which they did in the body of the text. But, left with no foreword, the Shackletons decided to fall back on the old blank page trick with Parkinson's signature underneath. In these circumstances, unfortunately, the device comes across as clumsy, confusing and decidedly unfunny. Unless, that is, they were trying to say something about busy old Parky.

Despite such hitches, the book was well received and the first print run sold out. 'I think we had two people that were adversely critical,' Roger reflected. 'Everybody else was full of praise. There's two 'phones in my house, plus a mobile 'phone, and I had to get a pal in to help me and my wife answer all the calls.' However, outside pressures are understood to have led to a costly reprint that did not go so well. Roger became very touchy when I began making enquiries about this aspect of the project, a reaction that suggested *Return of the Clown Prince* had not enjoyed anything like the raging commercial success of its famous predecessor.

But, as he was quick to point out, that was not really the purpose of the publishing venture he undertook with his father. 'People,' he said, 'were ringing up – this was before my dad died and not a nostalgic thing after he'd passed on – and saying: "We're really impressed. Well done, and please pass on our thanks to your father." That was my dad's object when we did the book. He wanted people to be pleased with the quality of it and not feel they were being ripped off – like having a £5 shirt for 50 quid – and they weren't.'

Despite the onset of heart trouble, Shack insisted on seeing the venture through to the end. Hospitalised about six weeks before he died, he'd struggled to autograph one or two things and sign thank-you notes. In fact, he was so weak, he could only hold a pen for about three signatures at a time. 'It's galling,' he told Roger. 'I feel absolutely worn out and I haven't done anything!' So imagine his son's surprise when Shack, having come home, worked his way through about 50 copies of *Return of the Clown Prince*, signing thank-you notes in all of them for family and friends.

'Obviously, with heart failure, you're left really debilitated,' recalled Roger. 'I'd never encountered anything like that before, and it was a hell of a shock, especially when it was your dad. I was aware that I didn't want to wear him out, but I was equally aware that he was keen to say thank you to people. So I said: "Well, here they are: you need to see them [the books], and it was great... Because of his ill-health, he'd have made Peter Cushing look robust, but I saw how pleased he was when his eyes lit up. So I told him I'd got a list made out and I'd leave the box of books next to his chair. "Any time you feel like doing a couple," I said, "have a go."

'By this stage, people had started ringing up saying they knew the book was available and wanting to order a copy. So we had 200-300 orders to fulfil immediately. But when you've got two youngish children and a wife who's working part-time, and I'm working full-time, how the hell do you do that? We couldn't have been more busy on all fronts, and I thought that if I left that box of books with my dad, I'd pop back in a couple of weeks' time, get them and send them out. But he was insistent on working his way through them.

'So one of us had the list, the other one had a box of books and Katie, my eldest, who was nine or ten then, was holding them for her granddad while he, in a shaky hand, did the autographs. And he worked his way through fifty of the bloody things, instead of just doing two or three! He was more or less worn out to start with, never mind at the finish. But he said to me: "I think we've achieved something there, Rog, don't you?" And I said: "Yes, Dad, I think we have." That is the first time I can remember him saying something as direct as that. So I knew at that time all the silly extra hours of working and whatnot had been the right thing to do. It had pleased him and given him something to do. It was also so well received that, whichever way you slant it, it was job done.'

You sense that was the closest the Shackletons, father and middle son, had ever been in their lives – and, more importantly, had articulated that closeness. As an appreciative Roger pointed out, there was something of a family tradition of not praising children for fear of giving them a swelled head. He quoted, as an example, his grandfather's dismissive reaction when his father scored a goal for England: 'Nay, lad, our Irene could have back-heeled that in!' 'My grandfather was very wont to be low-key,' he said. 'In fact, he was almost an archetypal, dour Yorkshireman. He wouldn't give much praise, and I don't think my father was ever praised by him. I don't think it was a compulsory familial thing: it must be cultural, rather than genetic. But my dad was never one for giving too much praise, either.'

Shack's final illness began on Wednesday 16 August 2000, when he suffered a heart attack mid-morning. An ambulance crew kept him alive and he was rushed into hospital, where he stayed for five weeks. 'LFS was very grateful that the prompt attentions of the Grange-over-Sands paramedics had saved him from instant demise,' said Roger in that sort of deliberately jokey, matter-of-fact way designed to disguise deep emotion. 'He was also very philosophical about the position: as far as he was concerned, life owed him nothing further. He considered himself very fortunate to have been paid to keep himself fit and to have travelled widely during his playing and subsequent columnist days, while managing to raise a family in the process.

`He didn't want anyone in our family, or his friends, to feel sorry for him in passing. Rather, he believed that you would really only be feeling sorry for oneself because of being the one or ones left behind. He was extremely ill during the final week of his life and, I guess, normally frightened, too. But he was very pleased with our publishing effort and, as far as I'm concerned, that's the job done.'

One old friend who met Shack by chance in the last few months of his life was Ivor Broadis, his inside-forward partner at Sunderland. 'Brian Moore, who was interviewing old players, came up to do some stuff for Sky TV and I arranged to meet him near Carlisle,' explained Broadis. 'When I got there, Shack was just finishing his interview and we had a good crack. I noticed, though, that he was helped on with his jacket. I knew Len played golf because he used to come over to Carlisle to play with Bob Stokoe quite a lot. In fact, he was quite well known at the golf club here when he and Bob were on the go. So I asked him if he was still playing. "No," he said, "I've had to pack it up." I was surprised, but I didn't know then that he'd had a heart attack; and, maybe a month after that, he died. It was a real shock because he'd always been a fit fellow, Shack.'

Leonard Francis Shackleton finally passed away on Tuesday 28 November 2000, after his condition had suddenly worsened and he had been taken back into hospital. Fittingly, somehow, one of the last people outside the family to speak to him was Tom Finney. 'Somebody had come on the 'phone to tell me that Len wasn't very well,' he recalled. 'The caller gave me his number at Grange and I rang him. He told me he was really gasping for breath and finding it difficult to breathe. Three days after that, he was dead. It was very sad.' Shack was cremated, a week after his death, at Lancaster, on the other side of Morecambe Bay from his home in the Lake District. Unlike the funerals of some famous footballers, Shack's was a small, quiet affair. That was not because people did not want to attend, but because his family were anxious that it did not turn into a major event.

'I knew my mother just couldn't cope with it, and we were having to tell people: "Please don't come",' explained Roger Shackleton. 'She's a little old lady almost as deaf as a post and she would have been completely overwhelmed by it. As far as my father was concerned – he wasn't an especially religious person, more agnostic than anything else – his attitude was: "Stick me in the back of the car and take me up to the tip! I won't know anything about it." So he wouldn't have wanted any sort of fuss.'

Thus, the Clown Prince of Soccer, the footballer who loved nothing more than to play to a huge crowd, made his final appearance in front of a small audience of family and close friends. His youngest son, David, came home from Australia for the funeral, and three of his former Newcastle United and Sunderland team-mates, Bob Stokoe, Billy Bingham and Johnny McSeveney, were among the mourners.

In attendance, too, was Vince Wilson, Shack's old travelling companion from his days on the road as a football writer. Wilson remembers it being a 'shocking day – cold and wet'. He also remembers, much more affectionately, the reply he received from Shack to the letter he had written when he had heard his old friend had fallen ill. Scribbled little more than six weeks before he died, and probably the last letter he wrote, it was full of the dry wit that had made the Clown Prince so popular with his colleagues as a footballer and a journalist.

Apologising for his poor handwriting, he said it was a Shackleton family trait. 'Indeed,' he added, 'our youngest is a doctor and his letters go to the chemist to get deciphered. I'm waiting for his last one to be delivered with my tablets!' Then, having brought Vince up to date proudly on the careers of his three sons, Shack joked: 'We're not having any more!' Finally, he signed off on a note that was as wistful as it was light-hearted. 'Like you say,' he concluded, 'it's one step at a time for me now. I find it hard work doing nothing – which I didn't at one time.'

That was the Clown Prince of Soccer – funny, entertaining and honest to the last.

INDEX